Great Job Stickers

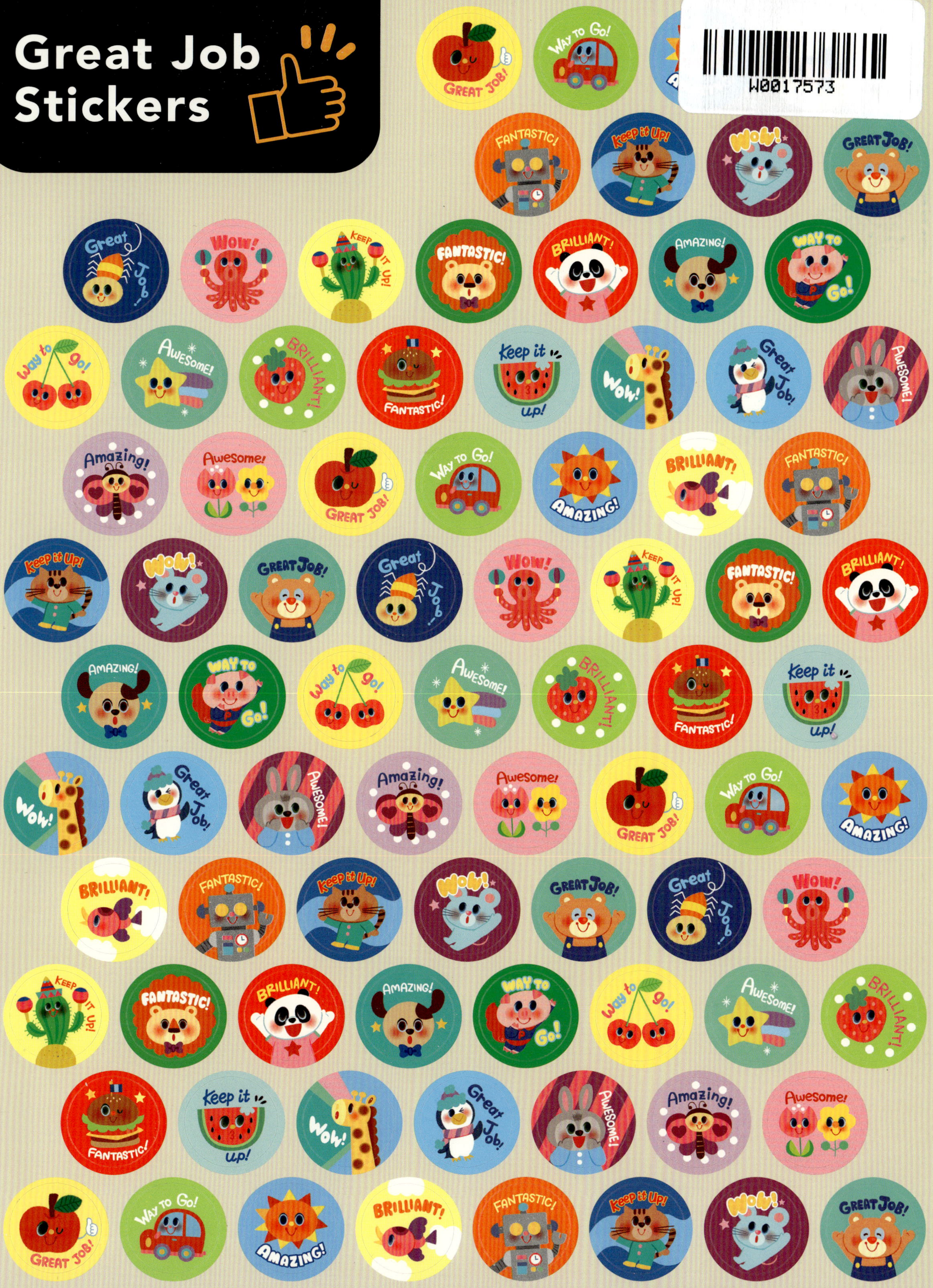

Great Job Stickers

 # Award Certificate

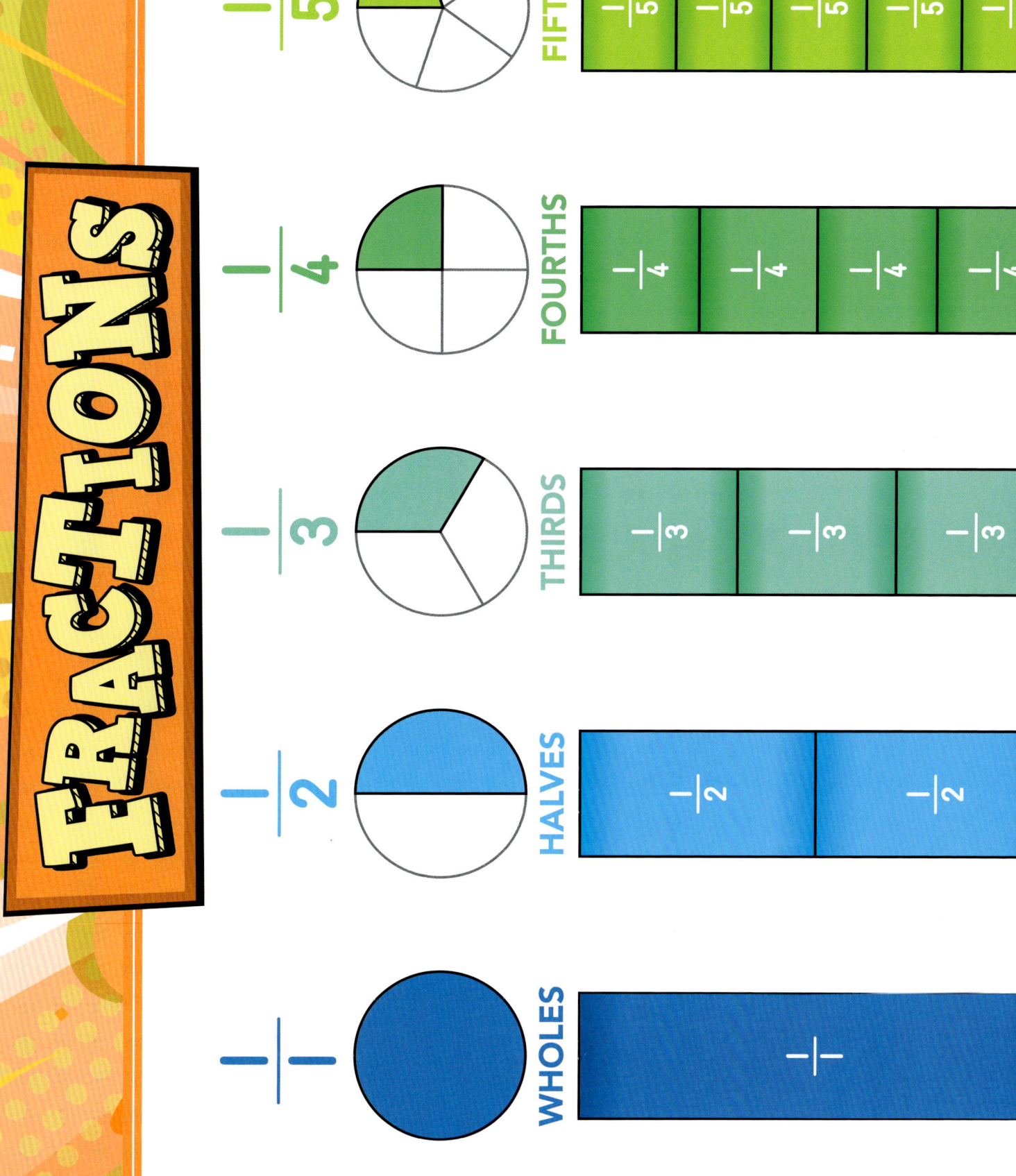

GEOMETRY

Angles

An angle is the space between two lines that meet at a point, like a corner.

Types of Angles

A right angle is an angle that measures 90°.

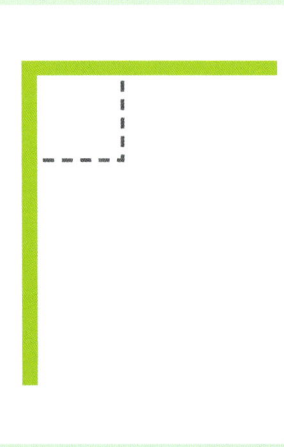

Right Angle

Lines

A line has no endpoints and extends indefinitely in both directions.

Types of Lines

A line segment represents the bounded area of a line. It has two endpoints with a defined length.

Line Segment

A ray is a portion of a line that has one endpoint but extends

Triangles

A triangle is a shape with three sides and three vertices.

Types of Triangles

An equilaterial triangle is a triangle with three equal sides.

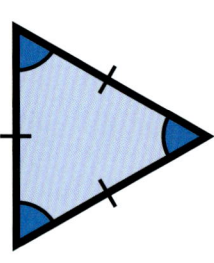

Equilateral Triangle

An isosceles triangle is a triangle with two equal sides.

An acute angle is an angle that measures less than 90°.

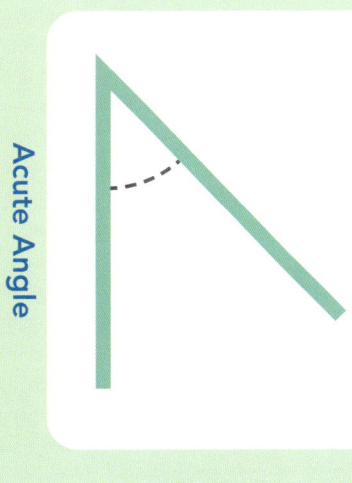

Acute Angle

An obtuse angle is an angle that measures greater than 90° and less than 180°.

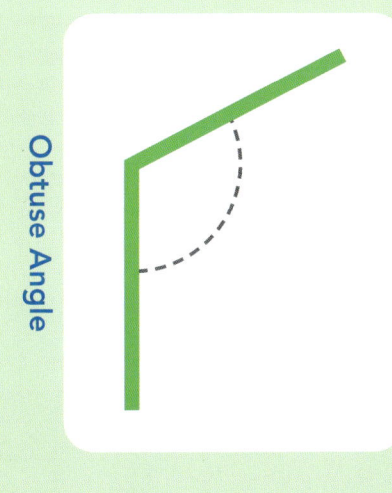

Obtuse Angle

...infinitely in a single direction.

Ray

Two lines are parallel when they do not intersect or cross.

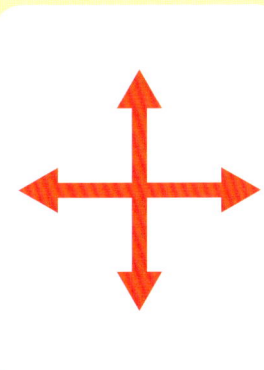

Parallel

Two lines are perpendicular when they intersect and create a right angle.

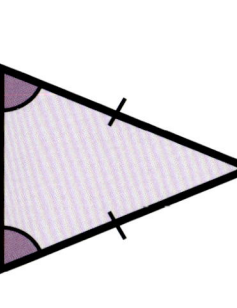

Perpendicular

A right triangle is a triangle with a right angle.

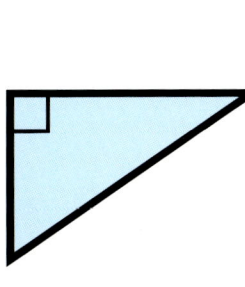

Isosceles Triangle

A scalene triangle is a triangle without any equal sides.

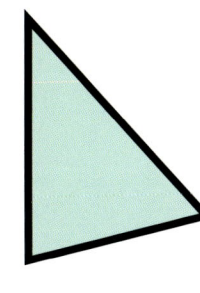

Right Triangle

Scalene Triangle

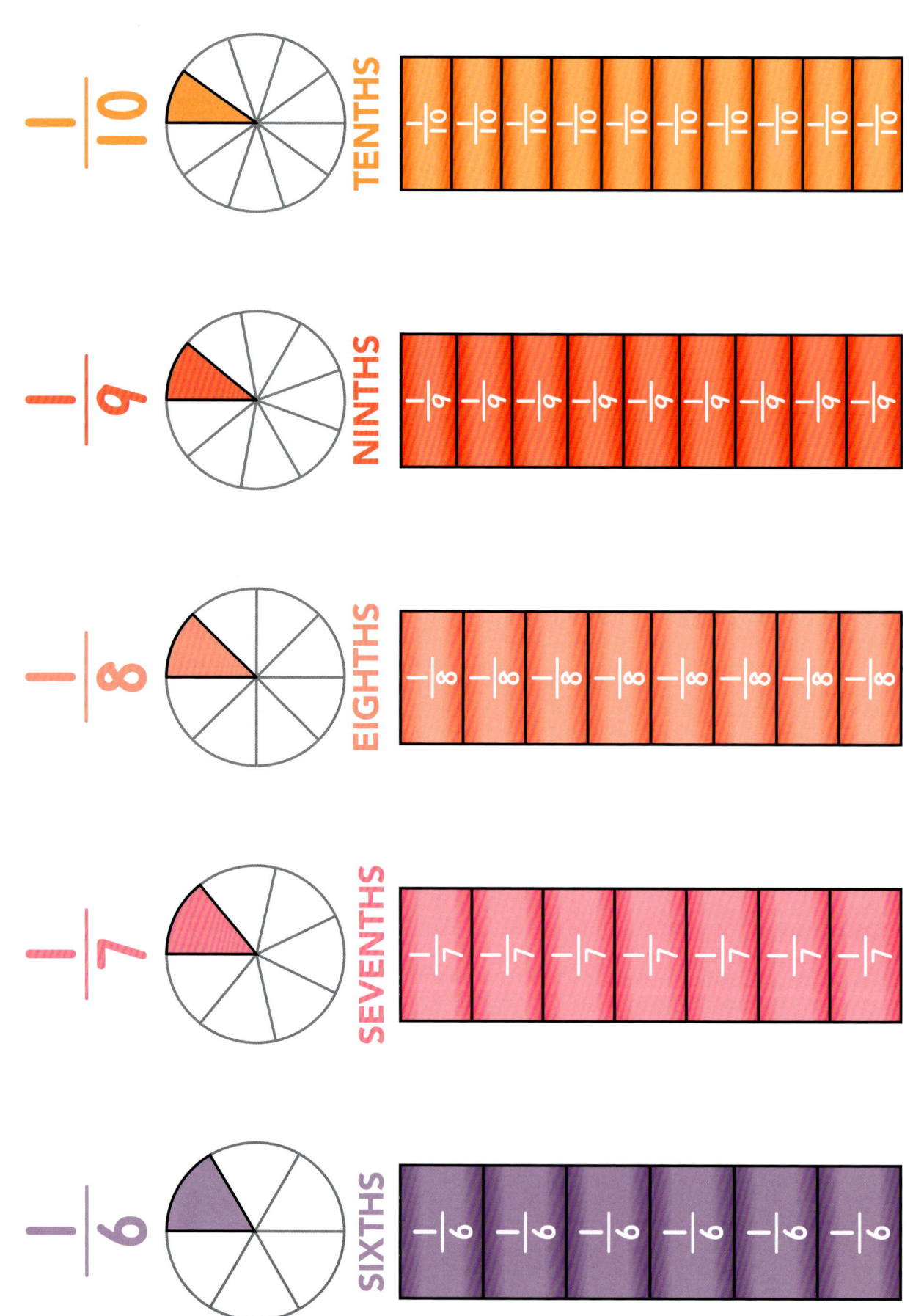

$\dfrac{1}{10}$ TENTHS

$\dfrac{1}{10}$ $\dfrac{1}{10}$ $\dfrac{1}{10}$ $\dfrac{1}{10}$ $\dfrac{1}{10}$ $\dfrac{1}{10}$ $\dfrac{1}{10}$ $\dfrac{1}{10}$ $\dfrac{1}{10}$ $\dfrac{1}{10}$

$\dfrac{1}{9}$ NINTHS

$\dfrac{1}{9}$ $\dfrac{1}{9}$ $\dfrac{1}{9}$ $\dfrac{1}{9}$ $\dfrac{1}{9}$ $\dfrac{1}{9}$ $\dfrac{1}{9}$ $\dfrac{1}{9}$ $\dfrac{1}{9}$

$\dfrac{1}{8}$ EIGHTHS

$\dfrac{1}{8}$ $\dfrac{1}{8}$ $\dfrac{1}{8}$ $\dfrac{1}{8}$ $\dfrac{1}{8}$ $\dfrac{1}{8}$ $\dfrac{1}{8}$ $\dfrac{1}{8}$

$\dfrac{1}{7}$ SEVENTHS

$\dfrac{1}{7}$ $\dfrac{1}{7}$ $\dfrac{1}{7}$ $\dfrac{1}{7}$ $\dfrac{1}{7}$ $\dfrac{1}{7}$ $\dfrac{1}{7}$

$\dfrac{1}{6}$ SIXTHS

$\dfrac{1}{6}$ $\dfrac{1}{6}$ $\dfrac{1}{6}$ $\dfrac{1}{6}$ $\dfrac{1}{6}$ $\dfrac{1}{6}$

KUMON

Skills for success in school and beyond!

Ace Fourth Grade

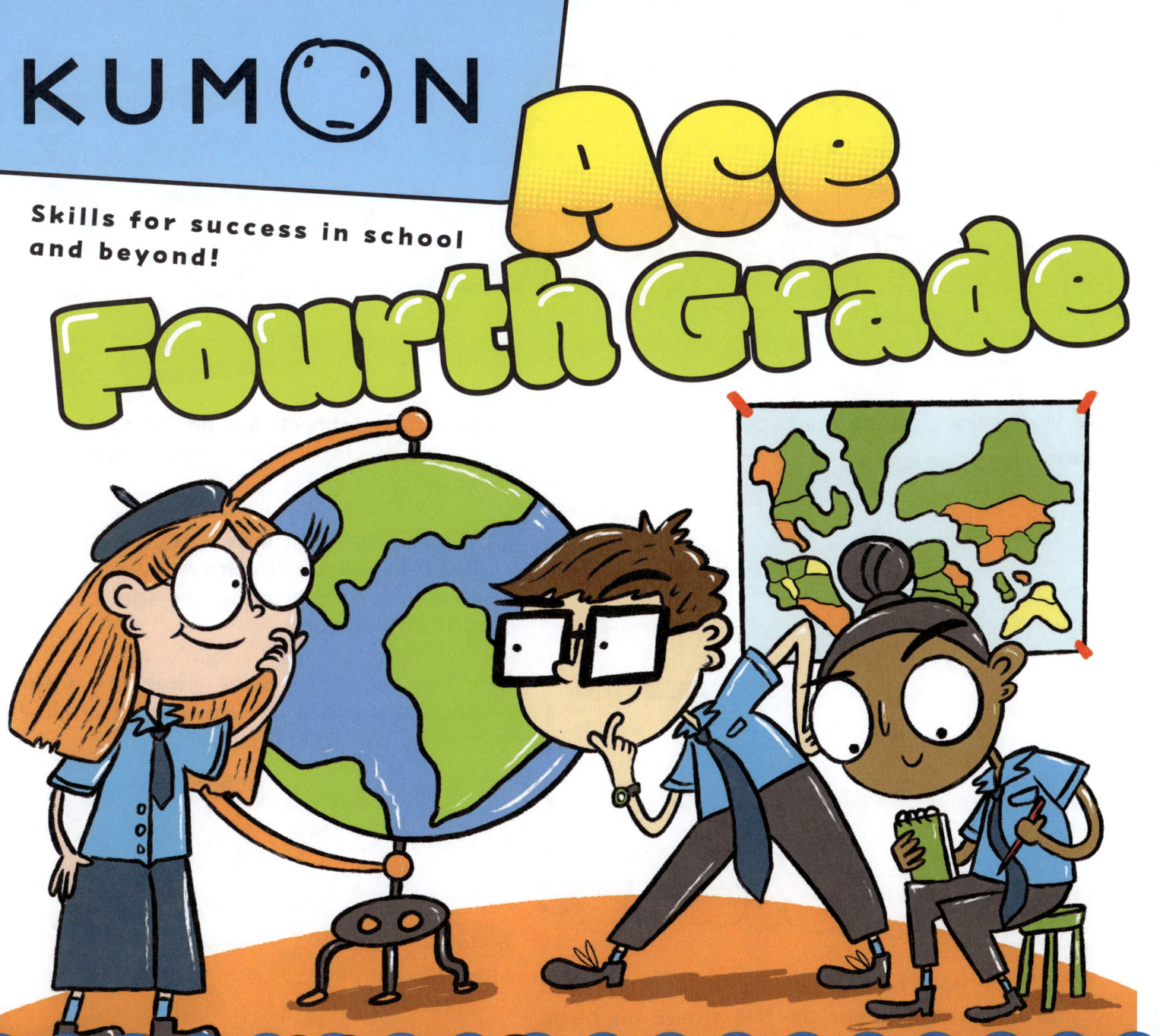

Table of Contents

Welcome to Kumon Ace Fourth Grade ... 2

Welcome to Kumon Ace Fourth Grade

❶ Write the date at the top of each page.

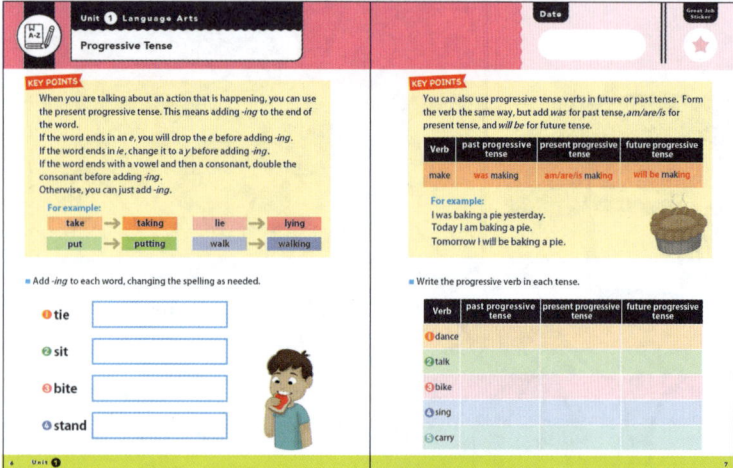

❷ Read the directions and Key Points on each page. Then complete each activity.

❸ When you complete a section, check your answers with the Answer Key in the back of the book. Try again if you got any wrong.

❹ When you are done checking your answers, place a "Great Job" sticker on the top of the page!

Let's study!

⭐ When you have finished studying each unit, put a sticker on the sheet on page 319.

⭐ When you have finished all of the units, place the largest sticker at the bottom of the same sheet.

⭐ Then have your parent or guardian sign the Certificate of Achievement and present it to you!

Cut out the study posters and hang them up for further study!

Unit **1** Table of Contents

Use this page to keep track of your progress throughout the book. Place a check mark in the box when you have completed a section.

Language Arts

Reading

Math

Science

Social Studies

Technology

Relative Pronouns and Adverbs

KEY POINTS

Relative pronouns link extra information, or subordinate clauses, to the main part of a sentence. Common relative pronouns include *who*, *whose*, *whom*, *which*, and *that*.

Relative pronoun	Meaning	Example
who	refers to a person, the subject of the sentence	This is the person *who* drove me to school.
whose	shows possession	She is the one *whose* backpack I borrowed.
whom	refers to a person, the object of a sentence	I told Lisa, the friend *whom* I was playing with.
which	refers to a thing or animal	This toy, *which* I was playing with yesterday, is now broken.
that	provides extra information about a noun	This is the book *that* I was reading at home.

■ Fill in the correct relative pronoun.

❶ Can we go to the store [   ] we saw yesterday?

❷ My coach is the one [   ] taught me that.

❸ I went with friends, one of [   ] is afraid of rollercoasters.

❹ The pencil, [   ] I got from my sister, is sparkly.

❺ Mary is the one [   ] sweater I wore to school.

Relative adverbs are adverbs that also add extra information to a sentence. Common relative adverbs are *where*, *when*, and *why*.

Relative pronoun	Meaning	Example
where	shows place	Do you remember where we parked the car?
when	shows time	That was when I didn't have a dog yet.
why	shows a reason	I'm not sure why she had to leave.

■ Fill in the correct relative pronoun.

❶ Is that _____ we were yesterday?

❷ Are you sure that is _____ we went to Ohio?

❸ I was having a hard time in math class. That was _____ I signed up for extra tutoring.

$$10 \div 2 =$$
$$20 + 7 =$$

Progressive Tense

When you are talking about an action that is happening, you can use the present progressive tense. This means adding *-ing* to the end of the word.

If the word ends in an *e*, you will drop the *e* before adding *-ing*.

If the word ends in *ie*, change it to a *y* before adding *-ing*.

If the word ends with a vowel and then a consonant, double the consonant before adding *-ing*.

Otherwise, you can just add *-ing*.

For example:

| take | → | taking | | lie | → | lying |
| put | → | putting | | walk | → | walking |

■ Add *-ing* to each word, changing the spelling as needed.

❶ tie

❷ sit

❸ bite

❹ stand

KEY POINTS

You can also use progressive tense verbs in future or past tense. Form the verb the same way, but add *was* for past tense, *am/are/is* for present tense, and *will be* for future tense.

Verb	past progressive tense	present progressive tense	future progressive tense
make	was making	am/are/is making	will be making

For example:

I was baking a pie yesterday.
Today I am baking a pie.
Tomorrow I will be baking a pie.

■ Write the progressive verb in each tense.

Verb	past progressive tense	present progressive tense	future progressive tense
❶ dance			
❷ talk			
❸ bike			
❹ sing			
❺ carry			

Commonly Misused Words

KEY POINTS

Some English words sound the same, but are spelled differently.

Word	Meaning	Example
There / They're / Their		
There	shows a place.	Let's go there!
They're	short for they are.	They're all very nice.
Their	shows possession.	This is their home.
To / Two / Too		
To	for something	This is the one to read.
Two	the number 2	I'd like two cookies, please.
Too	also	It's my birthday too!
Its / It's		
Its	shows possession	Our house is old, and its roof is leaking.
It's	short for it is	It's not fair!

■ Place the correct word in the blank

| there | they're | their |

❶ Are you sure it's over ⬚ ?

❷ Did you borrow ⬚ book?

❸ This is where ⬚ staying.

■ Place the correct word in the blank

| to | two | too |

❶ There are [   ] apples left over.

❷ Do you think this is [   ] sweet?

❸ Let's mail this [   ] her.

| its | it's |

❹ [   ] not my fault that she wasn't listening.

❺ I put the book on [   ] shelf.

KEY POINTS

Sometimes we use more than one adjective to describe a noun. The order of the adjectives matter. For example, we say the big red ball, not the red big ball. Let's look at some rules for ordering adjectives.

Number	three	some	all
Opinion	beautiful	cute	gross
Size	large	small	tiny
Age	new	old	ancient
Shape	round	square	boxy
Color	red	blue	white
Origin	American	Japanese	Italian
Material	glass	wood	plastic
Purpose	dining	shopping	travel

■ Let's say we want to use the adjective stinky, old, and cotton to describe a pair of socks. Which way is correct? Write a check (✓) or an x.

❶ My cotton stinky old socks.

❷ My stinky cotton old socks.

❸ My stinky old cotton socks.

■ Write a sentence describing each noun using the adjectives provided.

❶ doll, cute, tiny, new

_____

❷ cat, naughty, orange, young

_____

❸ shoes, leather, brown, old

_____

❹ book, cool, ancient, huge

_____

❺ house, small, yellow, wood

_____

Brain Break
Silly Story

■ Fill in the blanks to write a silly story.

On [_____], I called my friend
    day of the week

[_____]. "What are you doing?" I asked.
   name

"Oh, I'm just getting ready to [_____],"
                                    verb

she/he said. "Do you want to come with me to

[_____]?" I asked. "Only if I can bring
  place

[_____] and [_____] with me,"
  plural-noun   plural-noun

she answered. "That's no problem," I answered. "I will

be bringing [_____] [_____] and
              adjective   plural-noun

[_____] [_____].
  adjective   plural-noun

Mindfulness Break!

Praise is expressing admiration or approval of something or for someone's actions. It is important to praise ourselves, and also to praise people around us for their good actions. Praise is important, and how we praise each other and even ourselves makes all the difference!

■ Read each situation and write what you would say to praise each person.

1 "Congratulations, you aced your test!"

> **How would you praise yourself?**

2 Your best friend didn't make the soccer team they tried out for.

> **How would you praise them?**

3 Your younger sibling is afraid to go down the slide, but they try anyway.

> **How would you praise them?**

4 Your mom made your favorite dinner.

> **How would you praise her?**

5 Your pet dog learned a new trick on the first try!

> **How would you praise them?**

Story Elements 1

Learning to identify story elements in a text is an important skill to master. When reading a work of literature, non-fiction, or poetry, picking out key details like the main point, setting, and character descriptions can help you better understand the passage.

Almost every story you read will have the following five key elements: plot, setting, characters, conflict, and theme.

Story Elements

Plot refers to the events that happen in a story. It consists of an introduction, rising action, climax, falling action, and resolution.

Setting refers to where and when the story takes place.

Characters refer to who or what the story is about. Characters are most often people or animals. Characters say the dialogue and perform the actions in a story that moves a story's plot forward.

Conflict refers to the problem or challenge that drives the story.

Theme refers to the overall message or point the story is trying to tell. It usually must be inferred from events and dialogue in the story.

■ Read the story below and fill in the chart with the main story elements.

One sunny afternoon, Lila was playing in her backyard garden when she saw something small and brown nestled in between two of the large rose bushes. Lila moved to take a closer look and smiled in delight at what she saw. A tiny fawn asleep in the grass! Its fur was speckled with white spots and its big ears looked soft and fuzzy. Lila knelt down quietly to get a better look and the fawn suddenly opened its eyes. It wobbled and stood up in front of her. She had never seen an animal so beautiful up close before. She really wanted to reach out and pet its soft fur.

Lila then remembered that her grandmother had told her it was best to leave wild animals alone. Lila didn't want to scare the fawn so she moved away carefully. The fawn then turned and walked slowly to the edge of the garden where it met the forest. Before it disappeared, it looked back at Lila one last time, as if to say thank you for letting it be.
Lila smiled and gave the fawn a little wave. She felt so happy that she had seen something special. She knew the fawn would be safe with its family in the forest, but she would always remember the magical moment they had shared in the garden.

Plot

Setting	Characters	Conflict	Theme

Story Elements 2

KEY POINTS

The plot is what happens in a story. It usually has an introduction, rising action, climax, falling action, and resolution. Each part is essential to the story and helps the reader follow what is going on. Most stories tell each part in the order it happens in.

See an example below that shows the plot elements of "Goldilocks and the Three Bears."

Beginning or Introduction:
Goldilocks is walking in the forest and comes across the home of the three bears. The bears are not home so she goes inside.

Rising Action:
Goldilocks tries their porridge, but Papa Bear's is too hot and Mama Bear's is too cold. She tries Baby Bear's and its just right. After eating the porridge, Goldilocks decides to take a nap. She tries Papa Bear's bed, but it's too hard. She tries Mama Bear's bed, but it's too soft. Finally, she tries Baby Bear's bed and it is just right. So she falls asleep.

Climax:
The Bears return home and find someone has been in their house!

Falling Action:
Papa Bear says, "Someone has been eating my porridge."
Mama Bear says, "Someone has been eating my porridge."
Baby Bear says, "Someone has been eating my porridge and its all gone!
Papa Bear says, "Someone has been sleeping in my bed."
Mama Bear says, "Someone has been sleeping in my bed."
Baby Bear says, "Someone has been sleeping in my bed and she's still here!"

Resolution or Ending:
Baby Bear finds Goldilocks asleep in his bed! She wakes up and sees the bears. This frightens her and she runs from their home.

■ Read the passage and fill in the chart with the five main parts of the plot.

It was Maverick's first baseball game, and he was excited but nervous. Finally, it was his turn to bat. He stepped up to the plate, gripping the bat tightly. The pitcher threw the ball, and Maverick swung as hard as he could. He missed. Maverick felt disappointed, but he knew he still had two more tries. The second pitch was thrown too wide and Maverick swung anyway. A second strike. The pitcher threw a final pitch and Maverick swung and missed a third time. He struck out. He walked back to the bench with his head low, even though his teammates were patting his back and telling him it was okay. He felt like he let his team down.

Maverick didn't want to give up. Every day after school, he practiced batting in his backyard. He asked his dad to help him. He worked on his timing, his stance, and on keeping his eye on the ball. When the next game came around, Maverick felt ready to try again. This time, he felt more confident when he was called up

to bat. The pitcher threw the first ball, and this time, Maverick made contact! The ball flew into the air and over the pitcher's head. Maverick ran to first base as fast as he could. He could hear his teammates shouting as he made it safely. Maverick turned back to them and smiled. He was happy his hard work had paid off!

Plot Chart

Beginning	Rising Action	Climax	Falling Action	Resolution

Story Elements 3

Characters are who or what the story is about. Characters are most often people or animals. Characters say the dialogue and perform the actions that move a story's plot forward. There are usually main characters who are most important to the story and side characters who interact with the main characters.

■ Read the story and list the characters.

Noah practiced for the last few weeks and today was the day he had been waiting for: tryouts for his school baseball team! Noah really wanted to earn the position of first base. He got to the field early to stretch and put his gear on. When he got to the field, he saw Coach Dan was already setting up the bases. Noah's best friend Riley was also there. Noah gave him a wave and the two boys warmed up together.

After a little while, more kids showed up for the tryouts. Noah recognized Dillon, who was on the team last year. This made Noah nervous because Dillon also played first base. "Don't worry," Riley said to Noah. "You can throw way harder than him! You can do this!" With Riley's confident words in his ears, Noah jogged to first base and waited. A few of the other boys took turns at bat and hit some balls far into left field. Noah stood patiently waiting for his chance.

The next batter came up to the plate and swung. Suddenly, the ball was in the air heading straight for Noah. He ran backwards a few feet and tipped his head up to spot the ball. He raised his glove and to his surprised the ball land right in the middle with a thud. Noah couldn't help but smile. He quickly ran to the base and tagged the batter out! He threw the ball back to the pitcher and gave his friend Riley a thumbs up. Noah realized that he would have fun whether or not he played first. He made the team and was happy to play third base alongside his friends.

❶ Main character(s)

_____

❷ Side character(s)

_____

■ Read the passage and identify three actions the main character takes that help move the story along.

One summer afternoon Emma and her brother Luke were exploring the woods behind their new house. They had only lived there for a few weeks and loved finding new paths and places to explore. As they walked deeper through the trees, Emma spotted something shiny on the ground. She picked it up. It was a small, rusty key. "I wonder what this could open, " Emma said to her brother. Luke grinned back at her. "Let's see if we can find out!" he said.
They continued to follow the path for several minutes. Then Emma saw something up ahead through the trees. It was an old wooden shed partially covered in creeping vines. The windows were covered in dust and cobwebs. Emma excitedly tried the key she found in the lock and to her and Luke's surprise the door opened!
She pushed the door open further with a creak. Inside she saw shelves full of dusty books and boxes. There were also boxes on the floor that held tools and garden supplies. Luke even found a box that contained dusty old maps! Emma was excited by this find. "Maybe one of these maps will lead to a treasure!" she said. Luke laughed, but said, "We should try and find it tomorrow!" Even if they didn't find a treasure, Emma and Luke knew they had found something special. They promised to keep the shed a secret between them and use it as their own hidden clubhouse.

❶ _____

_____

❷ _____

_____

❸ _____

_____

Story Elements 4

KEY POINTS

Theme refers to the overall message or point the story is trying to tell. It usually must be inferred from events and dialogue in the story.

Some examples of themes are:

"Never judge a book by its cover."

"Even the smallest person can make a difference."

"Actions speak louder than words."

"It's okay to be different."

Finding the Theme

1 Look at the main character's actions. Are their motives good or bad? What are they trying to accomplish?

2 What results do their actions have? Are they happy or unhappy? How do the other characters feel?

3 Does the character change at the end of the story?

■ Read the story and answer the questions about the theme.

Olivia had always dreamed of playing the role of Wendy in her school's performance of Peter Pan. She practiced every day, imagining herself on stage as the star. But when the cast list was posted, Olivia was shocked to see her best friend Zarah had gotten the part of Wendy instead. Olivia felt angry and upset. She didn't understand why Zarah was chosen over her. Instead of congratulating her friend, Olivia started saying mean things and said Zarah only got the part because the teacher liked her. Zarah was hurt by Olivia's actions and she said she didn't want to talk to her again!

After a few days, Olivia missed Zarah and began to feel bad about the things she said. She realized it wasn't right to be mean to her friend just because she was upset. Olivia realized hurting Zarah didn't make her feel any better about losing the part in the play. So she decided to apologizes to Zarah.

"I'm sorry," Olivia said to her friend. "I was upset and jealous and I shouldn't have said those mean things to you." Zarah smiled and forgave Olivia. She gave her friend a big hug. From then on, Olivia cheered for Zarah on stage. She learned that true friends support each other no matter what.

❶ What is the overall theme of this story?

_____

❷ Write one or two lines from the story that support the theme.

_____

_____

❸ What can you learn from the theme and use in your own life?

_____

Brain Break
Plot it Out!

■ Choose your favorite book or even movie and see if you can identify all the story elements!

Plot

Setting

Characters

Conflict

Theme

Mindfulness Break!

KEY POINTS

Mindfulness is about listening to your body and your feelings. It can help you know when you are happy, stressed, excited or worried.

Worrying is when you think a lot about something that makes you scared, nervous, or anxious. It is important to be aware of when you feel worried so you can try and stay calm or overcome that feeling.

Worrying is normal. Everyone worries! You might worry about a spelling test or going to a new place for the first time or going to the doctor's office.

One way to be mindful of your worries and to keep them controlled is to practice writing them down.

■ Write down your worries in the box.

Addition with 2-digit and 3-digit Numbers

■ Add.

1
$$\begin{array}{r} 124 \\ + 13 \\ \hline \end{array}$$

2
$$\begin{array}{r} 365 \\ + 24 \\ \hline \end{array}$$

3
$$\begin{array}{r} 732 \\ + 56 \\ \hline \end{array}$$

4
$$\begin{array}{r} \overset{1}{1}36 \\ + 24 \\ \hline \end{array}$$

5
$$\begin{array}{r} 315 \\ + 36 \\ \hline \end{array}$$

6
$$\begin{array}{r} 527 \\ + 54 \\ \hline \end{array}$$

7
$$\begin{array}{r} \overset{1}{1}83 \\ + 34 \\ \hline \end{array}$$

8
$$\begin{array}{r} 256 \\ + 51 \\ \hline \end{array}$$

9
$$\begin{array}{r} 93 \\ +423 \\ \hline \end{array}$$

10
$$\begin{array}{r} \overset{11}{1}67 \\ + 59 \\ \hline \end{array}$$

11
$$\begin{array}{r} 249 \\ + 64 \\ \hline \end{array}$$

12
$$\begin{array}{r} 675 \\ + 78 \\ \hline \end{array}$$

■ Add.

① 253
  +514

② 326
  +341

③ 117
  +762

④ 1̇66
  +125

⑤ 428
  +246

⑥ 163
  +619

⑦ 2̇51
  +153

⑧ 342
  +286

⑨ 185
  +793

⑩ 2̇8̇4
  +227

⑪ 578
  +268

⑫ 437
  +496

Addition with 3-digit and 4-digit Numbers

■ Add.

① $\begin{array}{r} 1353 \\ +\ 142 \\ \hline \end{array}$ ② $\begin{array}{r} 2426 \\ +\ 142 \\ \hline \end{array}$ ③ $\begin{array}{r} 4157 \\ +\ 612 \\ \hline \end{array}$

④ $\begin{array}{r} 1376 \\ +\ 315 \\ \hline \end{array}$ ⑤ $\begin{array}{r} 2563 \\ +\ 227 \\ \hline \end{array}$ ⑥ $\begin{array}{r} 6445 \\ +\ 129 \\ \hline \end{array}$

⑦ $\begin{array}{r} 3543 \\ +\ 188 \\ \hline \end{array}$ ⑧ $\begin{array}{r} 286 \\ +6137 \\ \hline \end{array}$ ⑨ $\begin{array}{r} 5279 \\ +\ 362 \\ \hline \end{array}$

⑩ $\begin{array}{r} 5687 \\ +\ 548 \\ \hline \end{array}$ ⑪ $\begin{array}{r} 3424 \\ +\ 878 \\ \hline \end{array}$ ⑫ $\begin{array}{r} 375 \\ +7625 \\ \hline \end{array}$

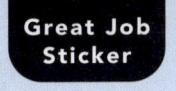

■ Add.

① 3415
  +1360

② 1256
  +7632

③ 4512
  +3365

④ 2137
  +2135

⑤ 6418
  +1209

⑥ 5326
  +3117

⑦ 1168
  +3178

⑧ 2342
  +6569

⑨ 3285
  +3467

⑩ 4328
  +1992

⑪ 3549
  +2582

⑫ 6418
  +1795

Subtraction with 3-digit and 2-digit Numbers

■ Subtract.

①
$$\begin{array}{r} 147 \\ -35 \\ \hline \end{array}$$

②
$$\begin{array}{r} 236 \\ -14 \\ \hline \end{array}$$

③
$$\begin{array}{r} 587 \\ -42 \\ \hline \end{array}$$

④
$$\begin{array}{r} 1\,\overset{4}{\cancel{5}}\,\overset{13}{\cancel{3}} \\ -26 \\ \hline \end{array}$$

⑤
$$\begin{array}{r} 247 \\ -29 \\ \hline \end{array}$$

⑥
$$\begin{array}{r} 736 \\ -18 \\ \hline \end{array}$$

⑦
$$\begin{array}{r} \overset{3}{\cancel{4}}\,\overset{16}{\cancel{7}}\,\overset{12}{\cancel{2}} \\ -88 \\ \hline \end{array}$$

⑧
$$\begin{array}{r} 563 \\ -95 \\ \hline \end{array}$$

⑨
$$\begin{array}{r} 284 \\ -87 \\ \hline \end{array}$$

⑩
$$\begin{array}{r} 1\,\overset{14}{\cancel{5}}\,\overset{12}{\cancel{2}} \\ -76 \\ \hline \end{array}$$

⑪
$$\begin{array}{r} 114 \\ -25 \\ \hline \end{array}$$

⑫
$$\begin{array}{r} 176 \\ -89 \\ \hline \end{array}$$

■ Subtract.

❶   352
    − 141

❷   486
    − 363

❸   725
    − 212

❹   2 17
    4 3̶ 7̶
    − 1 1 9

❺   685
    − 258

❻   293
    − 174

❼   2 13 16
    3̶ 4̶ 6̶
    − 1 7 8

❽   527
    − 289

❾   763
    − 364

❿   1 14 11
    2̶ 5̶ 1̶
    − 1 6 5

⓫   637
    − 548

⓬   843
    − 776

Subtraction with 4-digit and 3-digit Numbers

■ Subtract.

①
$$\begin{array}{r} 1328 \\ -\ 216 \\ \hline \end{array}$$

②
$$\begin{array}{r} 2567 \\ -\ 351 \\ \hline \end{array}$$

③
$$\begin{array}{r} 5612 \\ -\ 402 \\ \hline \end{array}$$

④
$$\begin{array}{r} 1\overset{3}{\cancel{3}}\overset{16}{\cancel{4}}6 \\ -\ 118 \\ \hline \end{array}$$

⑤
$$\begin{array}{r} 3524 \\ -\ 207 \\ \hline \end{array}$$

⑥
$$\begin{array}{r} 7241 \\ -\ 119 \\ \hline \end{array}$$

⑦
$$\begin{array}{r} 2\overset{3}{\cancel{4}}\overset{12}{\cancel{3}}\overset{17}{\cancel{7}} \\ -\ 168 \\ \hline \end{array}$$

⑧
$$\begin{array}{r} 4516 \\ -\ 349 \\ \hline \end{array}$$

⑨
$$\begin{array}{r} 6372 \\ -\ 296 \\ \hline \end{array}$$

⑩
$$\begin{array}{r} \overset{2}{\cancel{3}}\overset{11}{\cancel{2}}\overset{10}{\cancel{1}}\overset{14}{\cancel{4}} \\ -\ 328 \\ \hline \end{array}$$

⑪
$$\begin{array}{r} 2561 \\ -\ 793 \\ \hline \end{array}$$

⑫
$$\begin{array}{r} 1394 \\ -\ 596 \\ \hline \end{array}$$

■ Subtract.

①
```
  3458
- 1134
_____
```

②
```
  2876
- 1425
_____
```

③
```
  4931
- 3730
_____
```

④
```
    6 11
  26 7̸ 1̸
- 1437
_____
```

⑤
```
  4438
- 2119
_____
```

⑥
```
  6553
- 5134
_____
```

⑦
```
  4 17 14
  3 5̸ 8̸ 4̸
- 1298
_____
```

⑧
```
  7236
- 4157
_____
```

⑨
```
  8451
- 4275
_____
```

⑩
```
  2 16 10 16
  3̸ 7̸ 1̸ 6̸
- 1857
_____
```

⑪
```
  5137
- 2469
_____
```

⑫
```
  2345
- 1586
_____
```

Word Problems

■ Answer the following word problems.

❶ A community garden needs to buy supplies for the upcoming planting season. They have raised $3,235 from a local charity, and $2,146 from a plant sale. How much do they have in total to spend on supplies?

Ans. $ _____

❷ An animal shelter received $1,567 in donations from a local fundraiser, and $4,165 from a campaign. How much did the shelter receive in total?

Ans. $ _____

❸ A local band sold 5,368 tickets for their concert. Later, they sold an additional 2,689 tickets. How many tickets did they sell in total?

Ans. _____ tickets

4 A family's water tank held 2,542 gallons of water at the beginning of the week. By the end of the week, they used 1,028 gallons. How many gallons of water were left in the tank?

Ans.   gallons

5 Emma was in a 3,865-meter race, but she had to stop after 2,677 meters to take a break. How many meters does she have left to finish the race?

Ans.   meters

6 The library originally had 4,878 children's books. At the end of the day, 3,989 books were left on the shelves. How many books were borrowed that day?

Ans.   books

Brain Break
Place Value Quiz

■ Circle the number described by the text.

❶ The number that has 3 in the thousands place.

> **3,246**   1,359   7,830

❷ The number that has 5 in the ten-thousands place.

> 50,139   15,267   83,542

❸ The number that has 2 in the hundred-thousands place.

> 342,081   926,185   214,507

④ The number that has 8 in the ten-thousands place, and 7 in the tens place.

84,170   86,753   28,976

⑤ The number that has 1 in the hundred-thousands place, and 0 in the ones place.

145,302   186,570   329,150

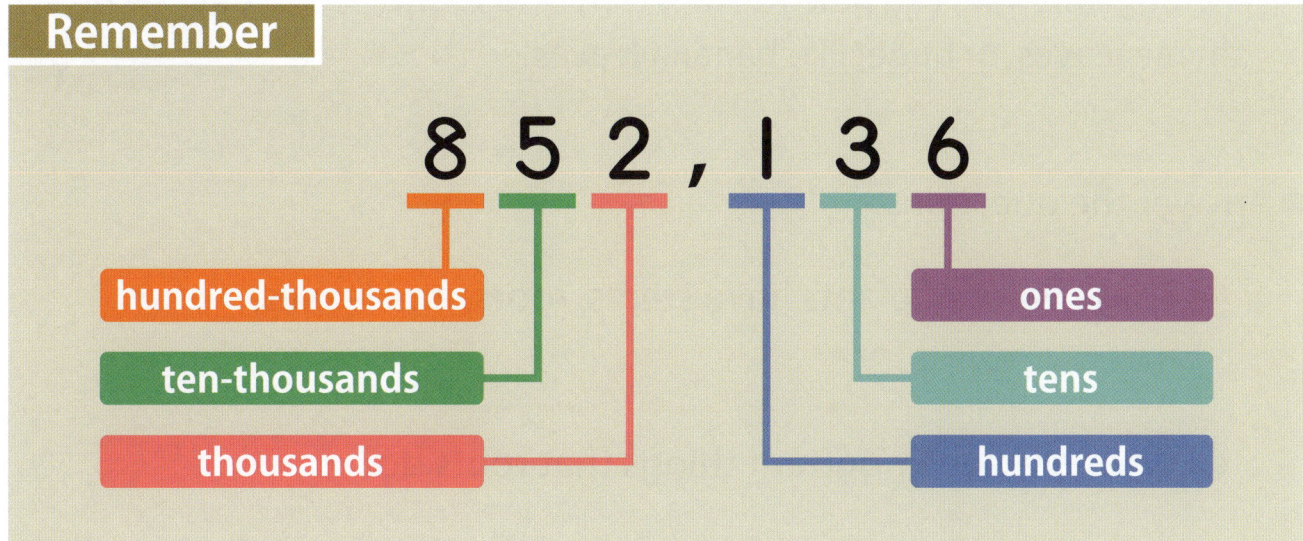

Remember

8 5 2 , 1 3 6

hundred-thousands
ten-thousands
thousands
ones
tens
hundreds

Living Things: Plants

KEY POINTS

Plants are either vascular or nonvascular. Nonvascular plants do not have roots, stems, or leaves. Mosses and algae are nonvascular. Nonvascular plants are usually small and typically grow in damp places where they do not need roots to reach down to find water. Vascular plants can move water and food from one part of the plant to another. They have roots, stems, and leaves. Many of them produce flowers and fruits. Maple trees, rose bushes, and holly bushes are examples of vascular plants.

Vascular plants have different parts that each have a role in helping them grow. Roots take in water and minerals that the plant uses to survive. They also help plants stay in place, even when there is strong wind or rain. Some plants' roots reach deep into the soil. Others are shallow. This depends on what is needed in a plant's habitat. Stems move water and food from one part of the plant to another. They often make plants stand upright, which can help them get more sunlight. Leaves absorb sunlight and water that is in the air. Leaves turn sunlight into food for the plant through a process called photosynthesis. Leaves can be long and thin, like pine needles, tiny and round, like thyme leaves, or huge, like banana leaves!

■ Answer the questions.

❶ These types of plants have stems, roots, and leaves.

_____

❷ What are two important things that roots do?

_____

■ Fill in the blanks with the correct words.

1 Plants that do not have roots, stems, or leaves are

 .

2 Plants that do have roots, stems and leaves are

 .

3 Plants with roots can move _____ from the soil

into their stems.

4 A plant's leaves take in _____ and

_____ to help it make food.

5 Plants use _____ to turn sunlight into food.

6 _____ help plants take water from the soil and

also holds them in place.

Plants Needs

KEY POINTS

Plants need water, sunlight, and air to grow and thrive. Most plants also need soil to grow. Plants use water to grow and to produce food. They get water through their roots and through their leaves.

Plants turn sunlight into food. They use some of this food to grow and reproduce. Plants need air. They take carbon dioxide from air and use it, along with water and sunlight, to make food. They release oxygen into the air. Humans and other animals need oxygen to survive. We breathe in oxygen and breathe out carbon dioxide. Plants and animals rely on each other to produce and receive the oxygen or carbon dioxide they need.

Some plants grow on hard surfaces like rocks or other plants and do not need soil. Most plants need soil. They get water and minerals from the soil. Minerals from the soil mix into the water, so when roots take water from the ground, they take minerals, too. Plants need space to thrive. If they are too crowded, they will not all have enough soil, water, minerals, or sunlight.

■ Answer the questions.

❶ What three things do all plants need to grow and thrive?

_____

❷ Plants take in [   ] from the air and release

[   ] into the air.

❸ True or false: All plants need soil to grow. [   ]

■ Fill in the diagram with the correct words.

carbon dioxide	water	oxygen	sunlight	minerals

1

2

3

4

5

①

②

③

④

⑤

How Plants Reproduce

KEY POINTS

Plants reproduce, or make more plants, using seeds or spores. Seeds and spores are both small and grow from each plant. Eventually they come off of the plants and can grow into new plants. Nonvascular plants like mosses, which do not have true stems, leaves, or roots, make spores to reproduce, as do some vascular plants like ferns. Spores are smaller and simpler than seeds. Spores can be spread by wind, water, or animals.

Most vascular plants reproduce by creating seeds. To get seeds to grow, many vascular plants need to go through a process called pollination. They often grow flowers that attract pollinators like insects and hummingbirds to pollinate them. Some flowers are pollinated by the wind, and others are pollinated by insects and hummingbirds.

Plants might attract pollinators with a particular smell or color, or even by looking like an insect themselves! Many flowers have nectar that pollinators can collect as food. Pollinators pollinate by bringing pollen from one flower to another. Most plants need the pollen of another plant in order to create seeds.

Once they are pollinated, flowers produce seeds that can eventually grow into new plants. Some seeds, like dandelion seeds, are tiny and blow away in the wind. Some plants grow seeds inside of fruits, like cherries, which can be distributed by animals that eat them. Some plants, like pine trees, produce seeds inside of cones instead of fruits.

■ Answer the questions.

❶ Do nonvascular plants reproduce using seeds or spores?

_____

❷ How can plants attract pollinators?

_____

❸ How do insects and hummingbirds pollinate plants?

_____

Date

■ Write true or false for each statement.

❶ All plants reproduce using seeds.

❷ Nonvascular plants reproduce using spores.

❸ Flowers are the part of a plant that makes the seeds.

❹ Many vascular plants need pollinators like bees or birds to help them reproduce.

❺ Plants only use the pollen from a single plant to be pollenated.

Plants Features for Survival

KEY POINTS

Plants have evolved to have many features that help them survive and thrive. These features can stop predators from eating them and help them deal with different kinds of weather. Prickles, spines, and thorns are all plant defenses. They can hurt animals that touch or eat them. Prickles are spikes on stems or branches, like on thistles' stems. Spines are tiny, spiky leaves like on cacti. Thorns are pointy stems or branches, like on hawthorn bushes.

Some plants have leaves or fruits that are poisonous. Some berries that are poisonous to humans are safe for birds to eat. Some caterpillars eat poisonous leaves that don't harm them but make them poisonous to predators that might otherwise eat them.

In places with cold winters, deciduous plants lose their leaves in the fall. If they didn't, the leaves would freeze and the liquid inside would burst the leaves' veins. The leaves would not be able to create food through photosynthesis, but the trees would still use energy to keep the leaves. So, deciduous plants drop their leaves in the fall to save energy. Evergreen plants like hollies and pines have thick, waxy coverings on their leaves that protect them from the cold, so they keep their leaves all year.

Plants have many adaptations to help them thrive in their particular climates. Rainforest plants, which get a lot of rain, often have waxy leaves that repel water so that the plants do not rot. Desert plants often have thick, waxy coverings on their leaves and stems to keep water inside of the plants. Leaves in places with strong sun often have tiny hairs to protect the leaves from the intense heat.

■ Answer the questions.

❶ Why do some plants have thorns, prickles, or spines?

_____

❷ Why do deciduous plants drop their leaves in the fall?

_____

❸ Why do rainforest plants have waxy leaves?

_____

■ Match the plant features with how they help the plant survive.

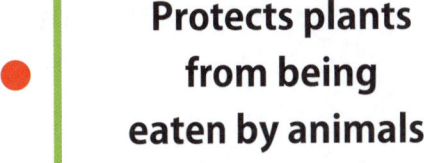

**Protects plants
from being
eaten by animals.**

**Protects plants
from too much
water and rot.**

**Protects plants losing
all their energy
in cold winters.**

**Are protected
from the cold by a thick
waxy cover.**

**Protects plants from
being eaten by animals
by making them sick.**

Brain Break
Science Journal 1

Create a new plant.

❶ What would it look like?

_____

_____

❷ What defenses does it have?

_____

❸ Is it vascular or nonvascular?

_____

❹ How does it reproduce?

_____

_____

Art Break!

■ Draw your new plant!

The American Revolution

KEY POINTS

The first thirteen states in the United States were previously colonies of Great Britain, starting in the early 1600s. By the 1760s and 1770s, many colonists were upset with Great Britain's rule.

To pay for the expensive French and Indian War (1754-1763), Great Britain imposed taxes and tariffs on the colonists. Colonists were angry that they had to pay these taxes without being represented in the British Parliament. They were also angry that the British government did not allow them to settle west of the Appalachian Mountains. The British government wanted to avoid more conflicts with the indigenous people who had been forced to move there.

In 1770, British soldiers shot at colonists who were protesting against British taxes in Boston, Massachusetts. They killed five people. This was called the Boston Massacre. It was difficult to unite the Thirteen Colonies, but they eventually banded together. Committees of correspondence met in towns and counties, writing letters to other groups about ways to resist British rule. Provincial congresses represented bigger areas, sometimes entire colonies. They helped gather money and recruit soldiers. The Continental Congress included representatives from all thirteen colonies. They made big decisions about resisting the British and fighting against them. George Washington was chosen as commander of the Continental Army.

The Revolutionary War officially started on April 19, 1775 with the Battles of Lexington and Concord in Massachusetts. The British army tried to take some of the revolutionaries' weapons. The revolutionaries were warned by Paul Revere and beat the British in the battles. On July 4, 1776, the Continental Congress signed the Declaration of Independence, written by Thomas Jefferson. It declared that the Thirteen Colonies were independent. The British had more weapons and better trained armies. The colonists knew the land better and were more motivated to win. In 1778, the French decided to help the colonists. The war's last battle was fought in Yorktown, Virginia, with the colonists and French beating the British. The British surrendered at the Battle of Yorktown on October 19, 1781. There were long negotiations between the colonists, Great Britain, France, and Spain about the control of North America. An agreement was made, officially ending the war on September 3, 1783, with the Treaty of Paris.

■ **Answer the questions.**

❶ Name two reasons the colonists were protesting again the British.

❷ Which European country helped the Thirteen Colonies win the Revolutionary War?

■ **Fill in the blanks to complete the statements.**

1 Great Britain imposed more taxes on the American colonies to pay

for the costs of [ ].

2 Five American colonists were shot by British soldiers while protesting

in Massachusetts. This was later called the [ ].

3 The [ ] was made up of a group of

representatives from all 13 colonies who made decisions about how

to fight the British at the start of the war.

4 These battles began the Revolutionary War: [ ]

and [ ].

5 On July 4th, 1776, the Continental Congress signed the

[ ], which declared the colonies independent.

6 The final battle of the Revolutionary War was fought in

[ ].

7 The war officially ended on Sept. 3rd, 1783 with the signing of the

[ ].

The American Civil War

The American Civil War was fought from 1861 to 1865 between the northern and southern states of the United States. Abraham Lincoln was elected president in 1860. His party, the Republicans, opposed, or were against, slavery, especially in new states that were being created in the western part of the country, like Kansas. Southern states allowed slavery and used the labor of enslaved Black people.

Powerful white southern slave owners thought that Lincoln would abolish, or get rid of, slavery in the whole country. The fear of slavery being outlawed caused eleven southern states seceded from, or officially left, the United States in 1861. They chose Richmond, Virginia as their capital and Jefferson Davis as their president. The remaining northern and border states were called the Union, with their capital in Washington, DC.

The first battle of the war was fought at Fort Sumter in South Carolina on April 12, 1861. The Confederacy captured the fort. Some other major battles were the Battle of Bull Run in Manassas, Virginia, which the Confederacy won, the Battle of Shiloh in Tennessee, which the Union won, and the Battle of Gettysburg in Pennsylvania, which the Union won. General Robert E. Lee led the Confederate army. General Ulysses S. Grant was eventually made the leader of the Union army.

On January 1, 1863, President Lincoln issued the Emancipation Proclamation, which said that all enslaved people in the Confederacy were free. Lincoln believed this would help the Union win the war because freed slaves would join the Union army. His plan worked and many of them fought for the Union. However, the Emancipation Proclamation did not free people in Union states that had slavery, like Maryland and Kentucky.

On April 9, 1865, Lee surrendered to Grant in Appomattox, Virginia. Grant had captured Richmond, and Lee had few soldiers or supplies left for fighting. Fighting continued in some parts of the country, but it was all over by the end of May 1865. Eventually, the states that had seceded rejoined the United States.

On June 19, 1865, the last enslaved people in the United States were freed when the news of the Emancipation Proclamation was brought to Texas. Today, the United States celebrates Juneteenth in honor of this event.

■ **Fill in the blanks to complete the statements.**

❶ The southern states that seceded from the United States called their

new country ☐ .

❷ ☐ led the Union army and ☐

led the Confederate army.

■ Write true or false for each statement.

❶ Abraham Lincoln was the president during the American Civil War.

❷ The southern states seceded or split from the northern states out of fear that President Lincoln would abolish slavery in the whole country.

❸ Jefferson Davis was elected president of the northern states during the Civil War.

❹ The northern states called themselves the Union and the southern states became the Confederacy during the Civil War.

❺ General Ulysses S. Grant was the leader of the Confederate Army.

❻ The Union won the Civil War and the Confederate states rejoined the country.

❼ The Emancipation Proclamation freed slaves throughout the entire United States.

World War I or The Great War

KEY POINTS

World War I was fought between 1914 and 1918. At the time, it was called The Great War. It was the biggest war ever fought at that point. World War I was fought between the Allies and the Central Powers. France, Great Britain, Russia, Italy, Japan, and the United States were the principal members of the Allies. Austria-Hungary, Germany, Bulgaria, the Ottoman Empire were the Central Powers. The war began with the murder of Archduke Francis Ferdinand, the Austro-Hungarian emperor's nephew, on June 28, 1914. He was killed in Bosnia and Herzegovina, which was controlled by Austria-Hungary, by someone who wanted Bosnia and Herzegovina to be part of Serbia instead of part of the Austrian-Hungarian Empire.

After this, Austria-Hungary declared war on Serbia. Russia, France, and Great Britain agreed to help Serbia and Germany agreed to help Austria-Hungary. Eventually the Ottoman Empire and Bulgaria joined Germany and Austria-Hungary.

World War I was fought on the Western Front along the border between Germany and France, on the Eastern Front along the border between Germany and Russia, and in the Middle East in the Ottoman Empire. On the Western Front, both sides dug trenches to protect themselves from the other side. Many people died but neither side made very much progress. Both sides used new technologies to try to win. The Germans invented and used poison gas against the Allies. The Allies created tanks that could drive over trenches. The Germans used warplanes to bomb Great Britain. The British created special guns that could shoot down warplanes. The Germans used submarines, also called U-boats, to sink ships. They sank the Allies' military ships but also ships with supplies and with civilians, or people who were not in the military.

The United States stayed out of the war until April 6, 1917, when it declared war on Germany. President Woodrow Wilson and Congress decided to declare war because Germany sank so many of the United States' ships. By 1917, Germany, Austria-Hungary, France, and the United Kingdom were all exhausted and running out of soldiers. Russia left the war in 1917 because the Russian Revolution changed who was in power. So, when the United States sent millions of soldiers and lots of supplies to Europe to fight against the Central Powers in 1917 and 1918, it made a huge difference. The Central Powers started surrendering in September 1918. The Germans were the last Central Power to surrender on November 11, 1918.

■ **Answer the questions.**

❶ Who were the main members of the Allied Powers?

❷ Why did the United States join the war on the side of the Allies?

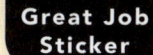

■ Use the Key Points to fill in the timeline.

1914

This event was the start of World War I.

①

1917

This country, that was part of the Central Powers left the war due to a revolution in its own borders.

②

April 6, the 1917

This was the day the United States joined the war by declaring war on Germany for:

③

Sept. 1918

The US sent millions of soldiers to fight in Europe and the

④

began to surrender.

This country was the last to surrender to the Allied Powers in November 1918.

⑤

1918

The Great Depression

The Great Depression was a period in US history from 1929 to 1941, when the economy of the country was very bad. It started in the United States but spread to most parts of the world. During the Great Depression, many people lost their jobs and couldn't get new ones. Many people did not have enough money for food, shelter, and other essentials.

In September and October 1929, prices of stocks fell. A lot of people had money invested in stocks, or small pieces of ownership of part of a company. The value of the stocks dropped very low and people lost a lot of money. Banks also lost money in the stock market crash. People worried about their money and tried to get it all out of the banks, but the banks didn't have enough to pay the people back. Many people lost all of their savings. Nowadays, the federal government protects people's savings in banks, but that was not the case in 1929.

People had less money, so they bought fewer goods and services. Because of that, many businesses closed, so people working there lost their jobs. They did not have money to buy goods and services, so the problem got worse and worse. There were also bad droughts in the United States' Great Plains area. It was so dry that it was called the Dust Bowl. Without rain, farms could not grow food. Farmers could not earn money either.

Herbert Hoover was the president when the Great Depression started. People thought he did not do enough to help them recover. In 1932, they elected Franklin Delano Roosevelt instead. He created the New Deal, a plan which gave jobs to people doing things that helped the country. For example, the New Deal made jobs for people to build roads and highways throughout the country. It also created the National Parks system and gave people jobs working in government owned parks.  It created programs that give money to people when they are out of work, like unemployment, or retired, like Social Security. It also made more rules for banks so that people would not lose their money in the future. The New Deal helped many people, but the Great Depression did not end until the United States entered World War II in 1941. The war required a lot of workers to make weapons and other goods, so there were jobs for everyone.

■ **Answer the questions.**

❶ What caused the Great Depression?

❷ What was the name of President Roosevelt's plan to help bring the country out of the Great Depression?

■ Match the Cause to the Effect using information from the Key Points.

Cause

Effect

The price of stocks fell and people and banks lost a lot of money.

People were able to get new jobs building roads and working for government parks.

Long droughts occurred in the mid-west of the United States.

The Great Depression began.

People lost their jobs.

The Great Depression ended because many jobs were created to make weapons and other goods.

The New Deal was created.

People had less money to buy things and businesses closed.

World War II started.

Farmers were unable to grow crops and make money to live.

Brain Break
Crossword Puzzle

■ Use the clues to fill in the puzzle.

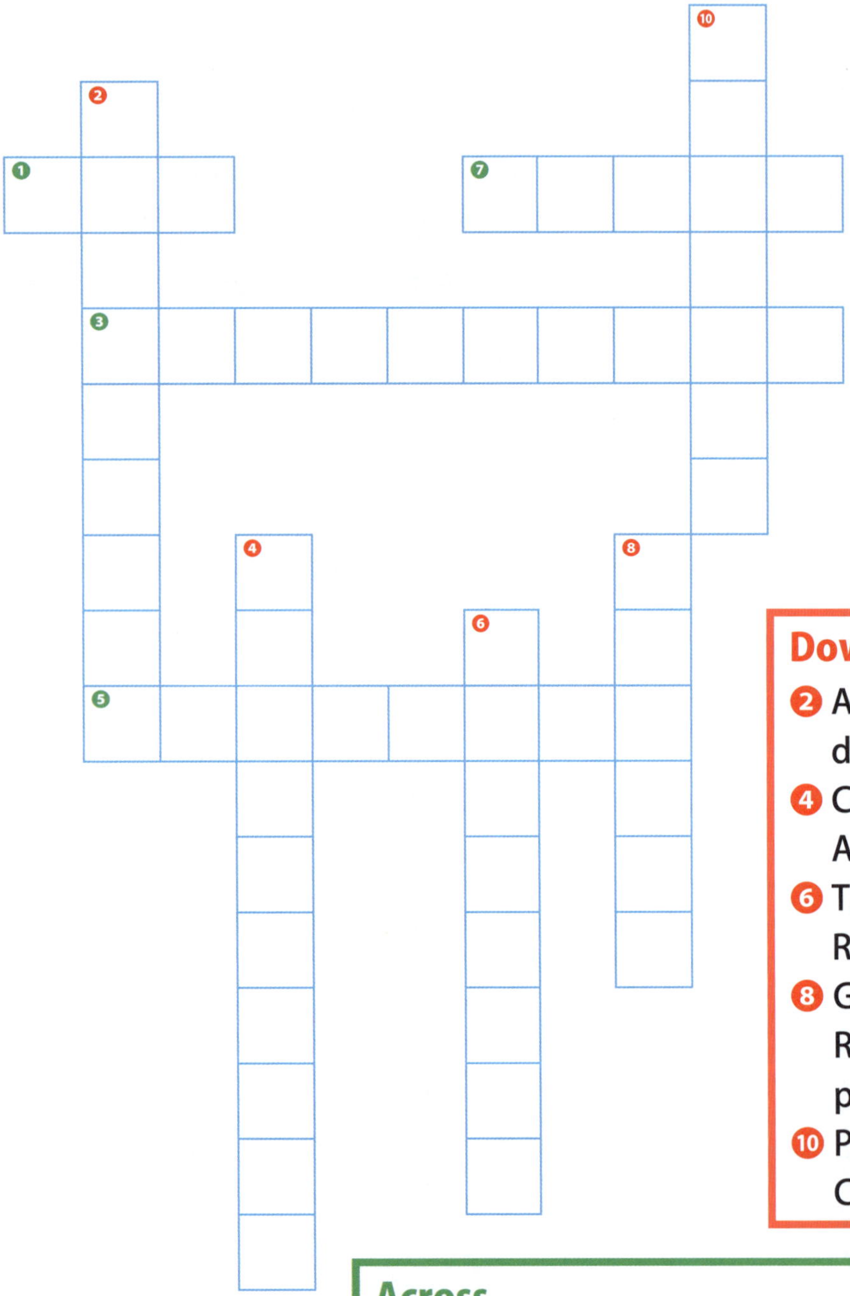

Down
2 Archduke of Austria-Hungary, his death began WWI.
4 Commander of the Continental Army, later US President.
6 The final battle of the American Revolution was fought here.
8 Great Britain, France, Italy, Russia, and the US made up these powers in WWI.
10 President during the American Civil War.

Across
1 Head of the Confederate Army during the American Civil War.
3 The Stock Market Crash caused this event, the Great _____.
5 Droughts in the American mid-west caused this.
7 Head of the Union Army during the American Civil War.

Mindfulness Break!

KEY POINTS

A mantra is a phrase you can say out loud or in your head to make yourself feel happy and confident.

■ Complete the mantras below.

1 "Today I will be [_____] and will do my best!"

2 "Today I will try something new and [_____]."

3 "If something upsets me I will [_____]."

4 "When I face a challenge I will [_____]."

5 "I will be [_____] and [_____] to everyone I meet today."

6 "I like [_____] about myself because [_____]."

Keyboard Skills

■ Which of the following three keyboard inputs will allow the letters to appear as shown in the screen below? Write the number that applies in the box.

Hello, my name is Eli.

1 Shift **+** H E L L O `<,` Backspace M Y

□ N A M E □ I S □

Shift **+** E L I `>.`

2 Shift **+** H E L L O `<,` □ M Y

□ N A M E Backspace □ I S

Enter E L I `>.`

3 Shift **+** H E L L O `<,` □ M Y

□ N A M E □ O Backspace I S

□ Shift **+** E L I `>.`

■ Draw a line to match the function keys to their explanation.

Enter ●

● Enables you to go to a
new line.

Shift ●

● Erases the characters that
come before the cursor.

 ●

● Enables you to write in
uppercase letters.

(**Spacebar Key**) ●

● Creates a space between
letters.

Backspace ●

● Move the cursor in the
four directions.

■ The four questions on the right hand page are written in secret code. Look at the table below and write your answers to the questions.

A	B	C	D	E	F	G
Secret code E	Q	M	U	G	C	P

H	I	J	K	L	M	N
Secret code K	Z	B	S	N	W	H

O	P	Q	R	S	T	U
Secret code X	F	J	V	D	Y	L

V	W	X	Y	Z
Secret code A	T	O	I	R

1 TKEY ZD IXLV CZVDY HEWG?

2 KXT XNU EVG IXL?

3 TKEY ZD IXLV CEAXVZYG CXXU?

4 EVG YKG JLGDYZXHD XH YKZD FEPG UZCCZMLNY CXV IXL?

Coding 1

■ The turtle robot follows the block's commands. ↑ and → represent the robot's direction.

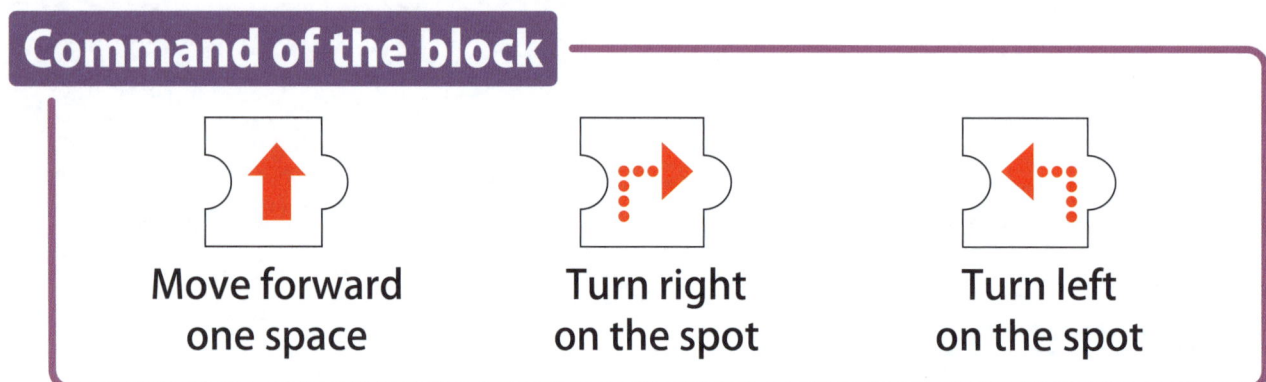

Command of the block

| Move forward one space | Turn right on the spot | Turn left on the spot |

Write in the box a command from Ⓐ to Ⓓ for the empty part of the blocks that will allow the robot to move to the goal.

❶ START ◀⋯ ⬜ ⬜ ⬜ ⬆ GOAL

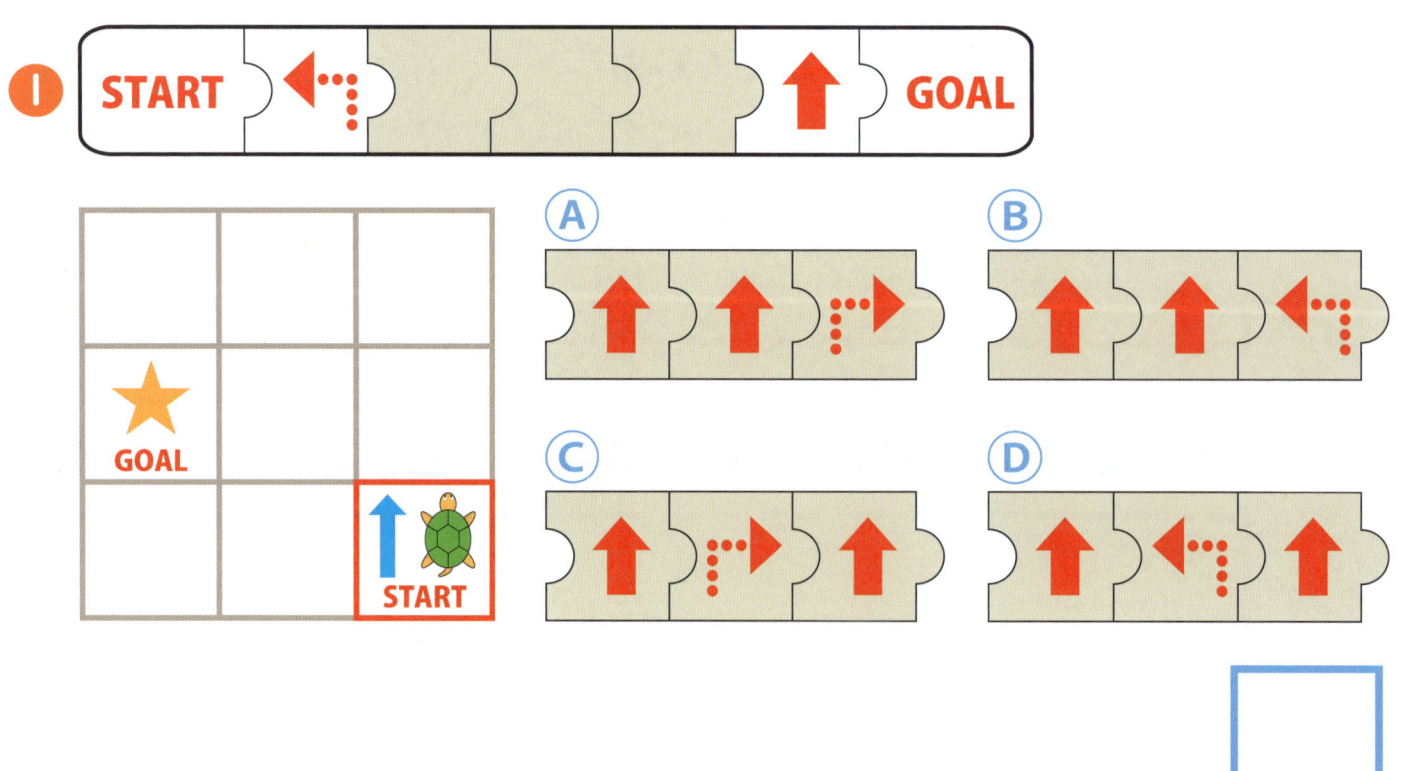

2 START   ⬅ ⬆ GOAL

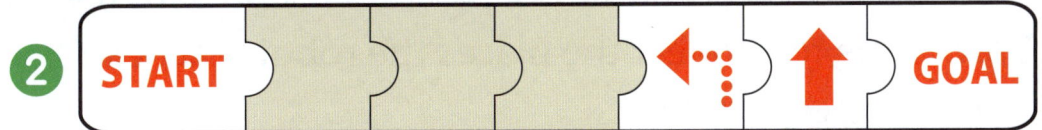

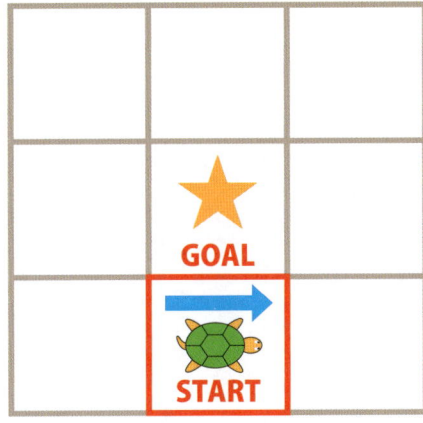

Ⓐ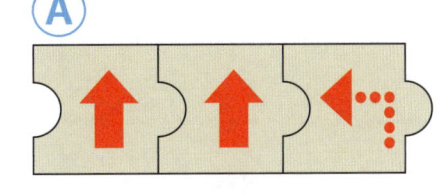

Ⓑ

Ⓒ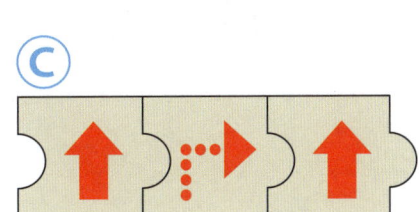

Ⓓ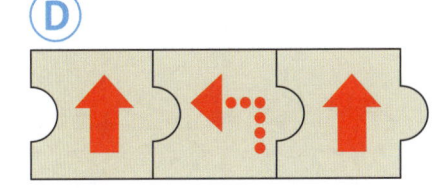

3 START ⬆ ⬆   GOAL

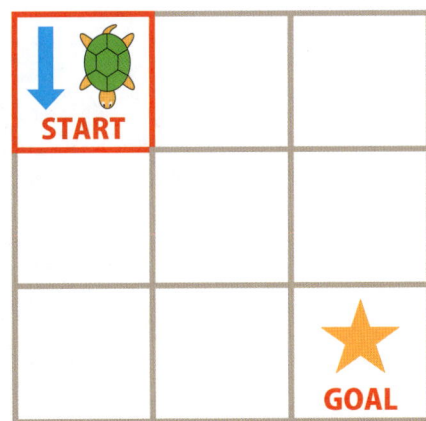

Ⓐ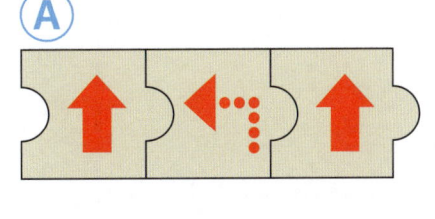

Ⓑ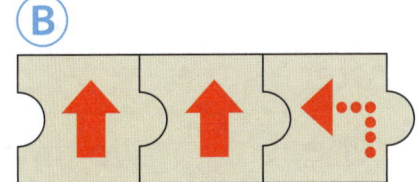

Ⓒ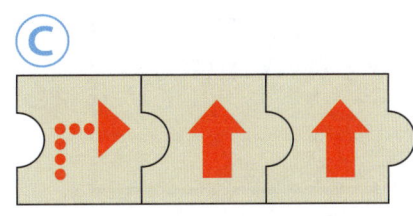

Ⓓ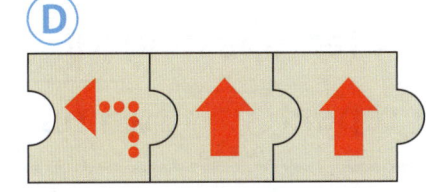

Coding 2

■ The turtle robot follows the block's commands. ↑ and ➡ represent the robot's direction. Draw a line to connect the places the robot reaches when you give the following commands.

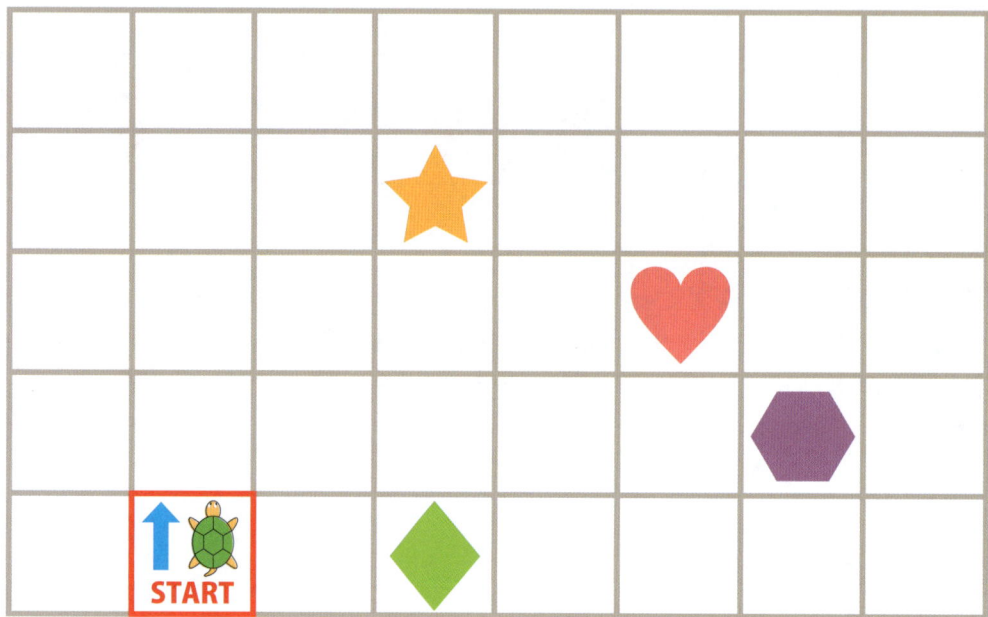

●   ●

●   ●

●   ●

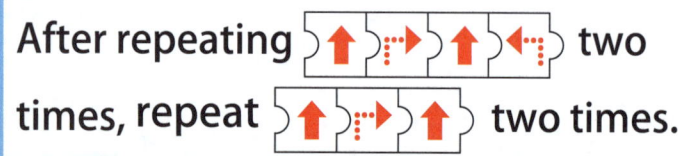

●   ●

■ The robot will travel the forked road with the following rules.
Choose the correct place for the robot to arrive and write one of the
letters Ⓐ to Ⓛ in the box.

Command of the block

When the robot sees a blue square ■ , it will go straight ahead.
If the robot sees a yellow circle ● , it will go right.
If neither of the above two applies, it will go left.

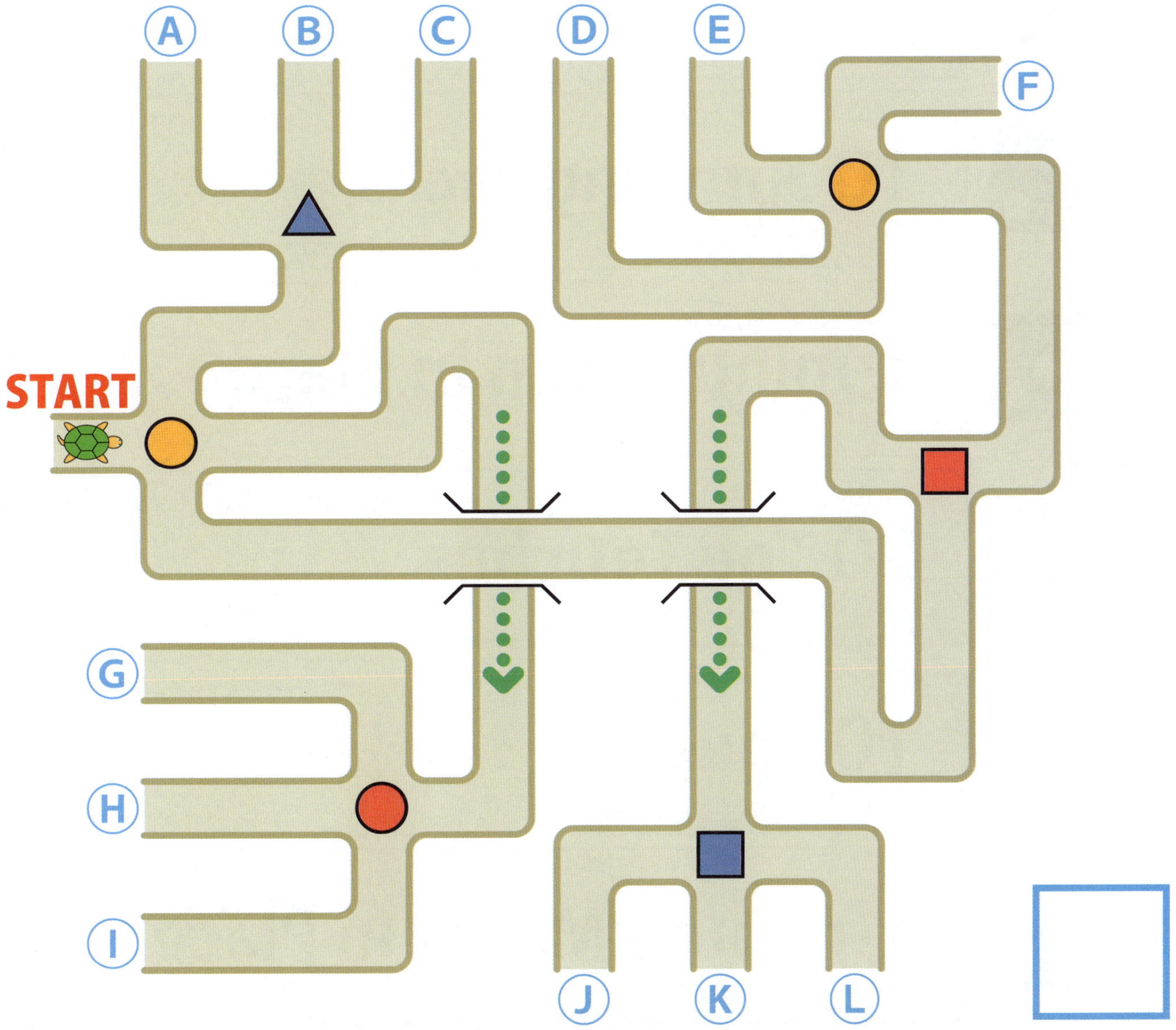

START

Physical Education Break!

It's important to move your body and exercise!
Try this fun activity below to break up your studying!

- Get a die or borrow a die from a board game.
  Roll the die and complete the exercise it lands on.
  Repeat at least 2 times or as many times as you want.

 **20 Arm Circles**

 **10 Jumping Jacks**

 **1-minute Run In Place**

 **20 Toe Touches**

 **10 Squats**

 **1-minute March In Place**

Unit **2** Table of Contents

Use this page to keep track of your progress throughout the book. Place a check mark in the box when you have completed a section.

Language Arts

Reading

Math

Science

Social Studies

Technology

Capitalization

The rules for when to capitalize certain words can be tricky. Let's review some common rules.

Capitalize names of people.

> **My friend Gertie.**

Capitalize a family member if you are using their relation instead of a name.

> **I went to the store with Mom.**
> **I went to the store with my mom.**
> **I was talking to Aunt Suzie.**
> **I was talking to my aunt.**

Capitalize the name of a country, state, or city.

> **I have been reading about France.**

Capitalize a nationality.

> **She is Italian.**

Capitalize days, months, and holidays.

> **This year, Halloween is on the last Friday of October.**

Capitalize the name of a historic event or document.

> **The Fourth of July celebrates the signing of the Declaration of Independence.**

■ If the sentence is correct, write a check (✔). If it is incorrect, write an x.
Then correct the sentence.

 I went to Pennsylvania to visit my grandparents.

 This book was printed in china.

 What does your family eat on thanksgiving?

 I played soccer with my friend emily.

 I jumped rope with my Mom.

 Can I ride with Aunt Vivian?

Quotations

KEY POINTS

Writers use quotation marks to show dialogue or an exact quote from someone. The quotation marks (" ") go around the thing the person said. Here is how to punctuate a sentence with quotes.

If the sentence begins with the quote, capitalize the first word of the quote.

"We won't need to bring anything," he said.

If the sentence doesn't begin with the quote, only capitalize the the beginning of the quote if it is a full sentence.

He asked, "Should I be writing this down?
"He said that the sandwich was "just ok."

If the quote comes at the end of the sentence, put the end punctuation inside the sentence.

She said, "I'd like to help you out."

Capitalize a nationality.

She is Italian.

If the quote doesn't come at the end of the sentence, use a comma inside the quote instead of a period.

"We can discuss it later," he said.

■ If the sentence is punctuated correctly, write a check. If not, write an x. Then write the sentence correctly.

1 My mom asked, "Do you need anything from the store?"

_____

2 "We can practice together." my sister said.

_____

3 My brother asked, "Can I borrow your soccer ball?"

_____

4 I didn't know how to answer, so I just said, "Ok."

_____

5 We yelled out to her, "can we come too"?

_____

6 "Let's pretend it's a sunny day" I said.

_____

Spelling Practice 1

■ Read the passage. Cirlce the misspelled words and write them correctly above the word.

1 Today we are learning how to cook! First up, we are making dumlpings. We will fill them with carots and onions. Next we are bakking sugar cookies. We will roll out the dough and cut it into shapes. Then we will add sprinlkes. After that, we bake them in the oven at 350 degres. But my favorit part is when we get to eat them!

2 Today my class is taking a feild trip to a science museum. Our teacher told us that we will see dinosors. I am also hoping we get to see the hall of cristals and gems. My freind Ravi is hoping we learn about electricity. And some of the students are hoping to learn more about how different types of whether, like tornados. There is so much for us to learn!

■ Read the passage. Cirlce the misspelled words and write them correctly above the word.

❶Everyone else at school knew how to ride a bike. But I never learned how, and I was a little nervous. I tired practicing at home, but every time I took my feet off the ground I started to tip. My dad saw me trieing, and he came out to help. He held the bike steady while I put my feet on the peddles. I started to petal the bike, and he gradually let go of me. I woblled a little at first, but I was moving! I kept going, and before I knew it I was halfway down the block!

2 It was my sister's bitrhday, and I forgot to get her a present. On my way home from school, I thought about what I culd get her. "I'll make her a card," I thougt to myself. But there wasn't enough time. "I know! She's always wanted a pupy," I thought. But wear would I get a dog? Finally I had an ideo. I raced home and told her, "For your birthday, I promiss I will let you pick what we watch on TV for the rest of the week!"

Brain Break
Write a Quote

■ Write a quote from your favorite book, movie, or tv show below. It can be a joke, or it can be something serious. Explain why you like it.

Mindfulness Break!

■ Fill in the boxes using the prompts. It's important to try and keep a positive mindset when things don't go our way! Use the chart below to practice changing your mindset about what happened.

Situation: You got a low grade on a test.

❶ What happened?

❷ Why did it happen?

❸ Can I change the outcome?

❹ If yes: how?

❺ If no: then what's next?

❻ How does it make me feel?

Story Craft Elements 1

KEY POINTS

Setting is an important element of a story. The setting tells where and when the story takes place. Most stories have one primary setting and other secondary settings. But books can have many different settings if the characters move around a lot. Often the setting can reflect the situation in the story and affect what the characters do.

The physical setting is where a story takes place: in a town, city, the jungle, or an imaginary world. The historical setting refers to whether the story takes place either in present day or any time in the past.

■ Read the passage and underline the sentences that describe the setting.

Aidan walked through the forest with the golden light of the sun shining through the trees. After a few minutes, he reached his favorite spot. The small lake shimmered and it was surrounded by tall, thick trees that seemed to touch the sky. Their leaves rustled in the soft breeze and cast shadows on the sandy shore. The water was clear and Aidan could see the smooth stones along the bottom. He sat down on a large rock that was along the water's edge and began to set up his fishing rod. Aidan cast his fishing line into the cool, clear water. He looked out into the woods and watched a few bluejays swooping along the shore. The sun warmed the air and fed the blue and purple wildflowers. Aidan felt at peace and happy. Suddenly, there was a tug on his line and he stood up to reel it in. Out of the water popped a shiny, silver fish with water glistening off its scales. Aidan marveled at the fish before taking out the hook and letting it back into the water. It was a successful trip to his fishing hole.

■ Read the story and answer the questions about the setting.

Kira woke up before the sun had come up, thrilled for what the day would bring. She was going on a trip with her family to a tropical island! The plane ride was long, but when they finally landed Kira was greeted by the most beautiful sights. The ocean was bright blue and the tall palm trees swayed with the breeze. Kira had never seen anything like it before. The air smelled sweet like coconuts and sun-tan lotion.

Her family drove to the small cottage they rented near the beach. The cottage was yellow with orange and pink shutters on the windows. And from her bedroom Kira could hear the ocean waves!

The next day, Kira and her family went on a boat ride to go snorkeling near a

coral reef. When Kira jumped into the water it was warm and the water that got in her mouth tasted salty. Swimming down under the water, Kira was met by an exciting surprise: a group of green sea turtles! She watched them until she had to go up for air. It was the best vacation she ever had.

❶ Where is the story set?

_____

❷ How does the setting effect Kira?

_____

❸ How does the setting make Kira feel?

_____

Story Craft Elements 2

Conflict is another important element of a story. Conflict is what drives the plot. Almost all stories have a central conflict which drives the main character or characters forward in the story.

Story Elements

Character vs Character:

This type of conflict happens when the main problem in a story or text is between two characters or two people.

Example: The main conflict of *Harry Potter and the Sorcerer's Stone* is character vs. character.

Character vs Self:

This type of conflict happens when the main problem a character faces is between them and themselves. For instance, it could be when someone has to make a difficult choice. They are usually told in the first person or third person. Sometimes they can be told in the second person, though this is not common.

Example: The main conflict of *The Lion, the Witch, and the Wardrobe* is character vs. self for Edmund.

Character vs Setting (Nature):

This type of conflict happens when the main problem in the story is between the main character and the natural world around them.

Example: The main conflict of *Hatchet* is character vs. nature for Brian.

■ **Answer the questions based on the reading passage.**

Ethan had always wanted a puppy, but he never thought he'd get to keep one. When his parents told him they were going to foster a little dog named Max, Ethan was excited but also nervous. Max was small with white, fluffy fur and big, brown eyes that made Ethan smile every time he looked at him. They spent every day together from that moment. Ethan would walk Max before and after school. He would play fetch with him in the backyard. They would even take naps together on the weekends. Ethan started to love Max like his own, and it was hard to imagine he would not get to keep him forever.

Then one day, Ethan's parents told him the shelter had found a permanent home for Max with a new family. Ethan felt a lump in his throat. He didn't want to say good-bye to Max. On the day Max was going to his new home, Ethan hugged him tightly and whispered, "I'll miss you, buddy. But I know you'll be happy with your new family."

As Max drove away with his new family, Ethan felt sad, but he knew Max would be happy in his new home. Even thought it was hard, Ethan knew he had helped give Max a chance for a happy future and loving home. Ethan felt proud of what he had done. He began to look forward to the next dog his family would foster.

❶ **What is the main conflict of this story?**

_____

❷ **What type of conflict does Ethan face?**

_____

❸ **What is the resolution of the conflict?**

_____

Story Craft Elements 3

All stories have a point of view. Point of view is the view through which the story is told. They are usually told in the first person or third person. Sometimes they can be told in the second person, though this is not common.

First person is when a narrator or main character uses pronouns like *I* and *me*.

Second person is when a narrator uses second person voice with pronouns like *you*.

Third person is the most common point of view where the narrator uses *she*, *he*, and *they*.

Examples of Point of View:

First Person:

Today, I learned how to ride a bike without training wheels! For me, it was a big accomplishment. My mom and dad were super proud!

Second Person:

One thing you need to know about taking care of a pet horse is that you have to give it a lot of your time. It is important that you clean its stall, give it fresh water and hay, and exercise it daily.

Third Person:

Marta and Emma were adopted together. Their new family was in the US. They had a long trip from Russia to New York before they settled into their new home for good.

■ **Answer the questions based on the reading passage.**

When I got in the car, I was so nervous. I looked out the open window for the entire ride from my old home to my new one. I was sad about leaving my old home, but was promised that my new home would be just as nice and safe. When the car finally stopped my tail started to wag a little in excitement even though I wasn't sure what was waiting for me.

I had been at the shelter for a while and before that I was all alone for a long time. I didn't know what a "forever home" was, but I hoped it was a place where I could run and play, and maybe have a soft, safe place to sleep. The man driving smiled at me and opened the car door.

"Welcome home, Charlie. You're going to be happy here!" I wanted to believe him, but I was still scared. I jumped out of the car and took a deep sniff. The yard smelled like fresh grass. Suddenly, I saw a small girl running toward me from the open front door. She had a huge smile on her face and when she reached me she wrapped her arms around me in a hug. I backed away at first, but the little girl's smile made me feel at ease. I gave her face a lick and her smile grew. It felt nice to be wanted and loved.

"Welcome home, Charlie!" the little girl exclaimed. I realized this was my new home and that this little girl would take care of me forever.

❶ What point of view is the story written in?

_____

❷ Who or what is the narrator?

_____

❸ Does the point of view make it easier or harder to understand the story?

_____

❹ How does the point of view affect the plot twist in this story?

_____

Let's try to identify all the story elements in one story.
Remember key story elements are:
Setting, Plot, Characters, Conflict, Point of View, and theme.

■ Read the passage below and answer the questions on the right hand page.

Luna and Evie were both excited and nervous as they trotted their horses out into the ring. Today was the big jumping competition they had been training for. Their horses, Thunder and Carrot, were ready to go and eagerly stamping the ground. Luna and Carrot were up first and the crowd cheered as she rode up to the starting place. Luna gave Evie a quick smile before turning to face the course. She knew they had both worked hard training for today's event, but also that only one of them could win. As the whistle blew she spurred Carrot forward towards the first hurdle. Carrot soared over the first obstacle with ease and Luna could hear Evie cheering her on. When Luna went over the last jump, she turned back to see her time. She finished the course in under six minutes! Luna was proud of her time and rode over to the fence. She dismounted and got ready to watch Evie and Thunder's run. The whistle sounded again and Evie and Thunder took off. They cleared the first two jumps with ease, but then Thunder hesitated at the water jump and Evie had to guide him back around to try again. Luna knew this would affect Evie's time. In the end, Evie's time was just over six minutes. This made Luna and Carrot the winners! But Evie wasn't upset. She was happy for her friend. The two girls hugged and started talking about their next competition right away.

❶ Where is the story set?

_____

❷ Who are the main characters?

_____

❸ Who are the supporting characters?

_____

❹ What point of view is the story told in?

_____

❺ What is the main conflict of this story?

_____

❻ How does the conflict affect the main characters?

_____

❼ What is the main theme?

_____

Brain Break
Writing Your Own Story!

■ Imagine you are writing your own story! What elements would you use? Fill in the chart below with your own ideas!

Plot

Characters

Setting

Conflict

Theme

Point of View

Mindfulness Break!

There are different ways to practice mindfulness. Focusing your attention on one word can help you stay in the moment and be mindful.

■ Choose a word to help you focus your mind. Fill in the answers below.

❶ Choose a word that makes you feel calm and relaxed.

❷ My word is [   ] .

❸ This word makes me feel [   ] .

❹ The color of my word is [   ] .

❺ How do you feel after spending some time focusing on your mindful word?

[   ]

Multiplication & Division

■ Solve.

① $2 \times 3 =$ **②** $6 \times 7 =$ **③** $3 \times 10 =$

④
$$\begin{array}{r} 4 \\ \times 2 \\ \hline \end{array}$$

⑤
$$\begin{array}{r} 5 \\ \times 5 \\ \hline \end{array}$$

⑥
$$\begin{array}{r} 7 \\ \times 8 \\ \hline \end{array}$$

⑦
$$\begin{array}{r} 12 \\ \times 3 \\ \hline \end{array}$$

⑧
$$\begin{array}{r} 24 \\ \times 2 \\ \hline \end{array}$$

⑨
$$\begin{array}{r} 31 \\ \times 3 \\ \hline \end{array}$$

⑩
$$\begin{array}{r} 16 \\ \times 2 \\ \hline \end{array}$$

⑪
$$\begin{array}{r} 12 \\ \times 7 \\ \hline \end{array}$$

⑫
$$\begin{array}{r} 25 \\ \times 3 \\ \hline \end{array}$$

George is planting flowers in his garden. He buys 13 packets of seeds, and each packet contains 6 seeds. How many seeds does he have in all?

☐ × ☐ = ☐ seeds

■ Solve.

① $8 \div 4 =$ **②** $27 \div 9 =$ **③** $54 \div 6 =$

④ $1 \overline{)9}$ **⑤** $2 \overline{)8}$ **⑥** $3 \overline{)6}$

⑦ $4 \overline{)28}$ **⑧** $9 \overline{)81}$ **⑨** $7 \overline{)70}$

⑩ $7 \overline{)56}$ **⑪** $8 \overline{)48}$ **⑫** $2 \overline{)20}$

Sarah baked 36 cookies, and wants to share
them equally among 4 plates. How many
cookies will be on each plate?

$\boxed{} \div \boxed{} = \boxed{}$ cookies

Multiplication with and without Regrouping

How to multiply 3-digit × 1-digit without regrouping

Example:

142 × 2

```
  1 4 2          1 4 2          1 4 2
×     2        ×     2        ×     2
─────────      ─────────      ─────────
      4            8 4          2 8 4
```

Step 1: Multiply the digits in the ones place.
Step 2: Multiply the tens digit.
Step 3: Multiply the hundreds digit.

■ Solve.

1
```
  123
×   2
─────
```

2
```
  231
×   3
─────
```

3
```
  107
×   7
─────
```

4
```
  421
×   4
─────
```

5
```
  634
×   2
─────
```

6
```
  523
×   3
─────
```

7
```
  200
×   3
─────
```

8
```
  500
×   4
─────
```

9
```
  703
×   8
─────
```

KEY POINTS

How to multiply 3-digit × 1-digit with regrouping

Example:

234 × 6

$$
\begin{array}{r}
\overset{2}{}2\ 3\ 4 \\
\times\ \ \ \ \ 6 \\
\hline
4
\end{array}
\qquad
\begin{array}{r}
\overset{2}{2}\ \overset{2}{3}\ 4 \\
\times\ \ \ \ \ 6 \\
\hline
0\ 4
\end{array}
\qquad
\begin{array}{r}
\overset{2}{2}\ \overset{2}{3}\ 4 \\
\times\ \ \ \ \ 6 \\
\hline
1\ 4\ 0\ 4
\end{array}
$$

Step 1: Multiply the digits in the ones place and regroup.
Step 2: Multiply the tens digit, and add the digit that was regrouped.
Step 3: Multiply the hundreds digit and add the digit that was regrouped.

■ Solve.

①
$$
\begin{array}{r}
\overset{2}{4}\ 1\ 7 \\
\times\ \ \ \ \ 4 \\
\hline
\end{array}
$$

②
$$
\begin{array}{r}
7\ 2\ 7 \\
\times\ \ \ \ \ 2 \\
\hline
\end{array}
$$

③
$$
\begin{array}{r}
5\ 2\ 8 \\
\times\ \ \ \ \ 3 \\
\hline
\end{array}
$$

④
$$
\begin{array}{r}
\overset{2}{3}\ 7\ 2 \\
\times\ \ \ \ \ 4 \\
\hline
\end{array}
$$

⑤
$$
\begin{array}{r}
2\ 4\ 1 \\
\times\ \ \ \ \ 6 \\
\hline
\end{array}
$$

⑥
$$
\begin{array}{r}
8\ 6\ 3 \\
\times\ \ \ \ \ 2 \\
\hline
\end{array}
$$

⑦
$$
\begin{array}{r}
\overset{2}{6}\ \overset{2}{3}\ 3 \\
\times\ \ \ \ \ 7 \\
\hline
\end{array}
$$

⑧
$$
\begin{array}{r}
1\ 5\ 2 \\
\times\ \ \ \ \ 8 \\
\hline
\end{array}
$$

⑨
$$
\begin{array}{r}
2\ 7\ 5 \\
\times\ \ \ \ \ 5 \\
\hline
\end{array}
$$

Multiplication 2-digit x 2-digit

KEY POINTS

How to multiply 2-digit × 2-digit

Example:
27 × 32

```
  ¹
  2̣7̣        27         ²          27
×3̣2̣       ×32      2̣7̣        ×32
─────      ─────   ×3̣2̣      ─────
  54         54    ─────        54
            0         54       810
                    810       ─────
                               864
```

Step 1: Multiply the top number and the ones digit of the bottom number.
Step 2: Put 0 in the ones place.
Step 3: Multiply the top number and the tens digit of the bottom number.
Step 4: Add the products.

■ **Solve.**

1
```
   12
 ×23
```

2
```
   53
 ×11
```

3
```
   21
 ×43
```

4
```
   60
 ×56
```

5
```
   25
 ×13
```

6
```
   18
 ×12
```

7
```
   26
 ×18
```

8
```
   67
 ×17
```

■ Solve.

❶ 34 × 46

```
  34
× 46
```

❷ 25 × 54

❸ 47 × 83

❹ 23 × 20

```
  23
× 20
  00
  46
```

❺ 41 × 30

❻ 65 × 40

Ms. Thompson's class is organizing a school fair, and needs to make gift bags. Each gift bag contains 27 stickers. If they need to prepare 63 bags, how many stickers do they need in total?

☐ × ☐ = ☐ stickers

Division 1

 Solve.

1

4)20

2

7)49

3

8)64

4

5)50

5

4 R 3

4)19
16
3

6

6 R

7)47
42

Sometimes the divisor doesn't fit into the dividend perfectly. The number left over is called the remainder.

7   R

8)57

8   R

5)52

9   R

2)19

10   R

6)50

11   R

3)25

12   R

6)44

13   R

9)17

14   R

4)34

KEY POINTS

Example: $72 \div 4$

Step 1: Divide the tens (7) by the divisor (4).

Step 2: The remainder (3) and the ones (2) makes the new number (32).

Step 3: Divide the new number (32) by the divisor (4).

```
   1              1             18
4)72          4)72          4)72
  4              4             4
  ‾              ‾             ‾
  3             32            32
                              32
                              ‾‾
                               0
```

■ **Solve.**

① 2)44

② 3)96

③ 4)84

④ 5)55

⑤ 5)75

⑥ 2)30

⑦ 8)96

⑧ 6)78

⑨ 4)90 R

⑩ 5)67 R

⑪ 3)49 R

⑫ 6)88 R

Division 2

Example: $762 \div 3$

$$
\begin{array}{r}
2 \\
3\overline{)762} \\
6 \\
\hline
1
\end{array}
\qquad
\begin{array}{r}
25 \\
3\overline{)762} \\
6 \\
\hline
16 \\
15 \\
\hline
1
\end{array}
\qquad
\begin{array}{r}
254 \\
3\overline{)762} \\
6 \\
\hline
16 \\
15 \\
\hline
12 \\
12 \\
\hline
0
\end{array}
$$

Step 1: Divide the hundreds by the divisor.

Step 2: The remainder and the tens makes the new number. Divide it by the divisor.

Step 3: The remainder and the ones makes the new number. Divide it by the divisor.

■ Solve.

① $4\overline{)864}$

② $2\overline{)578}$

③ $5\overline{)865}$

④ $6\overline{)984}$

⑤ R $2\overline{)775}$

⑥ R $3\overline{)734}$

⑦ R $4\overline{)619}$

⑧ R $6\overline{)857}$

■ Answer the following word problems.

① Maria baked 91 cookies, and wants to pack them into boxes. If each box holds 7 cookies, how many boxes does she need?

Ans. _____ boxes

② Tom has 70 books to place on 4 shelves. How many books will each shelf have, and how many will be left?

Ans. _____ books, _____ remaining

③ Mr. Parker has 438 colored pencils, and wants to distribute them equally among 3 art classes. How many colored pencils will each class receive?

Ans. _____ colored pencils

Brain Break
Telling Time Quiz

■ Write a check mark (✓) in the box of the correct time.

① Two hours after 9 a.m.

☐ 2:00 a.m.

☐ 7:00 a.m.

☐ 11:00 a.m.

④ Five hours after
11:45 p.m.

☐ 4:45 p.m.

☐ 4:45 a.m.

☐ 6:45 a.m.

② Half an hour before
7:00 p.m.

☐ 6:30 p.m.

☐ 7:30 p.m.

☐ 8:30 p.m.

⑤ An hour and a half before
1:00 a.m.

☐ 2:30 a.m.

☐ 2:30 p.m.

☐ 11:30 p.m.

③ 10 hours before noon

☐ 2:00 a.m.

☐ 2:00 p.m.

☐ 12:10 p.m.

⑥ 120 seconds after
5:38 p.m.

☐ 5:36 p.m.

☐ 5:40 p.m.

☐ 5:50 p.m.

Trace the path by following the clocks that move forward 3 minutes.

START

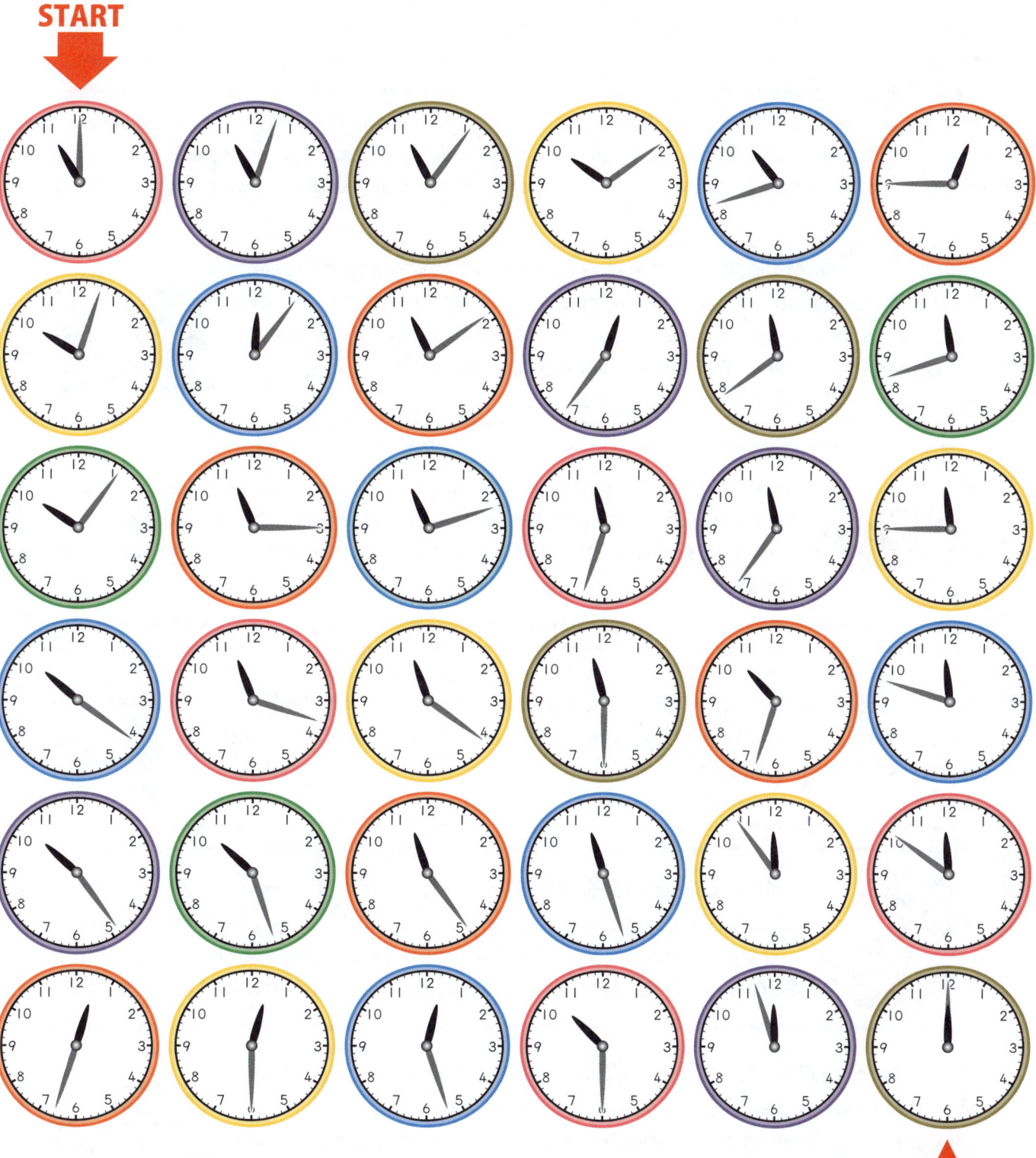

GOAL

Animals are Living Things

KEY POINTS

Living things, also called organisms, are things that can move, feel, grow, and create new life. Animals, plants, and fungi (like mushrooms, yeast, and mold) are all living things. Animals can move, feel, grow, and reproduce, or create new life. They have babies that can grow up to be adults and have their own babies. This continues the life cycle of the animal. Invertebrates are animals without backbones, like worms, jellyfish, insects, and spiders. Most animals on Earth are invertebrates. Vertebrates are animals with backbones. Vertebrates are separated into the categories of mammals, reptiles, amphibians, birds, and fish.

Mammals are warm-blooded, which means their bodies stay about the same temperature no matter what the air temperature is. Mammals have hair or fur. Most mammals give birth to live young instead of laying eggs. Mammals breastfeed their babies. They breathe air. Humans, dolphins, jaguars, platypuses, and mice are examples of mammals.

 Reptiles are cold-blooded, which means their body temperatures change depending on the air temperature. Reptiles lay eggs. They breathe air. They have scales. Turtles, snakes, alligators, and iguanas are all examples of reptiles.

Birds are warm-blooded. They all have wings and feathers, but not all of them can fly. Birds have bills. They lay eggs. Penguins, parrots, ostriches, and sparrows are all kinds of birds.

 Fish are cold-blooded. They live in water. Most of them have gills instead of lungs so they can breathe underwater. Most have scales. Most have fins instead of arms and legs. Fish lay eggs or produce eggs that hatch inside the fish's body. Trout, seahorses, eels, goldfish, and sharks are all kinds of fish.

Amphibians are cold-blooded. Amphibians can live in water or on land. Most live in water when they are young and grow lungs and live on land when they are adults. They do not have scales and they can breathe through their skin. Their skin is usually moist. They lay eggs. Frogs, toads, and salamanders are all kinds of amphibians.

■ Fill in the blanks with the correct words.

1 This type of animal is cold-blooded and covered in scales.

2 This type of animal is warm-blooded and covered in fur.

3 This type of animal is warm-blooded and covered in feathers.

4 This type of animal is cold-blooded and can live on land and in the water.

5 This type of animal is cold-blooded, covered in scales and breathes air.

Animals - Features for Life

KEY POINTS

Animals need food, water, shelter, space, and oxygen to grow and thrive. All animals have to eat food. Herbivores like cows and rabbits eat plants. Carnivores like lions and hawks eat other animals. Omnivores like humans and raccoons eat both plants and animals.

All animals must consume water. Some drink it from rivers, lakes, or kitchen sinks. Some get all of their water through foods that contain a lot of water, like koalas, who eat eucalyptus leaves.

Animals need shelter to protect them from weather and predators. Shelters can be caves, underground burrows, nests under tree branches, or buildings. Animals need space. Some animals, like wolves, need a lot of space to find enough food, water, and shelter to survive. Some animals find everything they need in a small area, so they need a smaller amount of space. Many animals need very specific resources to survive and can only live in particular kinds of habitats. That is one reason it is so important to protect different habitats.

Animals all breathe oxygen, either through lungs, gills, or their skin. If a fish, which breathes using gills, is out of the water for too long, it will die. If a mammal, which uses lungs to breathe, is underwater for too long, it will die.

■ Answer the questions.

❶ What are five things that all animals need to survive and grow?

_____

❷ Why do animals need shelter?

_____

❸ What are three ways that different animals get oxygen?

_____

■ Write true or false for each statement.

❶ Herbivores eat only plants.

❷ Carnivores eat only plants.

❸ Omnivores, like humans, eat plants and animals.

❹ Animals need shelter to protect them from predators.

❺ Some animals do not need oxygen to survive.

❻ Fish breathe underwater with their gills.

❼ Animals cannot survive without food, water, oxygen, space, and shelter.

Animals and Offspring

KEY POINTS

All kinds of animals can reproduce, or create more animals of their kind. Most animals need a mate to reproduce, with a male and a female creating offspring. Some animals have special features to help them attract a mate so they can reproduce. For example, male peacocks have huge, colorful tails to help them attract female peahens. Male weaver birds build complex nests to show female weaver birds that they can be good co-parents.

Some animals, like frogs, turtles, and rabbits, have a lot of offspring but many of the offspring do not survive to adulthood. These animal parents do not spend a lot of energy taking care of their young. Other animals, like elephants, eagles, and humans, have few offspring but spend a lot of energy raising their young and more of their young survive to adulthood. They might only have one or two babies every few years so that they can give more resources to each baby.

Some animals lay eggs in order to reproduce. Most fish, reptiles, amphibians, insects, and birds lay eggs. Some animals have eggs that hatch inside of them. Some kinds of sharks create eggs, but do not lay them. The eggs hatch inside of the shark and the shark gives birth to live young. Seahorse mothers lay eggs, but the fathers carry the eggs in a special pouch until the eggs hatch.

Almost all mammals give birth to live young instead of laying eggs. Platypuses and spiny anteaters are the only mammals that lay eggs. Mammals breastfeed their babies. The mothers feed their babies with milk they make in their bodies.

Marsupials are a kind of mammal that give birth to their young when they are very small and not very developed. These babies live in their mothers' pouches until they are developed enough to survive outside of it. Kangaroos, opossums, and koalas are all examples of marsupials.

■ **Answer the questions.**

1 What type of animals have live babies?

_____

2 What type of animals lay eggs?

_____

3 How are marsupial babies different from other mammals?

_____

■ Sort the animals below into egg-laying or giving birth to live young.

bear	dog	alligator	sea turtle	platypus
hawk	snake	giraffe	frog	bass	whale
tiger	bald eagle	penguin	mouse	horse

Egg-laying	Non-egg laying

Animals - Features for Survival

Adaptations are traits that living things inherit from their parents that help them survive and reproduce. Adaptations can be physical, meaning they are a part of an animal's body, or behavioral, meaning they are something the animal does. Physical adaptations are traits in animals' bodies that help them survive and reproduce, like fur that helps an animal camouflage so that it can hide from predators or sneak up on prey. Hummingbirds' long, narrow beaks are a physical adaptation that allow them to drink nectar from inside flowers. Animals' claws help them climb trees, dig, groom themselves, and/or catch prey.

Different animals have very different kinds of teeth. You can often tell what kind of food an animal eats by looking at its teeth. Cows are herbivores who have adapted to eat grasses and hay. They have sharp, flat bottom teeth in the front, which they press against the hard top of their mouths to cut the plants they eat. They have flat molars in the back that they use to chew the plants before swallowing. Lions, who are carnivores, have huge, sharp teeth in the front that they use to kill their prey. Their other teeth are also sharp because they are used to tear apart meat when they chew. Omnivores like gorillas have sharp teeth in the front for biting off meat and flat molars in the back for chewing plants.

Behavioral adaptations are things that animals do that help them survive and reproduce. Schools of fish swim together in large groups as a behavioral adaptation to protect themselves from predators and to have a better chance of finding food. Many animals, including some kinds of frogs, birds, snakes, and opossums, "play dead" when a predator is pursuing them. Most predators will only eat animals that are freshly killed, so this behavior can help protect animals from predators.

■ **Answer the questions.**

❶ **What is a physical adaptation?**

_____

❷ **What kind of teeth do many omnivores have?**

_____

❸ **What is an example of a behavioral adaptation?**

_____

■ Fill in the blank with the correct animal.

① This animal plays 'dead' to stop predators from eating it.

② This type of animal has flat teeth that allow it to eat grasses.

③ This animal has sharp teeth and claws that help it eat meat.

④ Some types of this animal swim in schools to protect themselves from predators.

⑤ This animal has flat teeth for eating grass and hay.

⑥ This animal has sharp and flat teeth for biting off meat and chewing plants.

⑦ This animal has a long narrow beak to help it get nectar from flowers.

Brain Break
Science Journal 2

Use what you learned in this unit to create your own unique animal!

1 Animal name:

2 Type of animal:

3 How would it get food?
What type? Carnivore, herbivore, or omnivore?

4 How would it reproduce? Egg-laying or non-egg laying?

5 What kind of defenses would it have for survival?

6 Would it have an special adaptations?

Art Break!

■ Draw a picture of your new animal here! Make sure to include all the features from your Journal page!

Unit 2 Social Studies

The Northeast

KEY POINTS

The United States is made up of 50 states across different regions of the country. Connecticut, Maine, Massachusetts, New Hampshire, Rhode Island, and Vermont are in the Northeast, also called New England. New Jersey, New York, Pennsylvania, Delaware, Maryland, and Washington, DC make up the Mid-Atlantic region. Most of these states have some coastline on the Atlantic Ocean. The Northeast and Mid-Atlantic regions generally have cold, sometimes snowy winters and hot summers, with rain year round. Some of the Native American groups in the region include the Iroquois and Algonquin peoples.

Most of these states were part of the Thirteen Colonies that became the first states after the Revolutionary War. The first battles of the American Revolution were fought in Massachusetts, and the Continental Congress met in Philadelphia. This region has many important historical sites including battlefields and historic buildings.

The Northeast and Mid-Atlantic region is the most densely populated in the US. That means that there are more people per square mile than in any other region of the US. The region has the country's most populous city, New York City. Other large cities include Philadelphia, Pennsylvania; Boston, Massachusetts; Washington, DC; Baltimore, Maryland; and Newark, New Jersey.

Historically, the Northeast and Mid-Atlantic region manufactured a lot of goods such as textiles and steel. They needed a lot of people to work in the factories. Many immigrants entered the US through New York City and other cities in the region, finding work at factories. Today, New York City is considered the financial center of the US, with the stock exchange and many large banks based there. Many of the country's biggest companies are based in New York City, Philadelphia, or Boston. This region also has rural areas, especially in the western parts of many states. People in these rural areas often earn money through farming, logging, tourism, and mining.

■ **Answer the questions.**

❶ What is the most populous city in the United States?

_____

❷ Name one important historical event that took place in the Northeast and Mid-Atlantic region.

_____

❸ What is another name for the Northeast?

_____

■ Fill out the area profile using the Key Points.

List the states that make up the Northeast.

Typical climate

Historical Fact

Most Populated City

Main Industry

■ Pick one state to learn more about! Use the Internet or a book to fill in the blanks about the state you chose.

The State

State Capital   Most Populous City

State Flower   State Bird

Main Industry

Fun Fact

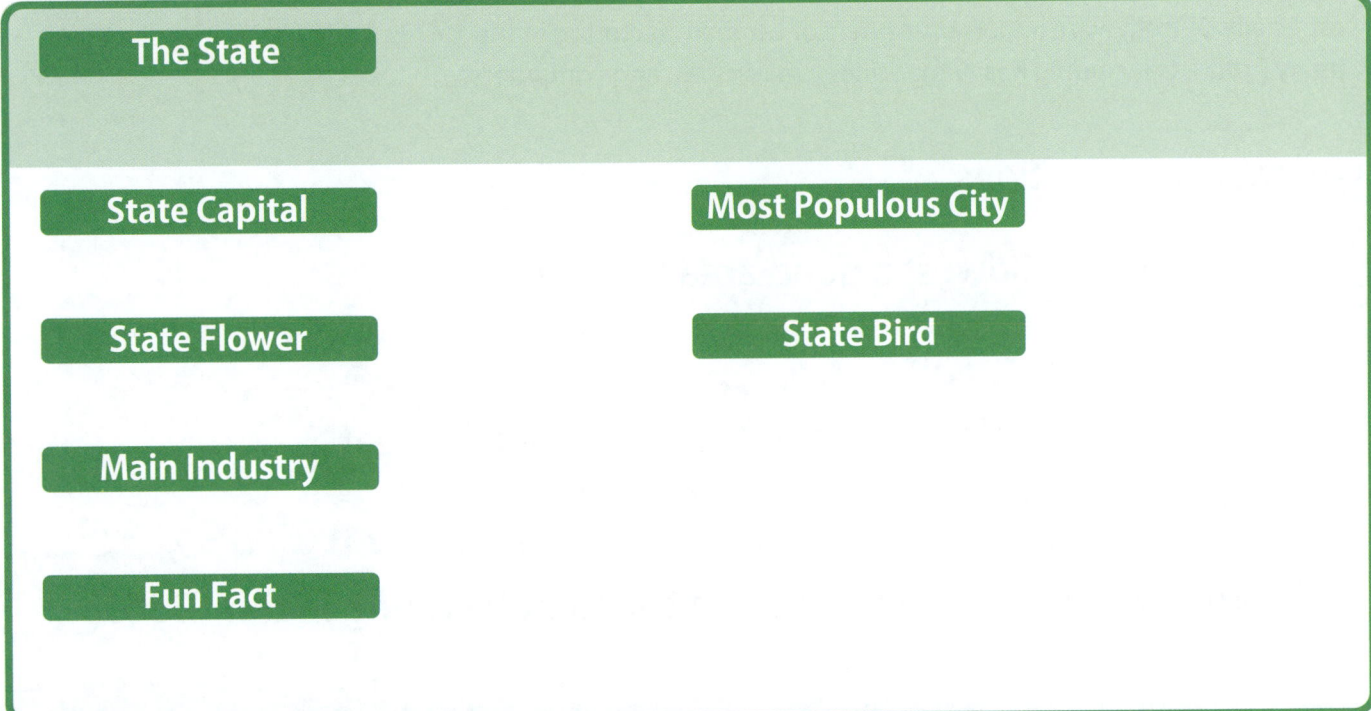

The Midwest

KEY POINTS

Illinois, Indiana, Michigan, Ohio, Wisconsin, Iowa, Kansas, Minnesota, Missouri, Nebraska, North Dakota, and South Dakota make up the Midwest of the United States.

When European-American settlers were first moving to this area in the late 1700s, it was farther west than other parts of the new country of the US. For this reason, it was called the Northwest and later the Midwest, even though today it lies in the middle, not the west, of the US. Native Americans lived in the Midwest for at least 10,000 years before European colonists arrived. The first European colonists in the region were French fur traders who often worked with the Native Americans. When the Midwest became part of the US, American settlers moved there and forced Native Americans to leave their land.

The Midwest has some hills and small mountains, but most of the land is fairly flat. The region's rich soil and flat landscape make it good for farming. A lot of the country's corn, wheat, and soybeans are grown here. In general, the Midwest has cold, snowy winters; wet springs; warm, humid summers; and dry autumns.

The Great Lakes are in the Midwest, mostly along the border with Canada to the north. There are five Great Lakes: Superior, Michigan, Huron, Erie, and Ontario. Together they are the biggest group of freshwater lakes on Earth. They are connected to important rivers via canals and have been used for many years to transport goods and people, as well as for fishing and recreation.

Much of the Midwest is rural, but it also has many big cities including Chicago, Illinois, which is the third most populous city in the country. Detroit, Michigan; St. Louis, Missouri; Indianapolis, Indiana; Columbus, Ohio; and Minneapolis, Minnesota are also important, big cities in the Midwest. Some of these cities, especially Detroit, were important centers of car manufacturing in the 1900s. Today, they manufacture many products including heavy machinery, medicines, and computers.

■ **Answer the questions.**

❶ Why is the Midwest a good area for farming?

❷ Why do you think the Great Lakes are called "great"?

❸ What city was a major center of car manufacturing in the 1900s?

■ Fill out the area profile using the Key Points.

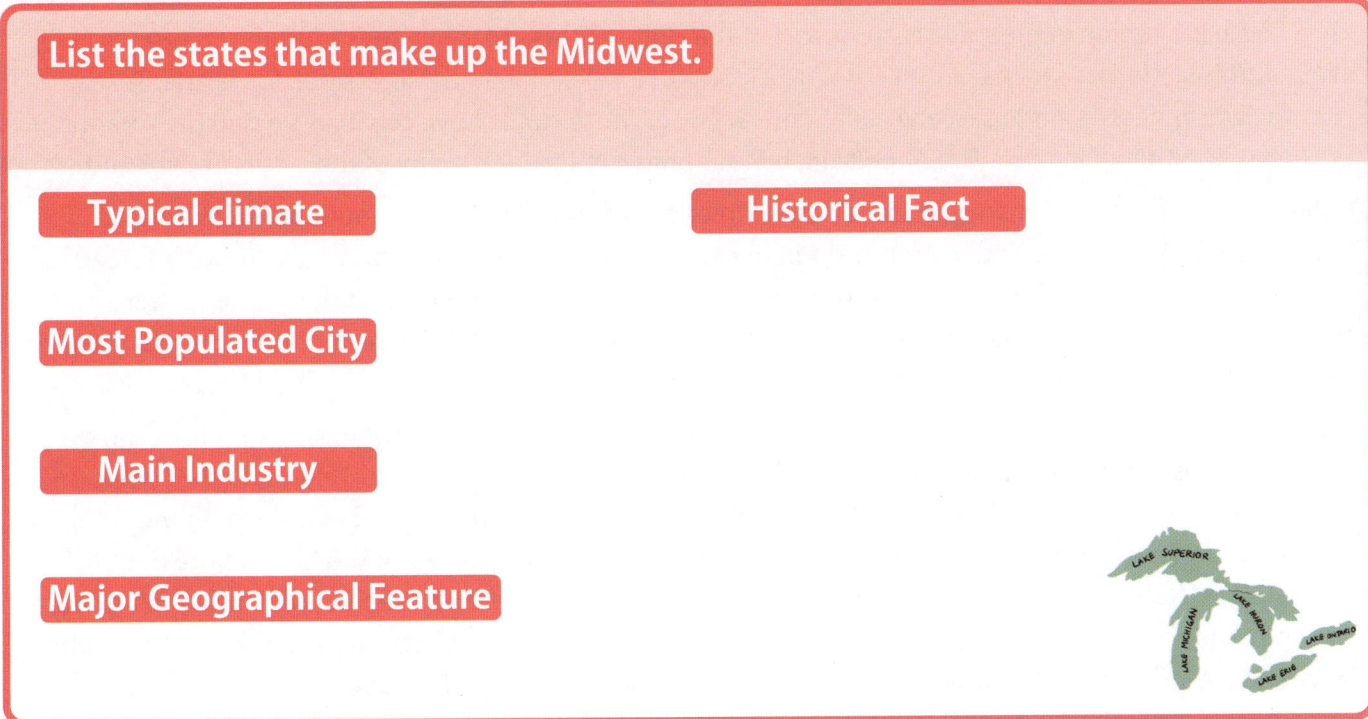

List the states that make up the Midwest.

Typical climate

Historical Fact

Most Populated City

Main Industry

Major Geographical Feature

■ Pick one state to learn more about! Use the Internet or a book to fill in the blanks about the state you chose.

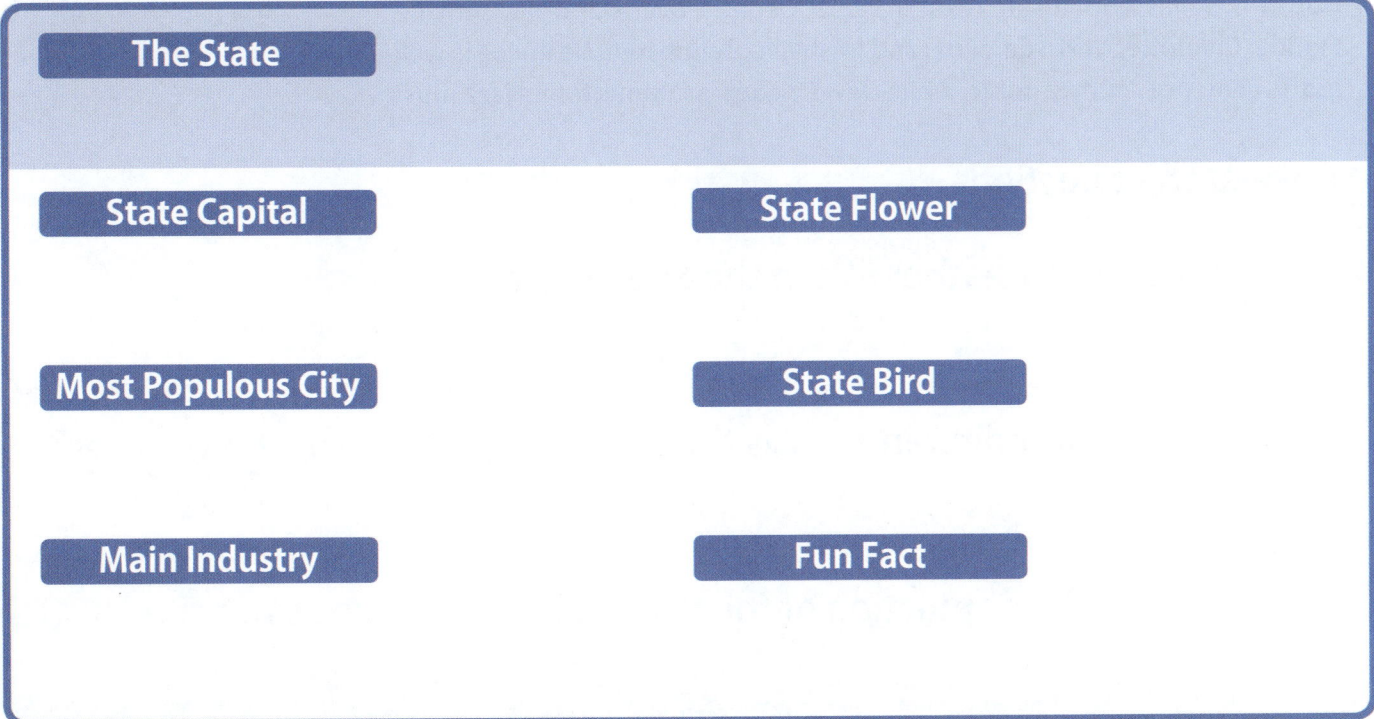

The State

State Capital

State Flower

Most Populous City

State Bird

Main Industry

Fun Fact

The South

The South is a region in the southeastern part of the United States that includes fourteen states: Virginia, West Virginia, North Carolina, South Carolina, Georgia, Florida, Alabama, Mississippi, Louisiana, Texas, Kentucky, Tennessee, Arkansas, and Oklahoma. Many of these states have coastlines along the Atlantic Ocean or the Gulf of Mexico. The Appalachian Mountains run through many of the states in the South.

Like in the rest of the US many different Native American groups lived in the South before European colonization. Most of the Native Americans in the southeast died due to war or disease or were forced to relocate to Oklahoma. The states bordering the Atlantic Ocean from Georgia north to Virginia were part of the original thirteen British colonies. Florida and Texas were originally Spanish colonies and Louisiana was a French colony. They became US states in the 1800s.

The southeastern states generally have hot, wet summers and mild winters, which means farms can grow crops for most of the year. European colonists started growing cotton, tobacco, rice, and other crops on large plantations. They needed a lot of workers for the farms and used enslaved people to do this difficult labor. Most of the states in the South had large-scale slavery on plantations in the time before the Civil War (1861-1865). For many years, cotton was the main product created by the South. This wasn't good for the economy or the soil. Eventually, people started also growing peanuts, soybeans, citrus fruits, and more. More industry was created in the South, like car manufacturing. Many southern states have oil drilling and coal mining.

The population of the South has grown a lot since the 1950s, when air conditioning became more common and affordable, making Southern summers much more pleasant. Much of the South is rural, but it contains many big cities, including Houston, Dallas, and Austin, Texas; Atlanta, Georgia; Miami and Jacksonville, Florida; Charlotte, North Carolina; and Nashville, Tennessee. Nashville is well-known as the center of country music, while New Orleans is famous for its jazz music.

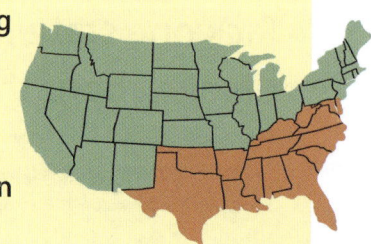

■ Answer the questions.

❶ What is the weather like in the Southeast?

_____

❷ Which mountain range runs through many of the southern states?

_____

❸ Why has the population of the South grown so much since the 1950s?

_____

■ Fill out the area profile using the Key Points.

List the states that make up the South.

Typical climate

Historical Fact

Most Populated City

Main Industry

■ Pick one state to learn more about! Use the Internet or a book to fill in the blanks about the state you chose.

The State

State Capital

State Flower

Most Populous City

State Bird

Main Industry

Fun Fact

The Southwest

KEY POINTS

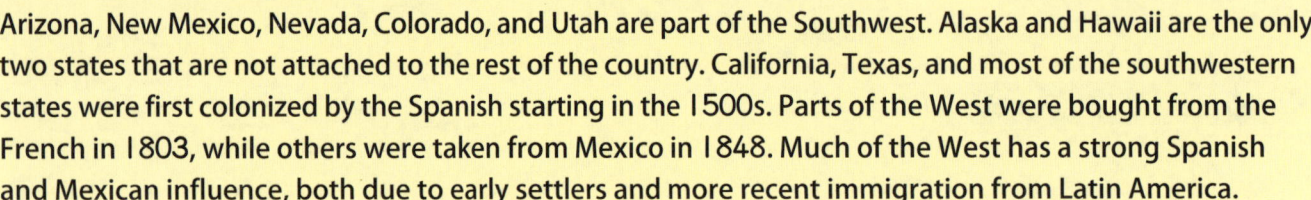

The American West includes thirteen states: Arizona, Colorado, Idaho, Montana, Nevada, New Mexico, Utah, Wyoming, Alaska, California, Hawaii, Oregon, and Washington.

The American West is huge - it takes up more than a third of the United States. California, Oregon, and Washington make up the West Coast, while Arizona, New Mexico, Nevada, Colorado, and Utah are part of the Southwest. Alaska and Hawaii are the only two states that are not attached to the rest of the country. California, Texas, and most of the southwestern states were first colonized by the Spanish starting in the 1500s. Parts of the West were bought from the French in 1803, while others were taken from Mexico in 1848. Much of the West has a strong Spanish and Mexican influence, both due to early settlers and more recent immigration from Latin America.

After gold was found there, California became the first area in the West that many settlers moved to, hoping to strike it rich. Today, California is the most populous state in the US with around thirty-eight million people. Its mild winters and rich soils make it one of the biggest producers of food in the US. It is also famous for its big cities like Los Angeles, the center of movie-making in the US, and the San Francisco area, the US's tech center. Much of the Pacific coasts of California, Oregon, and Washington are densely populated, as are cities like Phoenix, Arizona and Denver, Colorado. However, the West also has many of the nation's wide open spaces, with huge national parks, like the Grand Canyon in Arizona, Yosemite in California, and Yellowstone in Wyoming. There are many farms and cattle ranches there.

Because the West is such a big area, its weather greatly varies. Oregon's and Washington's coasts are rainy. Much of the West is dry and hot, with frequent wildfires in the summer. The Rocky Mountains run through the West, and the higher the elevation, the colder and wetter it generally is.

■ Answer the questions based on the Key Points.

❶ Why was California the first place in the West to have a lot of American settlers?

❷ Why does much of the West have Spanish and Mexican influences?

❸ What is the weather like on Oregon's and Washington's coasts?

■ Fill out the area profile using the Key Points.

List the states that make up the Southwest.

Typical climate

Historical Fact

Most Populated City

Main Industry

Major Geographic Feature

■ Pick one state to learn more about! Use the Internet or a book to fill in the blanks about the state you chose.

The State

State Capital

State Flower

Most Populous City

State Bird

Main Industry

Fun Fact

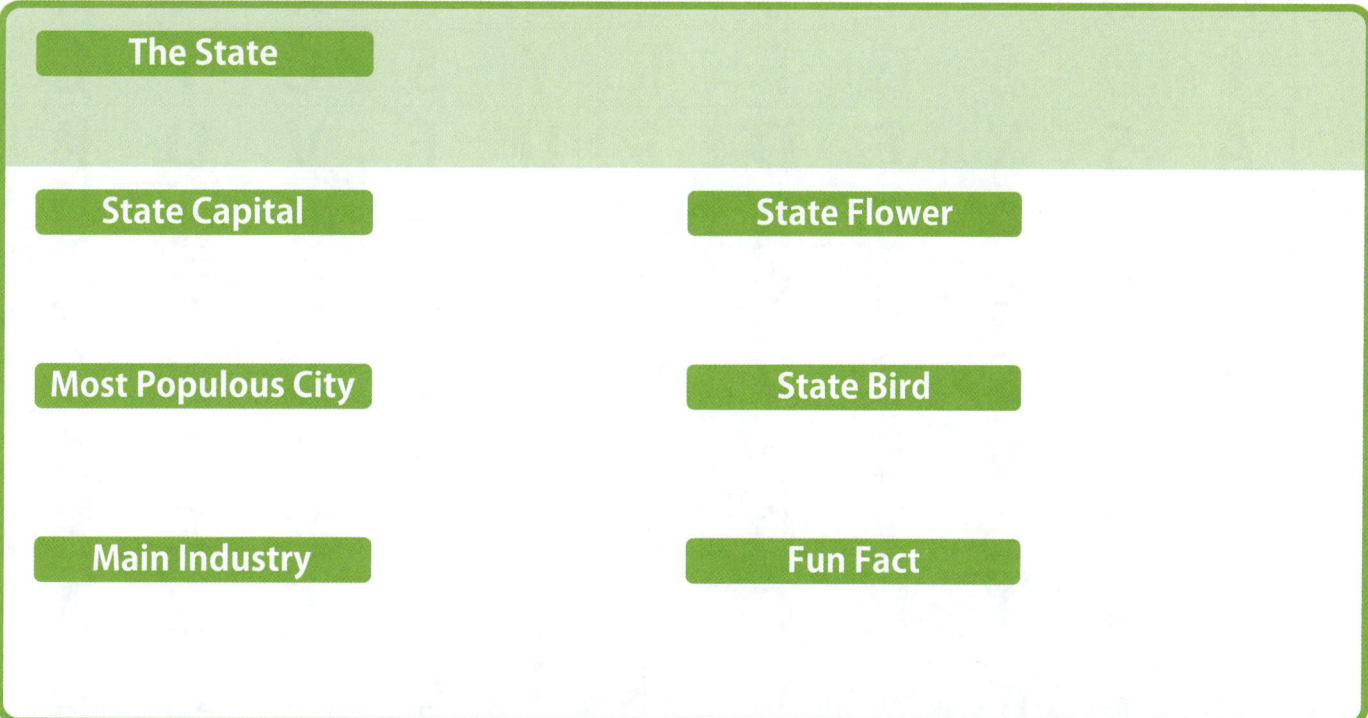

Brain Break
Word Search

■ Circle the words in the puzzle below.

New York	Maine	Vermont	Michigan	Ohio
Kansas	Virginia	Florida	Texas	Tennessee
	Alaska	California	Colorado	Utah

C	O	L	O	R	A	D	O	L	P	V
A	Q	W	H	E	R	T	Y	U	I	I
L	D	F	I	K	G	H	T	J	K	R
I	S	A	O	A	Z	X	E	C	V	G
F	J	K	L	N	P	M	N	B	F	I
O	H	G	F	S	D	S	N	A	L	N
R	W	E	M	A	I	N	E	Z	O	I
N	R	T	T	S	Y	U	S	X	R	A
I	O	E	G	F	T	Y	S	C	I	L
A	S	X	F	D	J	U	E	V	D	P
A	L	A	S	K	A	C	E	B	A	O
V	O	S	U	Y	K	L	A	N	M	U
B	I	S	Z	V	E	R	M	O	N	T
N	E	V	B	W	R	T	Y	K	L	A
N	E	W	Y	O	R	K	W	H	P	H
K	A	I	H	G	F	E	D	C	B	A
J	L	M	I	C	H	I	G	A	N	Q

Unit 2

Mindfulness Break!

KEY POINTS

Mindfulness is about listening to your body and your feelings. It can help you know when you are happy, stressed, excited, or worried.

Worrying is when you think a lot about something that makes you scared, nervous, or anxious. It is important to be aware of when you feel worried so you can try and stay calm or overcome that feeling.

Worrying is normal, everyone worries! You might worry about a spelling test or going to a new place for the first time or going to the doctor's office.

One way to be mindful of your worries and to keep them controlled is to practice writing them down.

■ Fill the box below with your worries to help get them off your mind. You can do this any time at home too in a journal or on extra paper.

Coding 3

■ Look at the flowchart. Follow the commands below to find out where the brown robot will end up. Write a check mark (✓) on the flag of the correct color.

①

Start
↓
Move 1 step
↓
Turn to the right
↓
Move 2 steps
↓
End

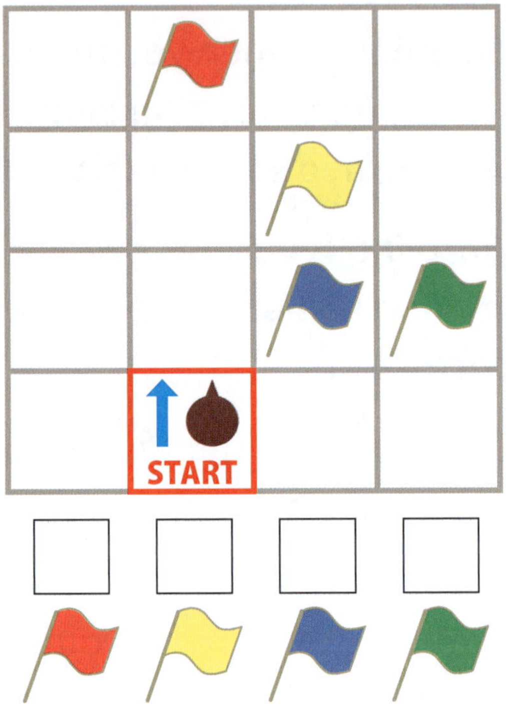

②

Start
↓
Turn to the left
↓
Move 2 steps
↓
Turn to the right
↓
Move 1 step
↓
End

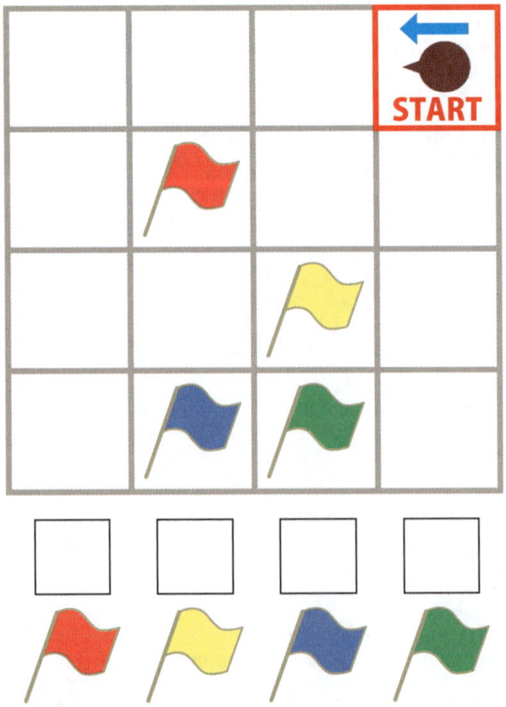

■ Using the flowchart, give the brown robot the command to move from start to the star. In the flowchart, choose the correct command to fill in the blanks and write one of the letters Ⓐ to Ⓓ in the box for each.

①

Start

?

Turn to the right

Move 1 step

End

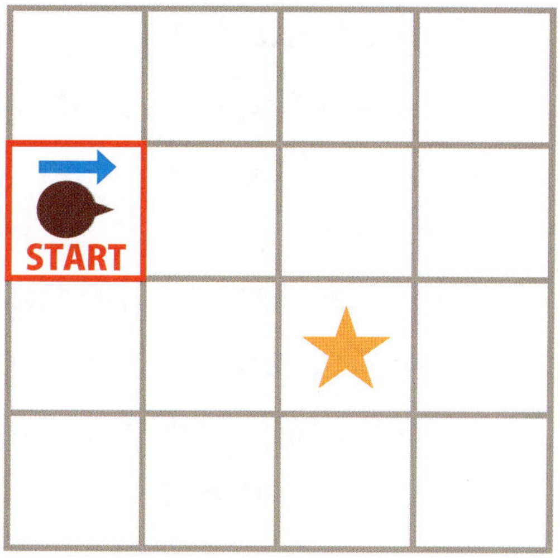

START

②

Start

?

Move 2 steps

Turn to the right

Move 3 steps

End

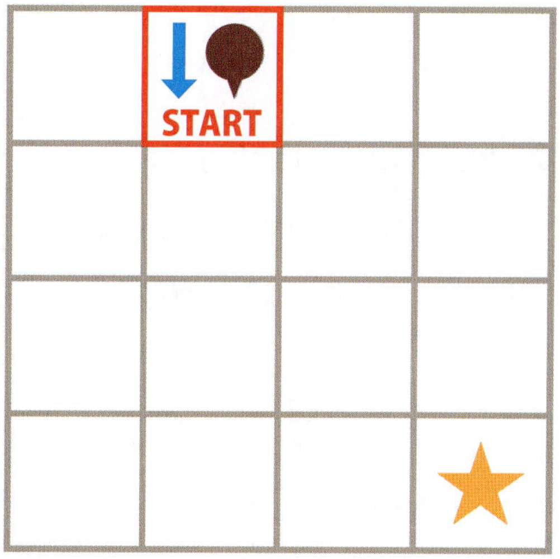

START

Ⓐ **Move 1 step**   Ⓑ **Move 2 steps**
Ⓒ **Turn to the right**   Ⓓ **Turn to the left**

Unit 2 Technology

Coding 4

KEY POINTS

If the same procedure is to be repeated, the flowchart can be shortened using [_____] and [_____] as shown on the right.

The robot draws the shapes from the left as commanded. Whichever flowchart you use to command the robot, the result is the same, but the length of the flowchart is different.

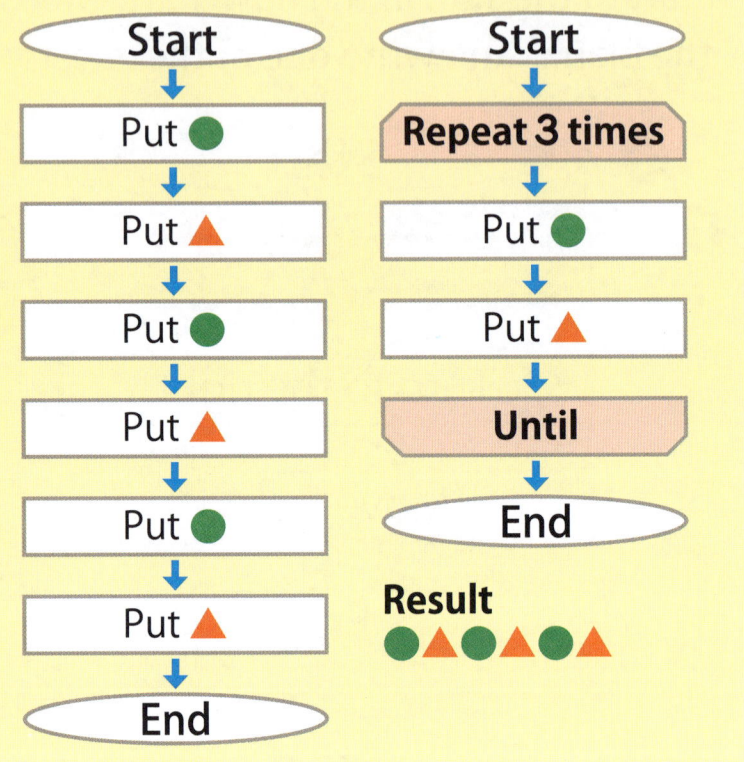

■ Use the flowchart to command the robot. The robot draws the shapes as commanded. When giving the following commands, write a check mark (✔) in the correct sequence of shapes put by the robot.

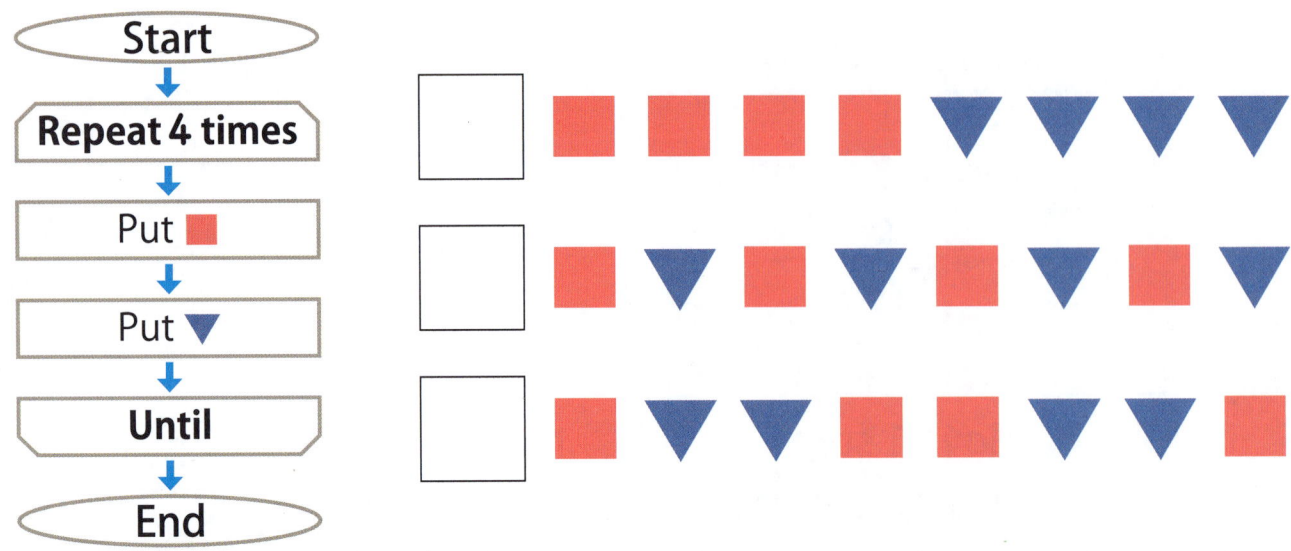

■ Use the flowchart to command the robot. The robot paints the color from the left as commanded. Choose a flowchart to color as follows and write one of the letters Ⓐ or Ⓑ in the box.

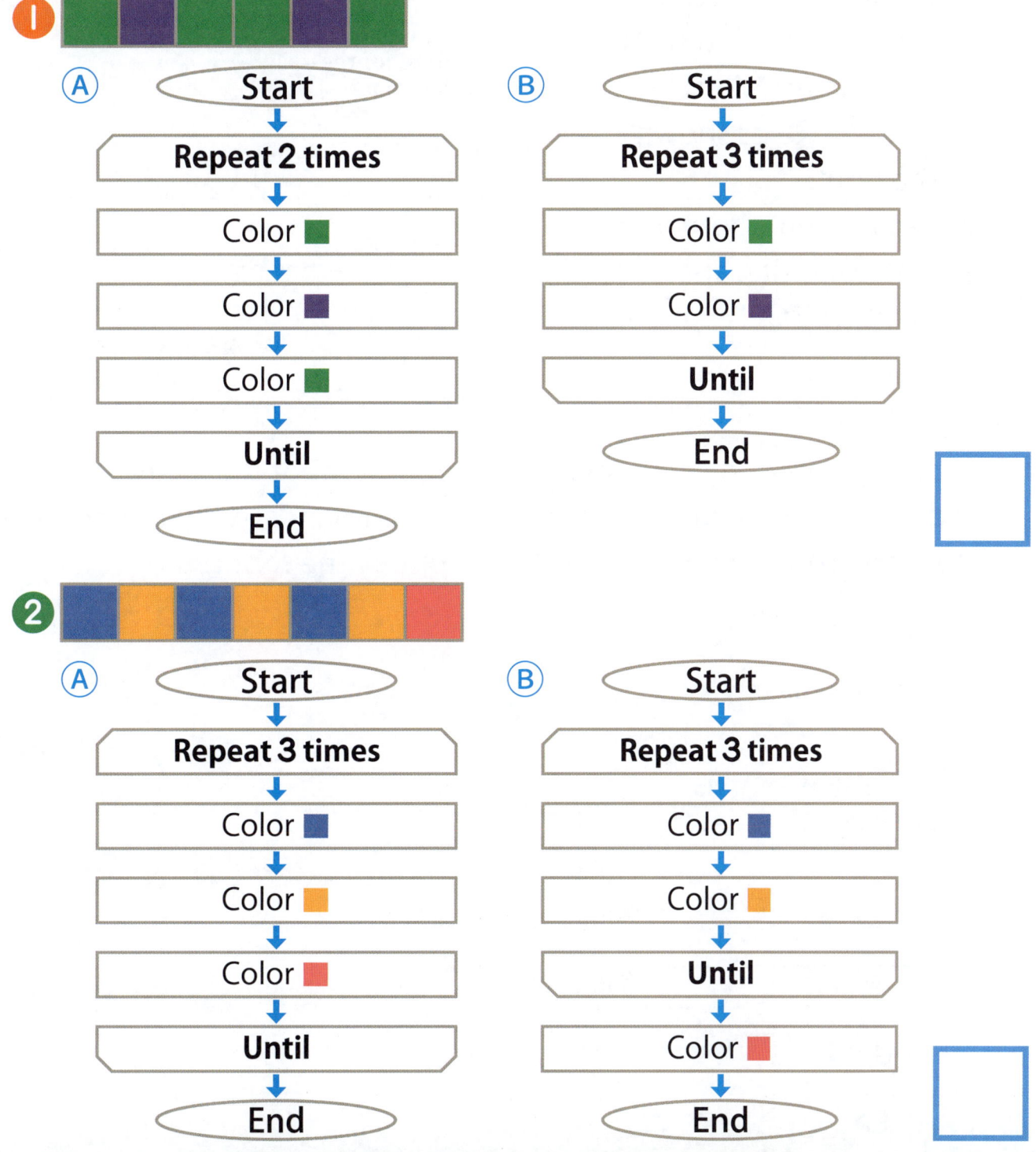

Unit ② Technology

Coding 5

When it is necessary to indicate that the next step to be executed depends on a condition, the flowchart can use the decision symbol ⬦ as shown on the right.
Depending on whether or not the condition applies, the next step will change.

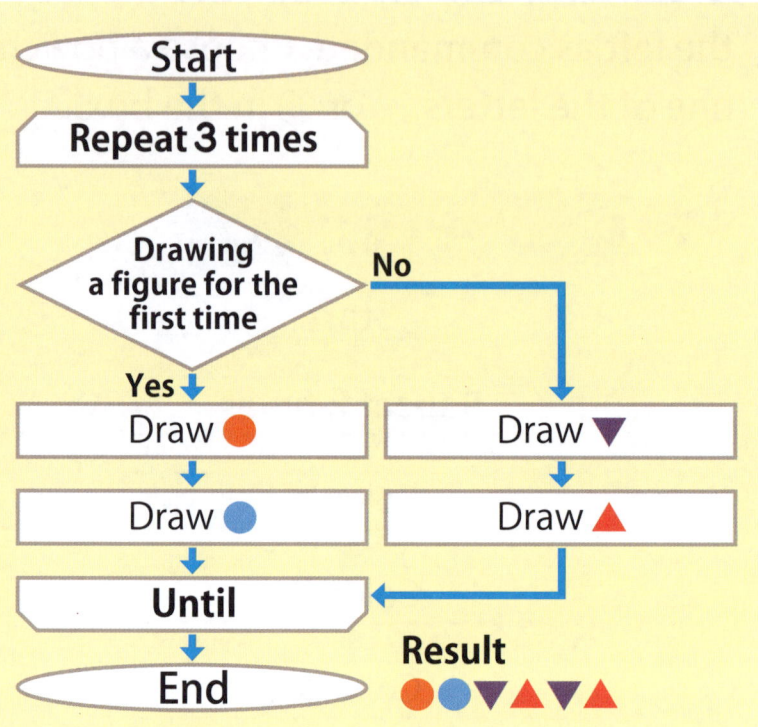

■ Use the flowchart to command the robot. The robot draws the shapes as commanded. When giving the following commands, write a check mark (✓) in the correct sequence of shapes put by the robot.

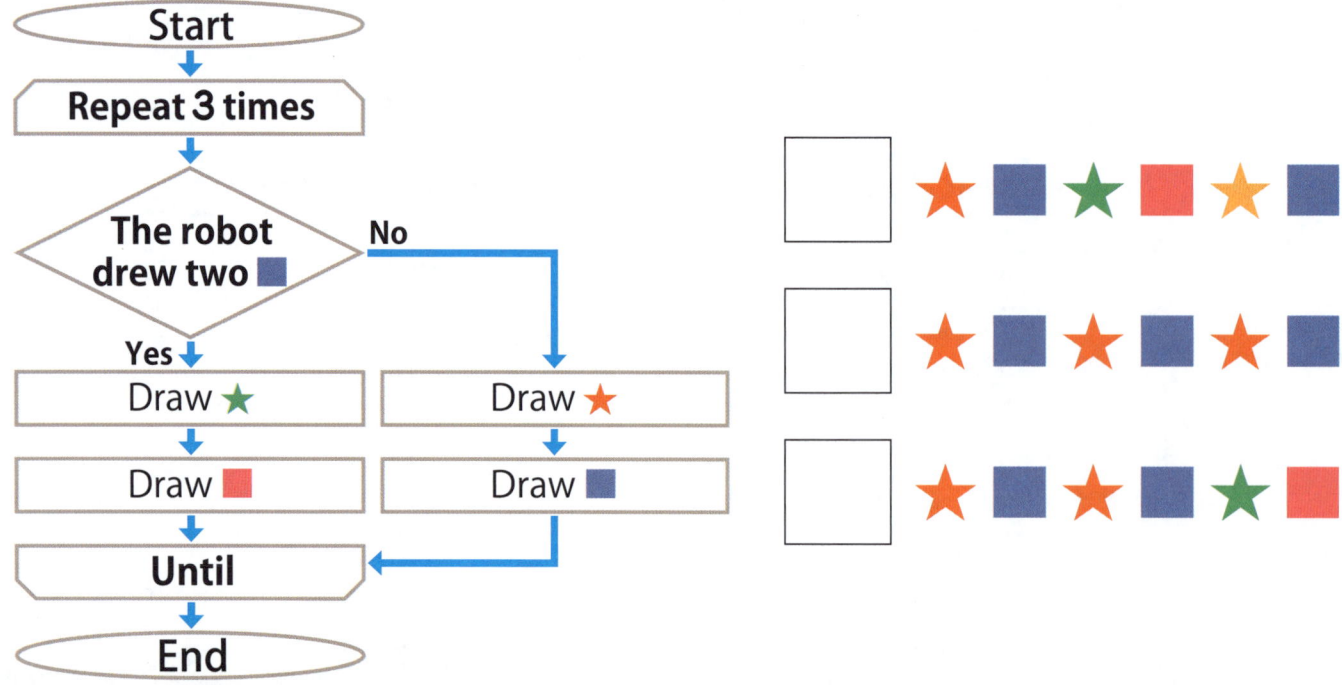

■ Use the flowchart to command the robot. The robot draws the shapes as commanded. When drawing figures like ❶ and ❷, choose a command from Ⓐ, Ⓑ, and Ⓒ that fits in the blank space in the flowchart and write it in the box.

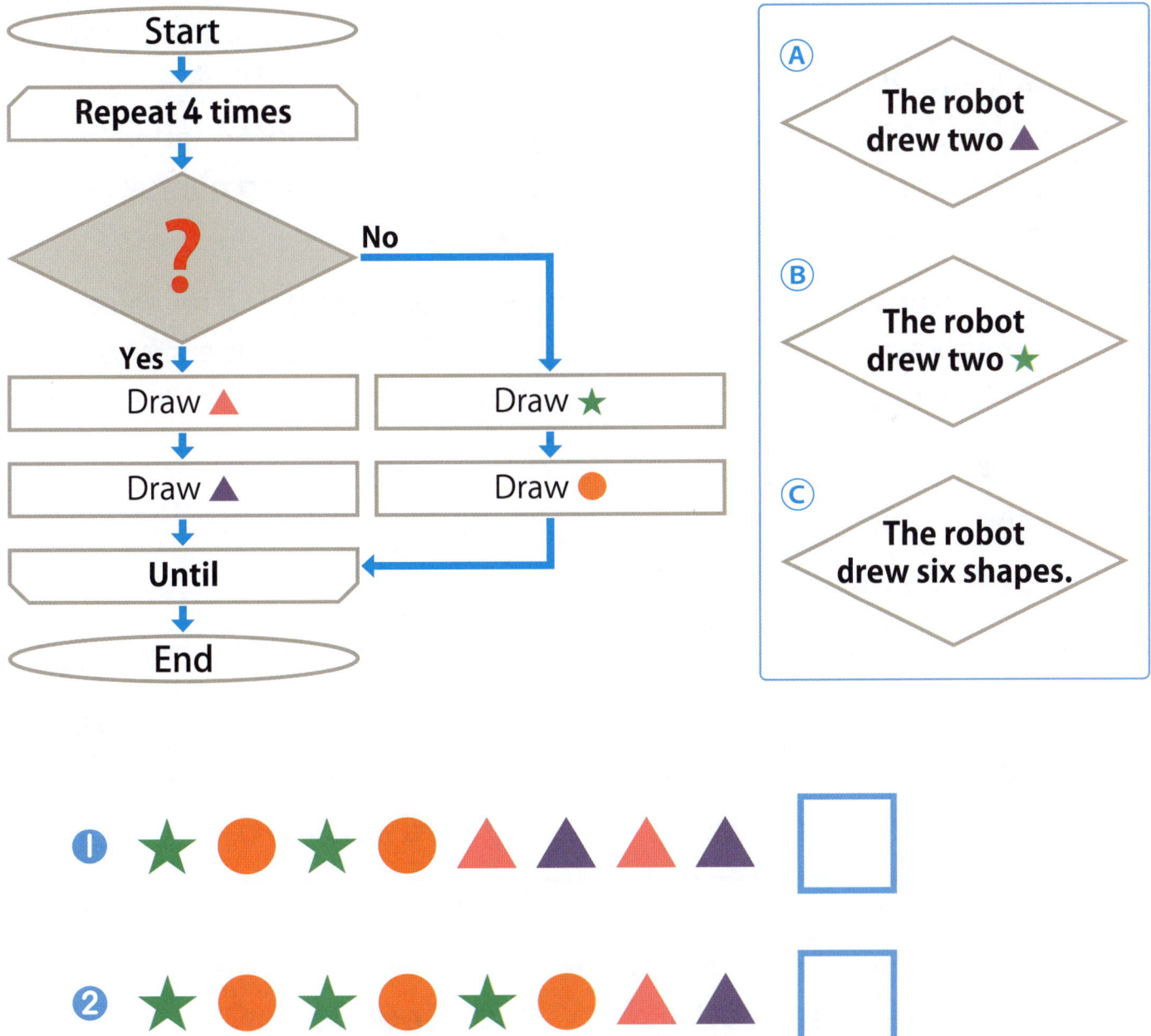

Online Safety

KEY POINTS

The Internet is used by many people around the world because it provides easy access to a wide variety of information.

It also allows you to spread a variety of information and share it with other people. However, we need to understand that there are dangers associated with being personally identified or having important information made known to others. It is important to avoid disclosing our full names, detailed addresses, passwords, and so on.

Passwords protect your important information from being revealed to others. Passwords should be a long mix of letters, numbers, and symbols to prevent others from guessing them.

■ Circle the stronger password.

❶ 123456789   4o0sZ_7@2

❷ password   Pdw5s@D6

❸ steven_2025   ep l egb4i6_r9sl

■ Read the questions below and check (✔) if the answer is true or false.

① When introducing yourself to strangers on the Internet, you should not share your address or phone number.

True False

② When deciding on a password, it is best to include your name or birthday so that you do not forget it.

True False

③ Whenever you receive a message from a stranger, you must respond.

True False

④ You should not believe all the news on the Internet.

True False

⑤ When showing photos to strangers on the Internet, you should be careful not to reveal personal information about yourself or others.

True False

Physical Education Break!

It's important to move your body and exercise!
Try this fun activity below to break up your studying!

■ Look at the images and read the text below. Try the yoga poses!

Tree Pose

Stand on one leg. Bend the knee of the leg you are not standing on, place the bottom of your foot on the inside of your leg, and then balance.

Butterfly Pose

Sit on your behind with your back straight. Bend your legs and place the bottom of your feet together.

Mountain Pose

Stand up straight with your feet apart and your arms out to the side with palms facing foward. Imagine being strong and unmovable like a mountain.

Frog Pose

Squat down with your knees apart and your arms resting between your knees. Touch your hands to the ground. Hold.

Unit ③ Table of Contents

Use this page to keep track of your progress throughout the book. Place a check mark in the box when you have completed a section.

KEY POINTS

When reading a story or any type of text, it is important to pay attention to details. What is the writer of the text trying to say? How does the main character feel about what's happening? What might happen next? How will the problem be resolved? When faced with these questions paying attention to details in the text can help you answer them.

Referring to details and examples in a text when explaining what the text says can help a reader better understand and help them draw inferences from the text.

■ Read the passage below and answer the questions on the right page using the passage.

Today was a day I had been waiting for for a month. It was the end of Ramadan and finally time to celebrate Eid al-Fitr! I woke up early and put on the new bright and colorful clothes my mom had laid out for me. Downstairs, I discovered my mom had made us a big breakfast with delicious treats like sweet pastries and dates. It was exciting to have treats for breakfast after a month of fasting.

After breakfast, my family went to the mosque to pray together. It felt special because the whole community was there smiling and and hugging each other. Then, we went home to greet our relatives! They come to visit every Eid. I couldn't wait to see my cousins.

Later, we gathered around our family's dining room table to enjoy the feast my grandmother and mom had cooked during the day. There were so many delicious dishes, like rice, chicken, bread, and sweets. Everyone laughed and talked about the month of fasting and renewal. I felt so lucky to be surrounded by my family.

After dinner, my grandparents gather all the kids and cousins to give us our "eidi" or little envelopes with money. Then my cousins and I ran outside to play games, while the adults shared stories in the house. At the end of the day, I felt thankful for my family and our traditions. It was a wonderful day.

1 What is the theme of this text?

2 How does the main character feel about what is happening?

3 What is the setting?

4 How does the setting affect the main character?

5 What did you learn from this story?

6 What can you take away from this story?

Reading Comprehension 2

All texts have a main idea or topic. You can determine the main topic of a piece by reading it and putting together the information and details. Details support the main idea by telling how, what, when, where, why, how much, or how many. Finding the topic, main idea, and supporting details helps you understand the points the writer is trying to express.

■ Read the passage below and answer the questions on the right page using the passage.

The Florida Everglades is a unique and important national park located in southern Florida. It is the largest tropical wilderness in the United States, spanning 1.5 million acres. The Everglades is a wetland ecosystem, which means it is made up of areas that are flooded with water for part of the year. This special park is home to many different types of plants and animals, some of which can only be found in here. Some examples are the endangered West Indian manatee and the American crocodile. The park also has a mix of swamps, marshes, and mangrove forests, which are the perfect home for these animals.

Visitors to the Everglades can explore the park by airboat, canoe, and even on foot. Some of the most popular activities are birdwatching, hiking, and taking guided tours to learn about the wildlife and history of the park. The

Everglades is also an important place for protecting the environment. It helps filter water and maintain the balance of the ecosystem in Florida. The park is designated a World Heritage Site, A Wetland of International Importance, and a UNESCO Biosphere Reserve because of its unique ecosystems.

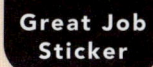

❶ What is the main topic of this text?

_____

❷ List three details to support the main topic.

_____

_____

_____

❸ What is the text trying to convey?

_____

❹ What conclusions can you draw from the key details of this text?

_____

❺ Name one takeaway from this text.

_____

Reading Comprehension 3

The structure, or how a text is written, can also tell the reader a lot about what the writer is trying to convey. Often writers will use chronology to shape the structure of a story and show how certain events happen over time. A writer might also discuss the main idea in terms of cause and effect to show how one thing affects something else.

■ **Read the story and then put the events in chronological order.**

Johnsonville Middle School was holding its annual bake sale to raise money for the school's extracurricular activities. Andi and Marco signed up to make cupcakes. Marco came over to the Andi's house after school to get started. Andi had all the ingredients on the counter - sugar, flour, butter, eggs and three tubs of bright colored frosting.

They carefully followed the recipe, but things started to go wrong right away.
Marco accidentally pour too much sugar into the bowl making the mixture too sweet. Then, Andi got distracted while stirring and spilled flour all over the kitchen floor. It made a big mess as they tried to clean it up and flour got everywhere. They both started laughing, even though they were beginning to get frustrated. They tried to fix everything, but it felt like nothing was going right.

When they finally got the cupcakes into the oven, they realized they forgot to add the baking powder! The cupcakes didn't rise like they were suppose to and turned out flat and hard. Andi and Marco agreed they couldn't bring these cupcakes to the bake sale. Instead, they decided to try again.

This time they worked together and double checked each step. Andi helped Marco pour the sugar and Marco checked off each ingredient as it was added. Andi stirred more carefully this time. The second batch came out perfectly! Andi and Marco gave each other an excited high-five and began the fun part - decorating the cupcakes.
At the bake sale, their cupcakes were a big hit. Even though their first batch was a disaster, they were proud of what they had made on their own and how they found a solution to each problem they faced.

(A) Andi and Marco decorated the cupcakes.

(B) Andi and Marco are baking cupcakes for their school bake sale.

(C) Marco double checked the measurements and checked off each ingredient.

(D) Andi and Marco's cupcakes didn't rise in the oven because they forgot the baking powder.

(E) Andi and Marco's cupcakes were the hit of the bake sale!

(F) Andi spilled flour all over the floor when mixing the cupcakes.

Event timeline

Comparing Reading Passages

Another important skill to develop when reading is the ability to compare and contrast the most important points and key details presented in different types of texts.

For example, reading an informational text about pandas will teach you something different than reading an opinion text about pandas. The details in informational texts are based on facts and the details in opinion texts are based on a person's opinion and interpretation of those facts.

■ Read the passages below and answer the questions on the right hand page.

Passage 1: Informational Text

Jazz music is a type of music that started in New Orleans, Louisiana in the early 1900's. It was created by African American musicians who originally blended African rhythms, blues, and European music styles. Jazz is known for its lively rhythms, improvisation, and its unique sound.  Some of the first jazz musicians were famous for their trumpet and clarinet playing, like Louis Armstrong and Sidney Bechet. As jazz spread to other cities in the US, like New York and Chicago, it grew into many different styles including swing, bebop, and cool jazz. Today, jazz music is still popular around the world and has influenced many musicians and current music trends.

Passage 2: Opinion Text

I really like jazz music because it's so fun and full of energy! I just started to learn to play the trumpet, and when I listen to jazz, I can hear all the cool notes a trumpet can play. It can even play notes faster and make unique noises that other instruments can't. It's amazing how the musicians get to improvise and  make up music as they go. It can make any music piece sound different and unique every time it's played. My favorite part is when the trumpet gets to play a solo, and all the other musicians stop to listen to the trumpet player. I think jazz is the best because it's creative and you can express yourself in your own way. The more I practice my trumpet, the more I try to find my own jazz style.

1 What is the main topic of both passages?

2 Which passage teaches you more about the topic?

3 What is the main difference between the informational text and the opinion text?

4 Which passage is more enjoyable to read? Why?

5 What facts does the informational passage provide about the topic?

6 What is the opinion writer's opinion of the topic? Positive or negative? Explain why you feel that way with a line from the text.

Brain Break
Create a Storyboard

Storyboarding is creating a picture by picture panel of a story to help show the events.

■ Take the Bake Sale story from page 132 and create a storyboard of the events.

Mindfulness Break!

An important part of being mindful is having self-awareness. Self-awareness is a person's ability to recognize and understand facts and feelings about themselves.

■ Fill in each bubble with a comment about yourself to practice self-awareness.

I am a good person because...

What I like most about myself is...

I am thoughtful when I...

I am unique because...

My special talent is...

I am helpful when I...

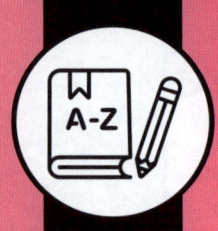

Narrative Writing: Elements of a Story

KEY POINTS

Narrative writing tells a story, and there are certain things that all stories have. Stories have characters, and events that happen to those characters. Those events are what make up the plot of the story.

■ Read the story below. Circle the characters and write three events below.

I couldn't believe it. I was flying on an airplane for the very first time. I sat down in my seat next to my mom, and listened to the flight attendant's announcements. After we were up in the air, I pulled down the tray in front of me and started watching a movie. Then I guess I must have dozed off, because the next thing I knew, we were about to land. My very first flight was over!

_____

_____

_____

■ In a few activities, you will write a story of your own. There is an optional prompt below. You can choose to use this prompt, or you can make up any story you wish. Use this page to choose your characters and events. Make sure to list the events in the order in which they happen.

Prompt (optional)

Imagine you are an alien who lands on Earth and can't get back to your home planet. What would you do?

Characters

Events

①

②

③

④

Narrative Writing: Dialogue

When a character in a story says something, that is called dialogue. Dialogue can help move the plot along, and it can also help the reader understand the character.

The words the person says should appear in quotation marks (" "). If the dialogue is the last part of the sentence, then the end punctuation should appear inside the quotation marks. If the sentence continues after the quotation mark, then use a comma inside the quotation marks instead.

"What a nice day," Harry said.
Harry said, "What a nice day."

■ If the sentence is correct, make a check. If it is incorrect, write an x and then fix it below.

❶ "I love going to the movies." Hannah told him.

☐ _____

❷ Sarah said, "I'd like to go to the library."

☐ _____

❸ "Let's go to the park," I suggested.

☐ _____

❹ Molly looked at me and said, "Let's go outside"!

☐ _____

Date

Great Job Sticker

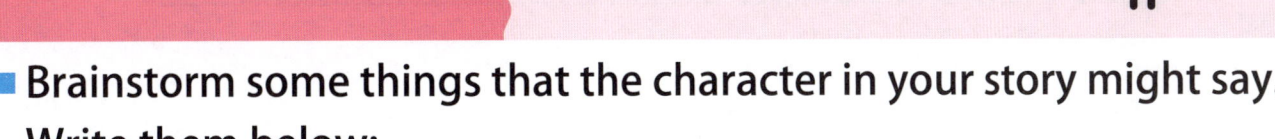

■ Brainstorm some things that the character in your story might say.
Write them below:

1

2

3

4

5

Narrative Writing: Sensory Details

Writers use descriptions to make their story feel real and easy for the reader to imagine. One way they do that is by using sensory details. Sensory details appeal to the five senses: sight, hearing, touch, smell, and taste.

Example: The sweater was rough and scratchy.

This details appeals to the reader's sense of touch.

■ Underline the sensory details in the text below.

I stepped out into the cool air. As I walked outside, I noticed that I could see my breath in front of me, like a little cloud. I heard birds singing loudly above my head. It smelled like it was about to rain, so I started walking quickly.

■ Write a sensory description of each thing below.

Taste

lemon ➡

Sight

lake ➡

Hearing

siren ➡

Touch

chalk ➡

Smell

coffee ➡

Writing a Story

■ Write your story, using the story elements and details that you wrote already, as well as sensory words.

Brain Break
My Favorite Character

■ Who is your favorite character from a book, movie, or tv show? Describe them and why they are your favorite.

Mindfulness Break!

■ Write a response for each sentence.

> Be in the present moment. Write what you see, hear, feel, and smell right now.

Right now I see...

Right now I feel...

Right now I hear...

Right now I smell...

Calculations with Fractions

■ Add the fractions.

1 $\dfrac{1}{5} + \dfrac{1}{5} = \dfrac{\square}{\square}$

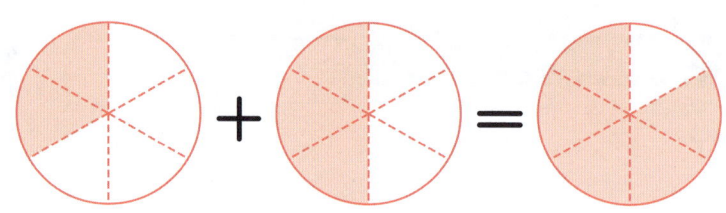

2 $\dfrac{2}{6} + \dfrac{3}{6} = \dfrac{\square}{\square}$

3 $\dfrac{1}{3} + \dfrac{1}{3} =$

4 $\dfrac{2}{4} + \dfrac{1}{4} =$

5 $\dfrac{3}{9} + \dfrac{2}{9} =$

6 $\dfrac{1}{8} + \dfrac{2}{8} =$

7 $\dfrac{4}{12} + \dfrac{3}{12} =$

8 $\dfrac{2}{10} + \dfrac{7}{10} =$

If the fractions
have the same denominator,
just add the numerators.

■ Subtract the fractions.

① $\dfrac{2}{4} - \dfrac{1}{4} = \dfrac{\square}{\square}$

② $\dfrac{6}{8} - \dfrac{3}{8} = \dfrac{\square}{\square}$

③ $\dfrac{4}{5} - \dfrac{2}{5} =$

④ $\dfrac{9}{9} - \dfrac{5}{9} =$

⑤ $\dfrac{3}{6} - \dfrac{2}{6} =$

⑥ $\dfrac{7}{10} - \dfrac{4}{10} =$

⑦ $\dfrac{3}{3} - \dfrac{2}{3} =$

⑧ $\dfrac{12}{12} - \dfrac{7}{12} =$

If the fractions
have the same denominator,
just subtract the numerators.

Greater than or Less than Fractions

■ Write > (greater than), < (less than), or = (equal to) to compare the fractions.

❶ $\dfrac{2}{3}$ ☐ $\dfrac{4}{6}$ 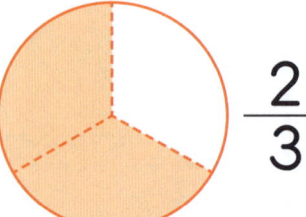 $\dfrac{2}{3}$ 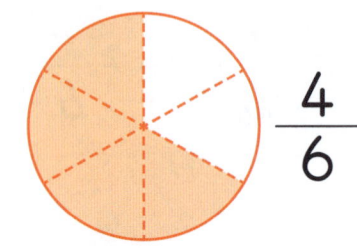 $\dfrac{4}{6}$

❷ $\dfrac{2}{5}$ ☐ $\dfrac{3}{5}$  $\dfrac{2}{5}$ 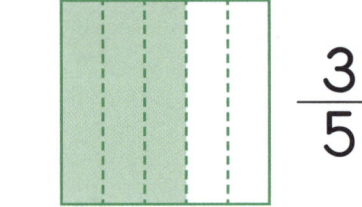 $\dfrac{3}{5}$

❸ 1 ☐ $\dfrac{4}{4}$  1 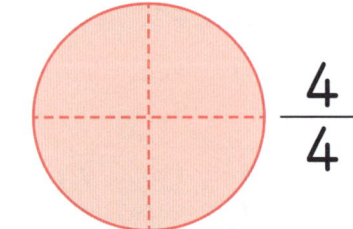 $\dfrac{4}{4}$

❹ $\dfrac{5}{8}$ ☐ $\dfrac{3}{8}$ $\dfrac{5}{8}$ $\dfrac{3}{8}$

❺ $\dfrac{5}{10}$ ☐ $\dfrac{1}{2}$ $\dfrac{5}{10}$ 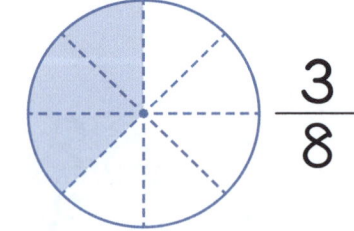 $\dfrac{1}{2}$

■ Draw a line to match the fractions that represent the same amount.

 $\dfrac{1}{2}$ •

• $\dfrac{2}{3}$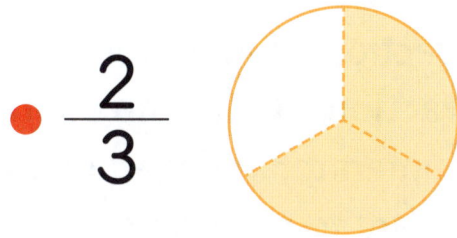

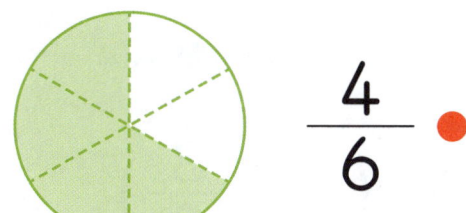 $\dfrac{4}{6}$ •

• $\dfrac{2}{5}$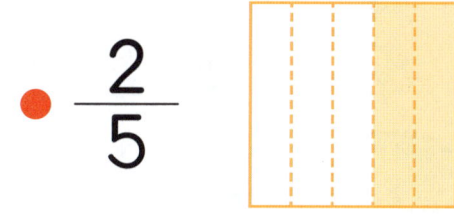

 $\dfrac{3}{4}$ •

• $\dfrac{6}{8}$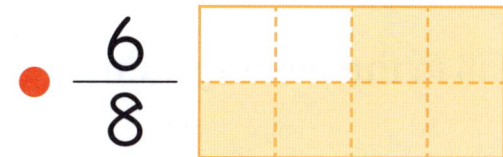

 $\dfrac{4}{10}$ •

• $\dfrac{2}{4}$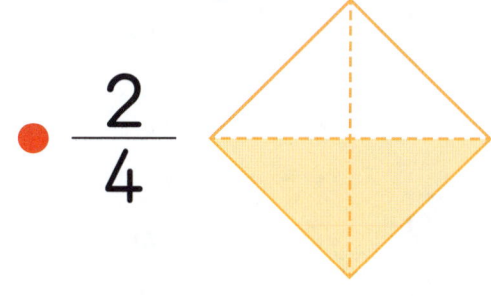

 $\dfrac{3}{12}$ •

• $\dfrac{1}{4}$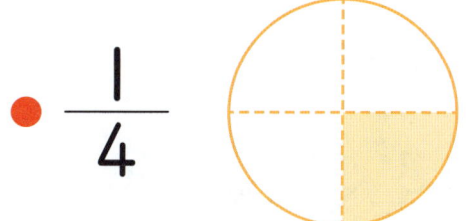

Equivalent Fractions

Fractions that represent the same amount are known as **equivalent fractions**. To find an equivalent fraction, you can multiply both the numerator and the denominator by the same number, which is meant to represent 1.

Ex.

$$\frac{1}{2} = \frac{3}{6}$$

$$\frac{1}{2} \times 1 = \frac{1}{2}$$

$$\frac{1}{2} \times \frac{3}{3} = \frac{3}{6}$$

Numerator

$$\left(1 = \frac{3}{3}\right)$$

Denominator

■ Fill in the missing number for each box.

① $\frac{1}{2} \times \dfrac{\square}{\square} = \frac{2}{4}$ ② $\frac{1}{2} \times \dfrac{\square}{\square} = \frac{3}{6}$ ③ $\frac{1}{4} \times \dfrac{\square}{\square} = \frac{2}{8}$

④ $\frac{2}{3} \times \dfrac{\square}{\square} = \frac{4}{6}$ ⑤ $\frac{1}{2} \times \dfrac{\square}{\square} = \frac{4}{8}$ ⑥ $\frac{1}{2} \times \dfrac{\square}{\square} = \frac{6}{12}$

⑦ $\frac{3}{4} \times \dfrac{\square}{\square} = \frac{9}{12}$ ⑧ $\frac{1}{5} \times \dfrac{\square}{\square} = \frac{2}{10}$ ⑨ $\frac{1}{3} \times \dfrac{\square}{\square} = \frac{4}{12}$

■ Fill in the missing number for each box. Then, circle the pairs of equivalent fractions you found in these problems.

① $\dfrac{1}{2} \times \dfrac{3}{3} = \dfrac{3}{6}$

② $\dfrac{\square}{\square} \times \dfrac{4}{4} = \dfrac{4}{8}$

③ $\dfrac{\square}{\square} \times \dfrac{2}{2} = \dfrac{2}{16}$

④ $\dfrac{\square}{\square} \times \dfrac{4}{4} = \dfrac{4}{12}$

⑤ $\dfrac{\square}{\square} \times \dfrac{2}{2} = \dfrac{6}{8}$

⑥ $\dfrac{\square}{\square} \times \dfrac{3}{3} = \dfrac{9}{12}$

⑦ $\dfrac{\square}{\square} \times \dfrac{2}{2} = \dfrac{4}{10}$

⑧ $\dfrac{\square}{\square} \times \dfrac{3}{3} = \dfrac{6}{9}$

⑨ $\dfrac{\square}{\square} \times \dfrac{4}{4} = \dfrac{8}{12}$

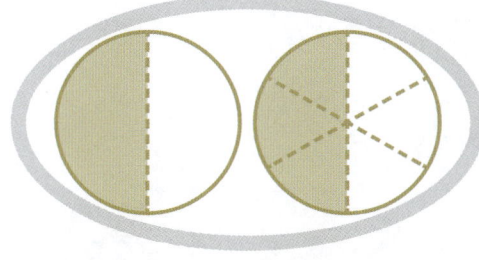
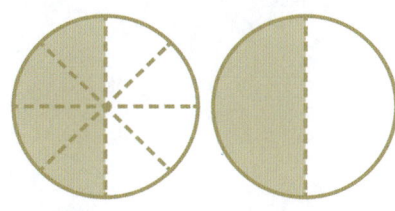
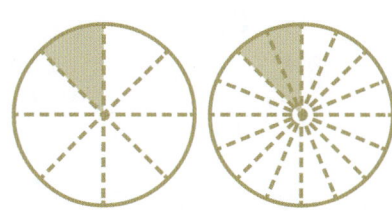
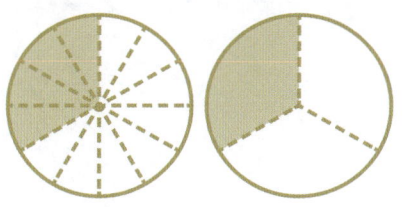
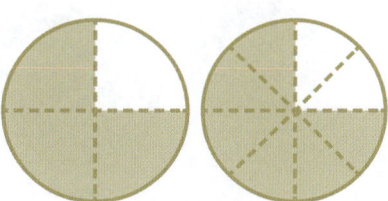
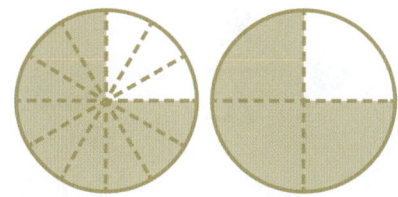
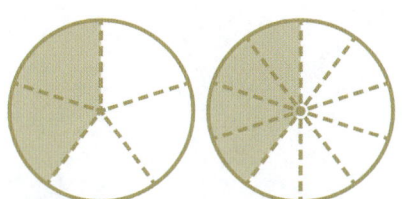
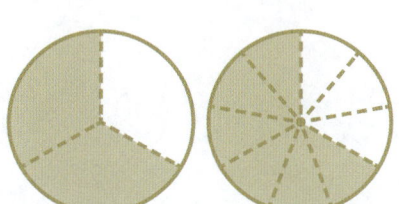
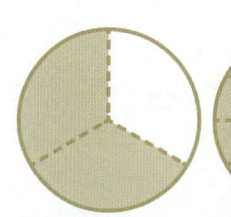

Proper and Improper Fractions

KEY POINTS

- **Proper Fraction:** The numerator is smaller than the denominator.

  Ex. $\dfrac{1}{3}$, $\dfrac{2}{3}$, $\dfrac{3}{4}$

- **Improper Fraction:** The numerator is equal to or larger than the denominator.

  Ex. $\dfrac{2}{2}$, $\dfrac{4}{3}$, $\dfrac{7}{5}$

- **Mixed Number:**
  Whole Number + Proper Fraction

  Ex. $1\dfrac{1}{3}$, $2\dfrac{3}{4}$

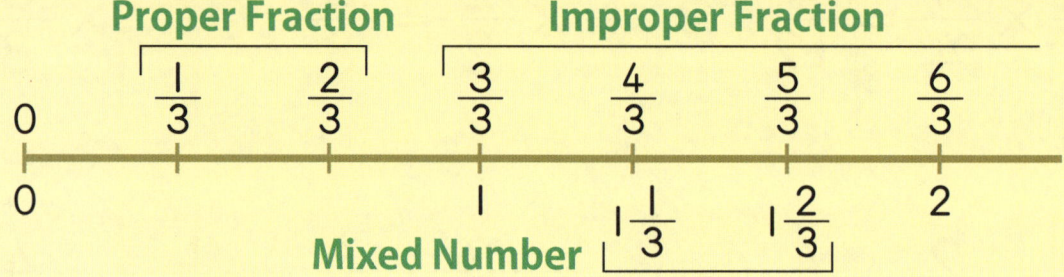

■ Convert the improper fraction to a mixed number, or a whole number.

❶ $\dfrac{5}{2} = 2\dfrac{\square}{2}$

$\dfrac{5}{2} \rightarrow 5 \div 2 = 2\,R\,1$
$\rightarrow 2\dfrac{1}{2}$

❷ $\dfrac{8}{4} = \square$

❸ $\dfrac{10}{3} = \square\dfrac{\square}{\square}$

■ Convert the mixed number to an improper fraction.

$$2\dfrac{1}{3} \rightarrow 2 \times 3 + 1 = 7$$
$$\dfrac{7}{3}$$

❶ $2\dfrac{1}{3} = \dfrac{7}{3}$

❷ $2\dfrac{2}{3} = \dfrac{\Box}{\Box}$

❸ $3\dfrac{1}{2} = \dfrac{\Box}{\Box}$

❹ $3\dfrac{3}{4} = \dfrac{\Box}{\Box}$

❺ $2\dfrac{2}{5} = \dfrac{\Box}{\Box}$

Calculations with Fractions

■ Add the fractions.

① $2\dfrac{1}{3} + 1\dfrac{1}{3} = 3\dfrac{\square}{\square}$

② $1\dfrac{1}{2} + 2 = 3\dfrac{\square}{\square}$

③ $1\dfrac{1}{4} + \dfrac{2}{4} = 1\dfrac{\square}{\square}$

④ $1\dfrac{2}{5} + 2\dfrac{1}{5} = \square\dfrac{\square}{\square}$

⑤ $2\dfrac{3}{8} + 3 = \square\dfrac{\square}{\square}$

⑥ $3\dfrac{2}{6} + \dfrac{3}{6} = \square\dfrac{\square}{\square}$

⑦ $4\dfrac{2}{9} + 5\dfrac{2}{9} = \square\dfrac{\square}{\square}$

⑧ $2 + 1\dfrac{2}{3} = \square\dfrac{\square}{\square}$

⑨ $\dfrac{3}{5} + 6\dfrac{1}{5} = \square\dfrac{\square}{\square}$

⑩ $4\dfrac{2}{7} + 3\dfrac{4}{7} = \square\dfrac{\square}{\square}$

Add the whole numbers.
Then add the fractions.

■ **Subtract the fractions.**

❶ $3\dfrac{3}{4} - 1\dfrac{2}{4} = 2\dfrac{\boxed{}}{\boxed{}}$

❷ $2\dfrac{2}{3} - 1 = 1\dfrac{\boxed{}}{\boxed{}}$

❸ $1\dfrac{3}{5} - \dfrac{2}{5} = 1\dfrac{\boxed{}}{\boxed{}}$

❹ $4\dfrac{7}{8} - 2\dfrac{4}{8} = \boxed{}\dfrac{\boxed{}}{\boxed{}}$

❺ $6\dfrac{7}{12} - 4 = \boxed{}\dfrac{\boxed{}}{\boxed{}}$

❻ $5\dfrac{2}{3} - \dfrac{1}{3} = \boxed{}\dfrac{\boxed{}}{\boxed{}}$

❼ $7\dfrac{8}{10} - 1\dfrac{5}{10} = \boxed{}\dfrac{\boxed{}}{\boxed{}}$

❽ $3\dfrac{1}{2} - 1 = \boxed{}\dfrac{\boxed{}}{\boxed{}}$

❾ $5\dfrac{4}{7} - 3\dfrac{2}{7} = \boxed{}\dfrac{\boxed{}}{\boxed{}}$

❿ $8\dfrac{4}{6} - \dfrac{3}{6} = \boxed{}\dfrac{\boxed{}}{\boxed{}}$

Subtract the whole numbers.
Then subtract the fractions.

Brain Break
Order of Operation Quiz

■ Write a number in each box to show the order of operation of each number sentence.

1

| 1 | 2 | 3 | 4 |

$$360 - 42 + 27 - 12 + 100$$

2

$$72 \div 8 \times 9 \times 10 \div 9$$

3

$$48 - (22 - 14) \times 6 \div 8$$

Remember

$$\underset{2}{3} \times \underset{1}{(10-2)} \underset{3}{\div} 4 \underset{4}{+} 1 = 3 \times 8 \div 4 + 1$$
$$= 24 \div 4 + 1$$
$$= 6 + 1$$

1 Parentheses

2 Multiplication and Division
3 (from left to right)

4 Addition and Subtraction
(from left to right)

■ Write a check mark (✓) in the box of the equation with the greatest answer.

1

A ☐ $10 + 4 \times 2 + 1$

B ☐ $(10 + 4) \times 2 + 1$

C ☐ $10 + 4 \times (2 + 1)$

2

A ☐ $120 - 24 \div 6 - 4 \times 3$

B ☐ $(120 - 24) \div 6 - 4 \times 3$

C ☐ $120 - 24 \div (6 - 4) \times 3$

D ☐ $120 - (24 \div 6 - 4) \times 3$

Geology - The Earth

KEY POINTS

The surface of the earth is covered in water and land. Land covers around 30% of Earth's surface and water covers approximately 70%. The land is split into seven continents and some smaller islands. The water is in oceans, lakes, rivers, and other bodies of water.

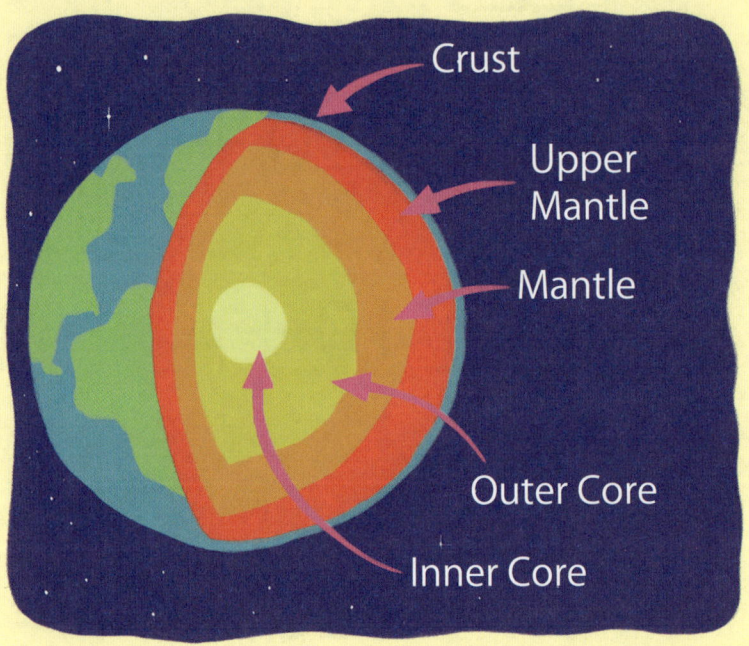

Underneath the water and land, Earth has three main layers – the core, the mantle, and the crust. As the name suggests, the core is in the center of the planet. The core is made almost completely of two metals, iron and nickel, as well as the element sulfur. The inner core is solid and the outer core is molten (melted) liquid metal. Both are extremely hot – the inner core is about 5,200° Celsius (9,392° Fahrenheit) and the outer core is between 4,500° and 5,500° Celsius (8,132° and 9,932° Fahrenheit). An incredible amount of pressure pushes on the core from all of the other layers of the Earth.

The mantle is the layer in between the core and the crust. It is the biggest of the layers and makes up 84% of the Earth's volume! The mantle is mostly solid rock but also includes molten rock that is pushed to the surface in volcanic eruptions. The closer to the core, the hotter the mantle gets – from 3700°C (6692°F) close to the core to 1000° C (1832°F) close to the crust. The mantle is made of a variety of minerals, most of which are silicates, or minerals that have silicon and oxygen, like quartz.

The crust is Earth's thin, rocky, outer layer. The crust below the ocean is thinner than the crust below land. Compared to the mantle and core, both are very thin. The crust only makes up 1% of Earth's mass. The deepest parts of the crust are solid rock. Above this are large, broken rocks, and above that are smaller and smaller broken rocks, including sand and soil. Humans have never gone below the crust of the earth. Scientists study the rocks, minerals, and fossils in the crust to learn more about Earth and its history.

■ Fill in the blank with the correct words.

❶ [_____] covers 70% of the Earth's surface.

❷ [_____] covers 30% of the Earth's surface.

❸ Earth has three main layers: the [_____], the [_____], and the [_____].

❹ The [_____] is the center of Earth and is the hottest layer.

❺ The [_____] is the layer between the core and the crust.

❻ The [_____] is the thinnest layer of Earth.

Types of Rocks

Rocks are hard materials made of minerals. Rocks are classified into three groups depending on how they are formed – either igneous, sedimentary, or metamorphic.

Igneous rocks are made from cooled, hardened magma. Magma is hot, liquid rock found below Earth's surface. Magma can come to the surface when volcanoes erupt or when there are cracks in Earth's surface. Magma can also cool very slowly right below the surface of the earth, taking thousands of years. Either way, when the magma cools, it turns into igneous rocks. Granite and basalt are both igneous rocks.

Sedimentary rocks are created from layers of tiny rocks, soil, and dead plants and animals. Tiny rocks and soil are washed into bodies of water by rain. They settle on the bottom of oceans, rivers, and valleys. They are covered by more and more things. The weight of the things on top eventually applies enough pressure that the layers underneath turn into sedimentary rocks. This process takes millions of years. Limestone and sandstone are both sedimentary rocks.

Metamorphic rocks form when existing rocks are subjected to intense heat and pressure. This can happen deep under Earth's crust. Metamorphic rocks are often very hard. Marble and schist are both metamorphic rocks. Limestone can turn into marble if the earth applies enough heat and pressure.

■ **Answer the questions.**

   ❶ How do igneous rocks form?

   ❷ Which type of rocks are created from layers of rock, soil, and dead plants and animals?

   ❸ Which type of rocks are created using heat and pressure?

■ Identifying rocks activity.

1

Granite is a(n)

[   ] rock.

2

Sandstone is a(n)

[   ] rock.

3

Limestone is a(n)

[   ] rock.

4

Marble is a(n)

[   ] rock.

5

Basalt is a(n)

[   ] rock.

6

Schist is a(n)

[   ] rock.

Minerals

A mineral is a solid that is formed in the earth and is always made of the same elements, or basic parts. For example, gold is always made of gold. Quartz is always made of the same mix of silicon and oxygen. Rocks are usually made of different types of minerals clumped together, sometimes mixed with other things like the remains of dead plants and animals. Unlike rocks, minerals are never made out of things that used to be alive. They are inorganic, which means they are not made of living things. Minerals vary. Some are metallic and others are not. They can be shiny, clear, translucent, or opaque. They can be hard or soft. Rocks, sand, and soil are made of minerals. Minerals can be formed in different ways. Extremely hot water can lead to hydrothermal formation. Very hot water dissolves and moves minerals. When the water cools, the minerals form veins or pockets of minerals on the surrounding rocks.

Just like rocks, some minerals are formed with igneous and metamorphic processes. Igneous minerals are made from cooled magma. Metamorphic minerals are created when existing minerals are put under intense heat and pressure. Plants and animals need minerals to live. For example, humans need the mineral calcium to grow strong bones and teeth. Plants usually get their minerals from the soil. People and other animals get minerals by eating plants and by eating animals that eat plants. Minerals are also used to make roads, buildings, machines, and more.

■ Answer the questions.

❶ What is the difference between minerals and rocks?

_____

❷ How do most plants get the minerals they need?

_____

■ Write true or false for each statement.

❶ A mineral is a solid that is formed in the earth.

❷ Minerals are always made of the same elements or basic parts.

❸ Rocks are made of different types of minerals clumped together.

❹ Minerals are only made out of things that used to be living like plants and animals.

❺ Igneous minerals are formed by pressure.

❻ Plants and animals need minerals to live.

Fossils

Fossils are the remains of plants or animals that lived long ago. They can be shells, teeth, bones, impressions in rocks, or even entire animals or plants. Most fossils are found preserved in sedimentary rocks. These rocks are formed when tiny bits of rock, soil, and dead plants and animals form layers at the bottom of a body of water. The pressure from the layers above causes the lower layers to turn into sedimentary rocks.

Sometimes, the hard parts (bones, shells, etc) of a plant or animal also become part of the rock instead of decomposing. This process creates fossils. Fossils help us understand what life was like on Earth millions of years ago. We can learn about plants and animals that no longer exist by studying their remains that have fossilized, or turned into fossils. Paleontologists are scientists who study animals, plants, and other living things from prehistoric times. They find and study fossils to learn about dinosaurs, wooly mammoths, and other ancient living things.

Animal footprints can also be fossilized if they stepped on a soft material like mud that later harden into rock. Small plants and animals can also be fossilized in resin, a sticky substance made by some trees. It hardens into amber, preserving the plant or animal inside.

■ **Answer the questions.**

❶ What are fossils?

_____

❷ Why do people study fossils?

_____

❸ Name one way fossils are made.

_____

■ Match the fossils with the plants or animals that they formed from.

A dinosaur

A fern

An ammonite

A mosquito

A spider

Got outside to your yard or local park. Find a rock that you think is cool. Take it home and research it.

1 My rock is likely a/an ⬚ rock.

2 Describe your rock:

_____

_____

3 What minerals is it made of?

_____

4 How did it form?

_____

_____

5 Is it made of one element or more than one?

_____

Art Break!

■ Try and recreate your rock as a drawing below!

Humans and the Earth

KEY POINTS

People live on almost all of Earth's land, in many kinds of places with many different geographical features. People live in deserts, arctic tundras, rainforests, by the ocean, next to lakes, on farms, and in big cities, to name a few. Where people live affects how they live. Some places have a lot of natural resources, while other places have fewer.

People often live near water. Water is necessary for human life. We drink it, water crops with it, give it to farm animals, use it to clean, and more. Most people live close to bodies of freshwater, like rivers or lakes. Most cities are next to rivers. Rivers are used for transportation. Boats can move people and goods along rivers. In the past and in some places still today, the rivers' water is used for drinking, bathing, and farming.

Historically, people who live in places with more fertile soil and easier access to water have farmed and stayed in one place. People who live in drier places with less fertile soil have been nomadic, moving from place to place to hunt and gather, often herding food animals with them such as goats, camels, cattle, sheep, or reindeer.

Different parts of the Earth have different natural resources. Places with oil reserves tend to have oil fields and people who work there. Places with gold often have gold mines and people who work there. Places with beautiful beaches often have tourist attractions and people who work there. Where someone lives determines what they are likely to do for work, what they are likely to eat, and many other things.

In places with cold winters and warm summers, people in the past had to store food for the winter, when most plants do not produce food. People in cold places wore more clothing than people in warm places. People's cultures adapted to fit the geography where they lived. This is still true today, even though we are much more connected to the rest of the world than people in the past were to each other.

Nowadays, many people can go to the store and buy food that has traveled from all over the world. In the past, it took much longer and was much more difficult to transport things. People mainly ate and used things that came from the areas where they lived. The geography of where we live still affects us, but in the past, it had a greater impact on how humans lived.

■ **Answer the questions.**

❶ Why did humans historically live by bodies of water?

❷ How does where a person lived affect their culture?

■ Fill in the blanks to complete the statement.

1 Humans live on almost all of [＿＿＿＿＿] land.

2 [＿＿＿＿＿] is necessary for human life.

3 Most cities are built next to [＿＿＿＿＿] to help transport goods and people.

4 In the past, humans tended to live near [＿＿＿＿＿] soil and stayed in one place.

5 [＿＿＿＿＿] people moved from place to place hunting and gathering, as well as herding animals.

6 Oil, gold, and beaches are examples of [＿＿＿＿＿].

7 Human culture was shaped by [＿＿＿＿＿].

Natural Resources

Natural means from nature, and resources are things that can be used. Natural resources are things that are found in nature and are used by people. Plants, animals, minerals, fossil fuels, soil, stone, wind, air, water, and sun are all natural resources.

People eat plants and animals. We use wood, stone, and minerals like copper and iron to build things. We grow plants to eat in soil, and those plants need sun, water, and air to grow. We burn fossil fuels to heat our homes, to power our cars, and to create electricity. We gather energy from wind using wind turbines. We gather energy from the Sun using solar panels. We gather energy from flowing water using turbines and generators. We drink water and breathe air. Natural resources make life on Earth possible.

■ Answer the questions.

1 What are natural resources?

_____

2 Name at least two natural resources used to build things.

_____

3 What do humans use fossil fuels for?

_____

■ Match the natural resource to the product humans use it for.

Metal ●

● Wood

Trees ●

● Diamond

Decomposed remains of plants and animals ●

● Gas

Coal ●

● Coins

Renewable and Nonrenewable Resources

KEY POINTS

Renewable resources are things that cannot be used up, like sunlight, air, water, and wind. They can't be used up, but it is possible to make them harder to use. For example, if we pollute water, it is harder to clean so that it is safe for us to drink or use to water plants. Plants and animals are also considered renewable resources because they can replace themselves as quickly as people use them. However, if people destroy habitats or hunt or gather too much of a kind of animal or plant, animals and plants can go extinct.

Nonrenewable resources are things that are used up faster than they can replace themselves. It takes thousands or millions of years to create soil, stone, or fossil fuels like coal, natural gas, and oil. Fossil fuels also create pollution when burned. We need to be careful about how quickly we use nonrenewable resources. We need to prepare for a time when we won't have any left, and we need to stop using so many so we can reduce the effects of climate change. We can do this by switching to renewable energy like solar power from the sun, wind power, and hydroelectric power from flowing water.

■ **Answer the questions.**

❶ Name two examples of a renewable resource.

❷ Name two examples of a nonrenewable resource.

❸ What is the difference between a renewable and nonrenewable resource?

Date

Great Job Sticker

■ Write renewable or nonrenewable next to each image of a natural resource.

1
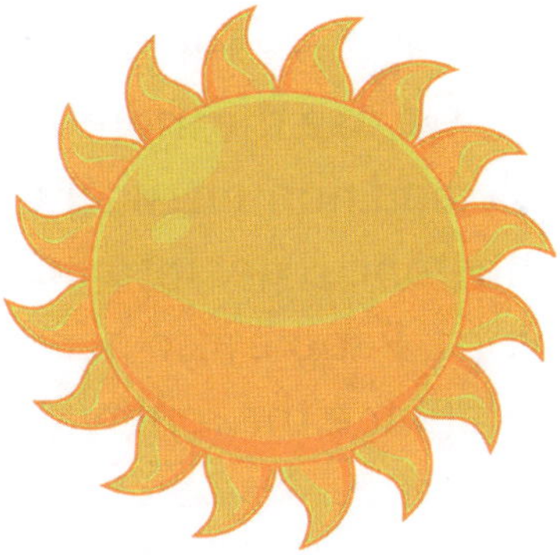

2
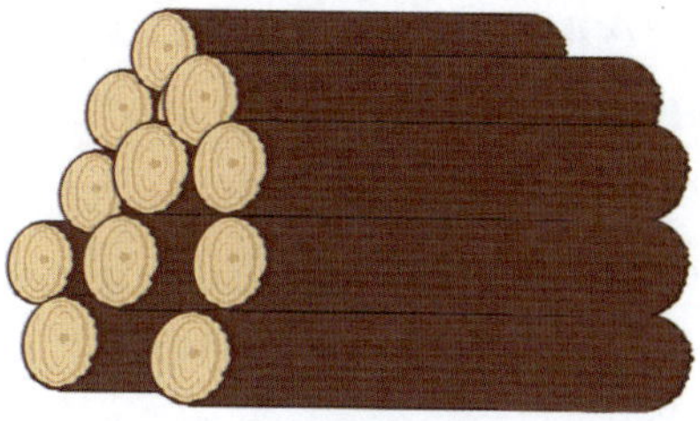

3
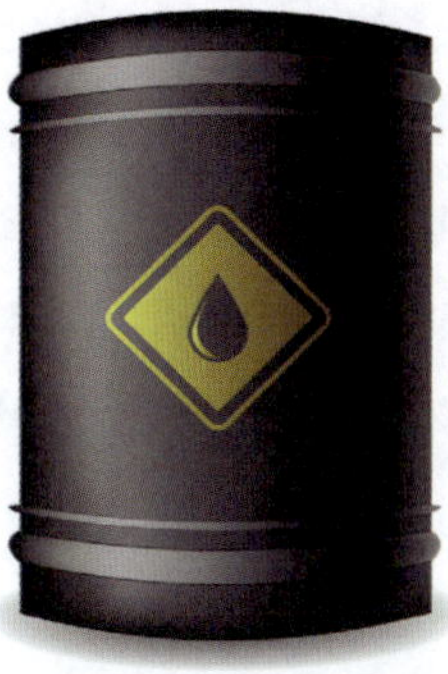

4
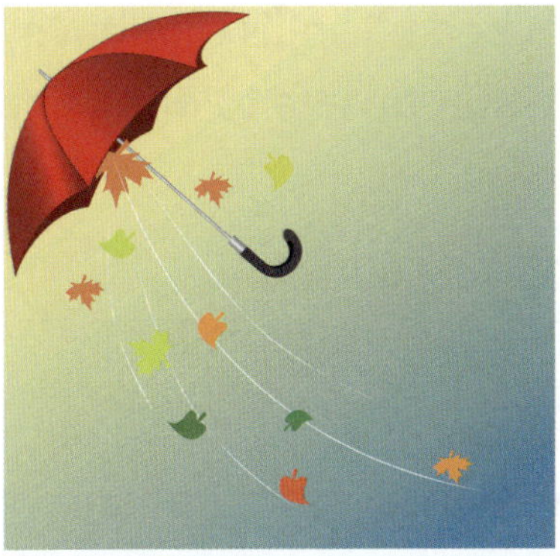

5
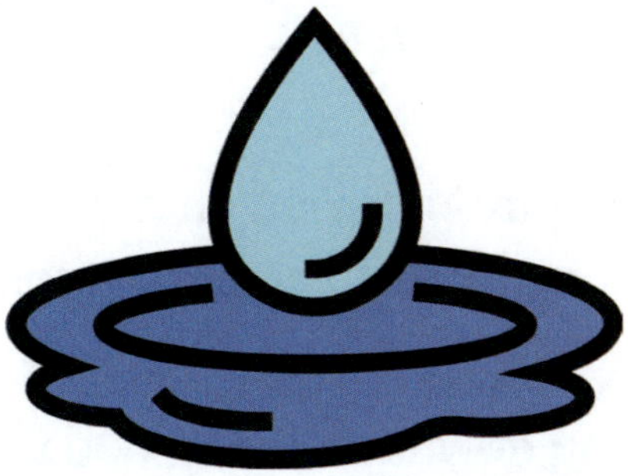

6
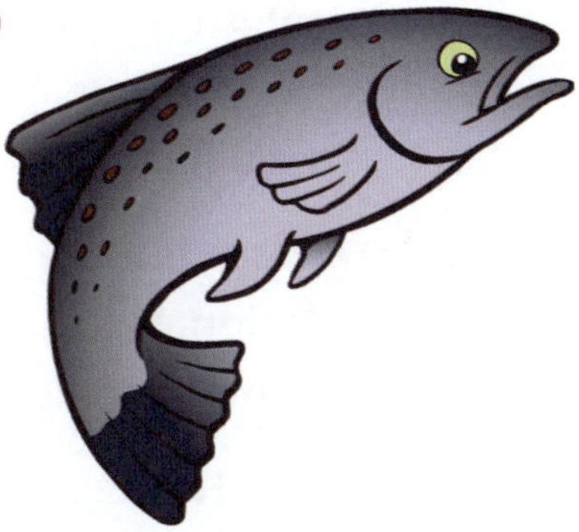

7
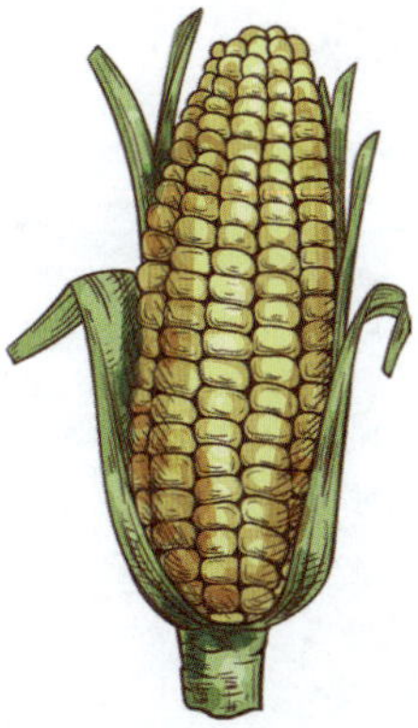

8
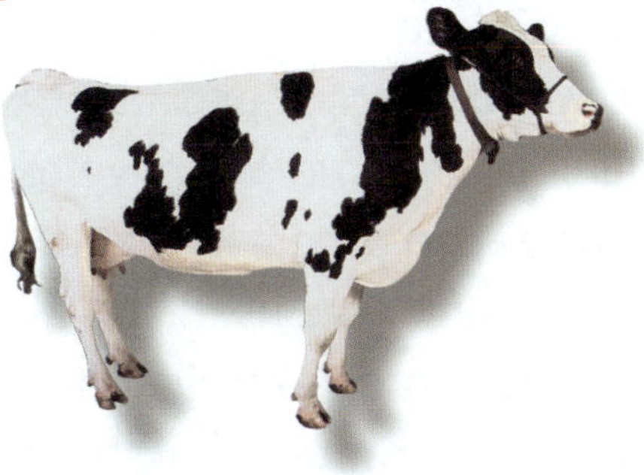

9
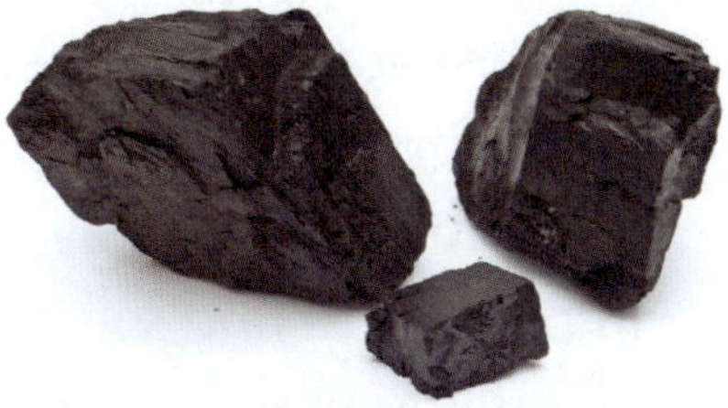

Human Impact on Resources

Throughout history humans have lived near bodies of water and other natural resources that were essential for daily life. Today, we have so many new technologies that help us move natural resources from one place to another that it is easier for humans to live anywhere. However, the more natural resources we use the more issues we can create for our environment. Collecting renewable and nonrenewable resources can cause pollution, which happens when unsafe substances get into the air, water or soil and make it unsafe or unhealthy for living things. People also need to be careful not to use too many nonrenewable resources or damage the renewable ones.

Some examples of human impact on natural resources are :
• **Air pollution** : This is the introduction of substances into the air that makes it harmful to people and can cause breathing problems.

• **Water pollution** : Collecting oil from the ocean floor has caused oil spills that have polluted rivers, lakes and springs of waters. This makes the water unsafe to drink and can harm wildlife.

• **Soil contamination** : Oil spills from drilling on the land can also cause soil contamination. It can cause negative effects on the soil, making it unusable for farming or other things.

• **Habitat destruction** : Cutting down trees for wood to make buildings and other products can also cause problems if it is done too quickly. Deforestation happens when too many trees are cut down from one area leaving no new trees to reproduce or provide shelter and food for animals. If too many trees are cut down in one area, it can also cause less oxygen to be released and lead to poor air quality.

It is up to humans to be responsible in the way we manage the natural resources in our environment especially those that are nonrenewable within our life time. We have to keep our environment safe for us and others in the future by controlling the way these resources are used. It is also important to find solutions to these problems like safer oil drilling practices, releasing less harmful pollutants into the air, water, and soil, and by planting new trees in areas where large amounts of trees are cut down.

■ Write true or false for each statement.

① New technologies have helped humans move natural resources from place to place more easily.

② Collecting nonrenewable resources can cause pollution.

③ Pollution is when harmful substances are removed from the environment.

④ Collecting natural resources has no negative effect on living things.

⑤ Drilling for oil can cause pollution in the water and on land.

⑥ Humans can help reverse deforestation by planting more trees in areas where many trees have been cut down.

■ Circle the words in the puzzle below.

resource	renewable	fuel	water
wind	wood	minerals	stone

R	E	S	O	U	R	C	E	T	O
A	P	O	I	U	E	Y	T	R	L
S	W	D	S	A	N	Q	W	E	M
D	I	F	G	H	E	J	K	L	I
F	N	X	C	V	W	B	N	M	N
G	D	Z	L	K	A	J	H	G	E
H	E	W	Q	A	B	S	D	F	R
J	R	T	Y	U	L	I	O	P	A
K	S	T	O	N	E	D	F	G	L
L	K	J	H	G	F	D	S	A	S
Z	M	N	Q	F	U	E	L	T	E
X	C	V	B	N	H	Y	J	P	K
W	A	T	E	R	O	I	E	A	P
C	T	T	B	A	U	Q	W	R	O
V	O	R	E	V	W	O	O	D	I
B	N	M	Q	W	E	R	T	Y	U

Mindfulness Break!

KEY POINTS

There are different ways to practice mindfulness. Focusing your attention on one word can help you stay in the moment and be mindful.

■ Choose a word to help you focus your mind. Fill in the answers below.

Choose a word that makes you feel calm and relaxed.

My word is _____ .

This word makes me feel _____ .

The color of my word is _____ .

How do you feel after spending some time focusing on your mindful word?

_____

Unit 3 Personal Finance

Counting Money

■ Count the money in each wallet. Then write the amount in the box below.

1

$ [   ]

2

$ [   ]

3

$ [   ]

4

$ [   ]

■ Circle the five wallets below that have the same amount of money.

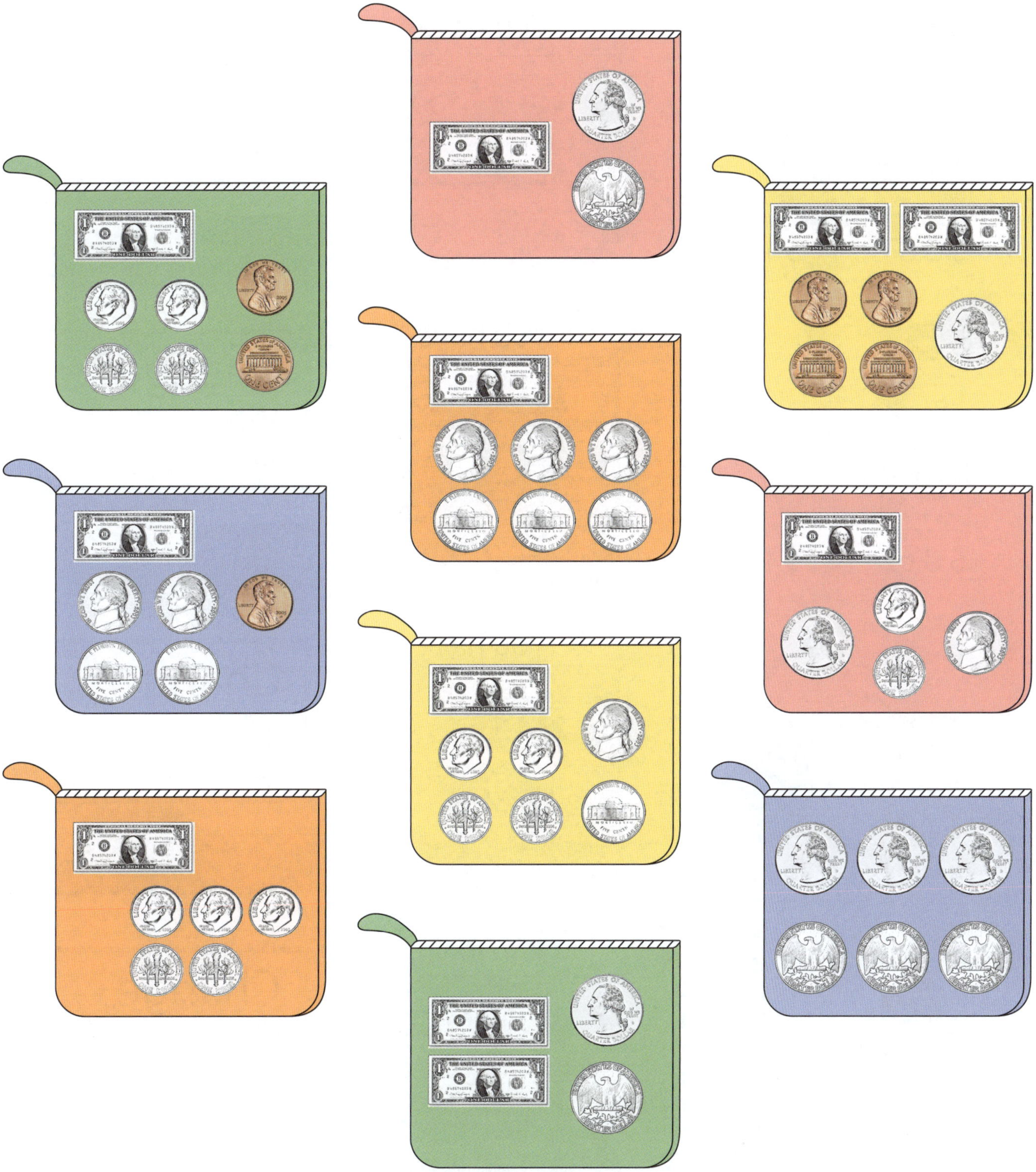

Making Change

■ How much change will you get back after paying? Write the number in the screen of each cash register.

① $ 3.87 $ 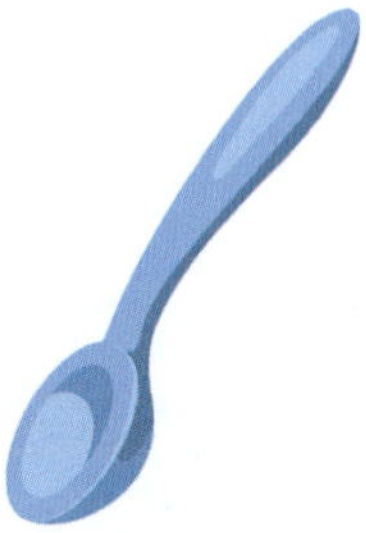 1.00   You have   Change $ 0.13

② 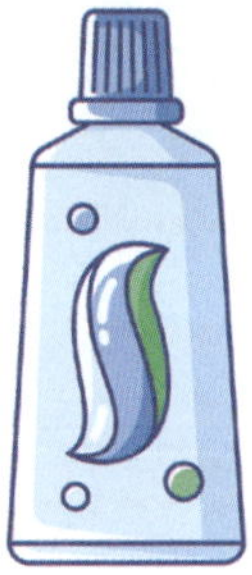 $ 3.62 $ 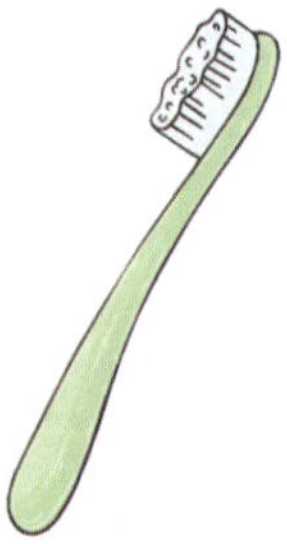 1.21   You have   Change $

③  $ 0.31 $  1.58   You have   Change $

④  $ 1.40 $ 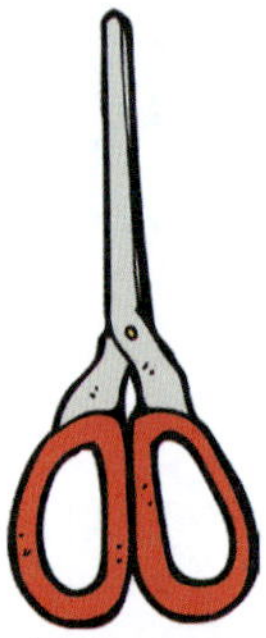 4.49   You have   Change $

■ **What did you buy? Choose two items from the menu.**

Hot Dog	Pancake	Hamburger
$2.23	$2.00	$3.29

French Fries	Salad	Ice Cream	Orange Juice
$1.40	$2.59	$1.85	$1.00

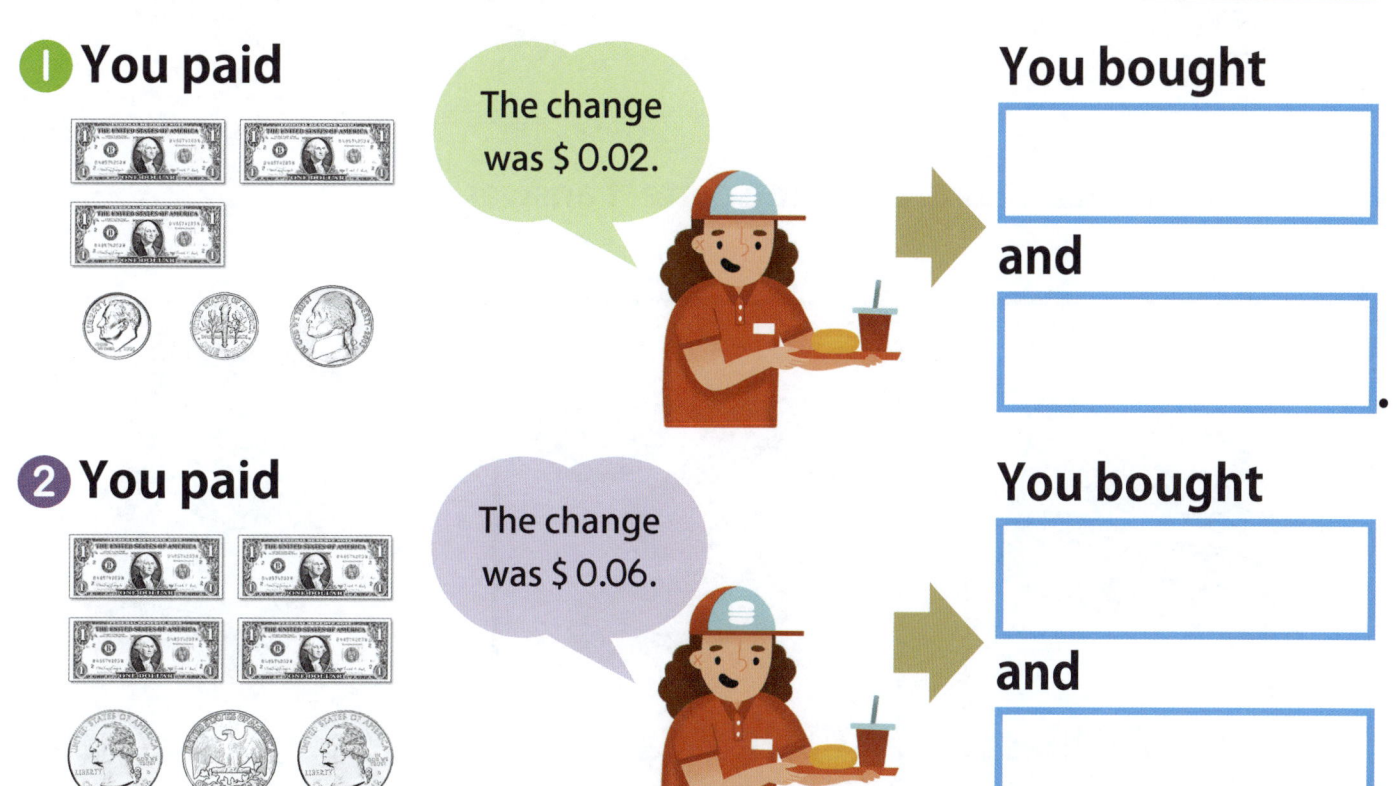

1 You paid

The change was $0.02.

You bought

_____

and

_____ .

2 You paid

The change was $0.06.

You bought

_____

and

_____ .

KEY POINTS

When purchasing things in stores or online, there are a variety of ways to pay.

Bills and coins are called **cash**. Debit cards, credit cards, and the use of smartphones are **cashless payments**.

A Debit card allows you to make purchases up to the amount in your bank account. If you don't have money in your account, you can't use this card to make purchases.

A Credit card allows you to make payments on a set date later. You need to be careful not to overspend, as it will be like borrowing money.

■ Look at each picture and circle the correct answer.

①

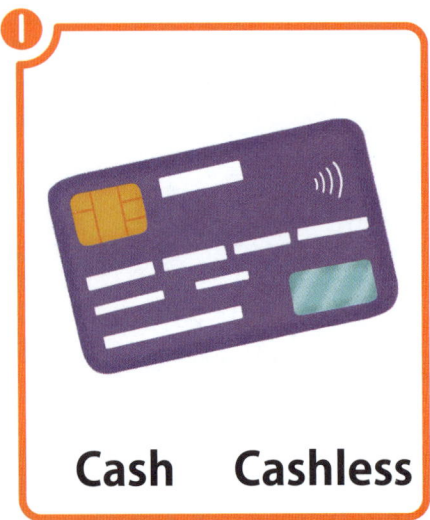

Cash   Cashless

②

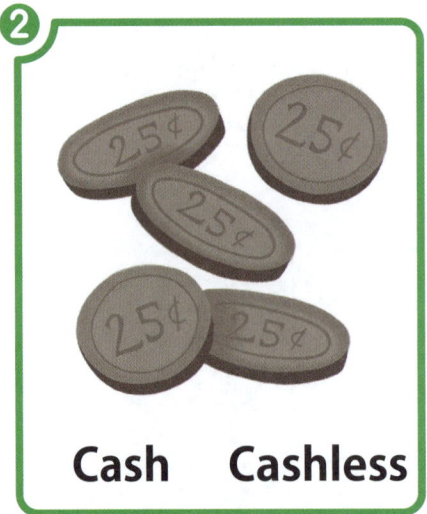

Cash   Cashless

③

Cash   Cashless

KEY POINTS

A **producer** is a person who makes and sells goods. It is also a person who provide services, such as teacher and firefighter.

A **consumer** is a person who buys goods and services from the producers.

Most people are producers and consumers.

■ Look at each picture and circle the correct answer.

①

Producer   Consumer

②

Producer   Consumer

③

Producer   Consumer

④

Producer   Consumer

Finance Words

■ Draw a line to match the finance words with the definition.

Debit Card ●	● Person who buy the goods and services from the producers.
Credit Card ●	● It is a plan you make to help spend or save money wisely.
Producer ●	● A card that allows people to borrow money within a preset limit.
Consumer ●	● The money you get for working a job or performing a task.
Budget ●	● A card that allows people to use money from their bank account.
Income ●	● Person who makes and sells goods or services.

■ Circle the words in the Word Search.

| cash | goods | services | needs | wants |

O	O	G	D	S	Q	I	W	B	K
A	V	F	X	W	G	Y	T	H	P
T	R	Z	L	W	O	N	T	S	C
J	E	K	M	L	O	E	N	E	D
K	S	G	U	O	D	G	V	C	U
M	T	R	C	A	S	H	E	I	Y
B	N	X	A	Z	R	W	S	V	K
F	A	Z	T	I	E	L	D	R	Q
Y	W	A	C	L	S	D	E	E	N
P	M	J	H	X	F	R	N	S	V

Physical Education Break!

It's important to move your body and exercise!
Try this fun activity below to break up your studying!

■ Pick a few of the options below to draw with sidewalk chalk and make your own "Activity Line."

Draw a bunch of bubbles and jump from one to the other to "pop" them.	Draw a flower vine and walk along the length. Make it as long or short as you want.	Draw a "lava" pit and jump over it. Add rocks you can hop on to be safe if you want to make it bigger.
Draw a few spirals and spin when you get to them.	Draw a few large circles along the path and stop for a "dance party" when you reach them.	Draw lily pads along the path and "frog hop" from one to the next.
Draw triangles along the path and stop and touch your toes in each one.	Draw a straight line as long as you want and run as fast as you can along it.	Draw a zigzag line and try and walk backwards along it.

Unit **4** Table of Contents

Use this page to keep track of your progress throughout the book. Place a check mark in the box when you have completed a section.

Figurative Language 1

KEY POINTS

Figurative language is a type of descriptive language used to convey meaning in a way that is different from its literal meaning. Words are used creatively to compare or exaggerate objects or situations.

Similes are a type of figurative language that compares two things using the words "like" or "as."

Example: Joel stands tall over his classmates like a giraffe.

Writers use figurative language to make strong points about characters looks, personality, and actions.

■ Match the simile to its meaning.

Tanya's dress sparkled like a star.	His eyes were the same color as the sky.
Gil's eyes were blue as the sky.	A wolf's howl is loud like an alarm.
The sunset looked like cotton candy.	Her dress was the color and brightness of the stars.
The wolf's howl was like a siren.	The sunset was pink like cotton candy is.

■ Read the passage below. Underline the similes.
   Then explain what each one means using the sentence lines.

Jared was excited to go stargazing with his family. Even though the night air was as cold as ice, he put on his hat and jacket and raced out into the field behind his grandparents house. His grandfather and parents were already standing by the telescope. Jared was jumping around like a rabbit with excitement. Finally it was his turn to look. His grandfather helped position the telescope down and Jared looked up at the stars. "Wow," he said. "The stars look like sequins!" He moved the telescope to look at the moon. "And the moon looks like Swiss cheese up close!" Jared stepped back to let his cousin have a turn at the telescope. He didn't stop smiling all night as he thought about how much fun he had.

①

②

③

④

Figurative Language 2

Metaphors are another type of figurative language that compares two things without using "like" or "as." Metaphors simply state that one thing is like another.

Example: Alex is a night owl.

This metaphor means that Alex stays up late at night like how owls are active during the night.

Another example would be, **"Kristen is a ray of sunshine."**

In this case, "ray of sunshine" is something warm that usually makes people feel happy. Saying that "Kristen is a ray of sunshine" is meant to convey that she is a warm and happy person.

■ Match the metaphors to the closet meaning.

The clouds sailed across the sky.	● ●	A voice like music
He was a couch potato.	● ●	Someone who doesn't do a lot of activity
Her smile lit up a room.	● ●	Moving across the sky the way ships move on water
Eloise's voice was music to their ears.	● ●	A smile that is so bright and happy it fills a room

■ Read the passage and underline the metaphors.
  Define what you think they mean on the lines below.

Franklin was going to the circus with his family. He could not

contain his excitement. Walking through the big, colorful entrance

felt like stepping into a dream. The tent was a giant rainbow

inside. The smell of popcorn filled the air with warmth. Franklin's

favorite part of the show were the acrobats. They flew through

the air like graceful birds. Then the elephants came in, each one a

gentle giant. The show ended with fireworks.

The sky was a sea of color. It was a day that

Franklin would remember forever.

①

②

③

④

Idioms

Not all figurative language uses clear comparisons like similes and metaphors do. Many languages, including English, use idioms to convey meaning in a creative way.

An idiom is a phrase that actually means something different from their literal meaning. For example, **"it's raining cats and dogs"** is an idiom. However, it does not mean cats and dogs are falling from the sky. Instead, it means it is raining very hard.

Another example is to say something is **"a piece of cake"** has come to mean that "something is very easy."

Many idioms are not literal and figuring out the meaning can be challenging. It's important to think about words and feelings that the idiom makes you think of. These word associations can help you figure out the intended meaning of an idiom you do not know.

■ Read the idioms and write what you think they mean.

① When Katie knocked over her mom's vase she was upset. But her mom just said, "Don't cry over spilled milk."

_____

② Henry had a big test coming up. He needed to hit the books!

_____

③ After winning the baking contest, Sam was so shocked she was tongue tied.

_____

④ Petra was feeling blue when she didn't get a part in the school play.

_____

■ Match the idioms to the closet meaning.

When pigs fly.	●	●	To be in agreement with someone about something.
Hit the nail on the head.	●	●	To feel uncomfortable in a situation.
Head in the clouds.	●	●	Something is impossible.
Cool as a cucumber.	●	●	Two people who are always together.
On the same page.	●	●	To let out a secret or share secret information.
Two peas in a pod.	●	●	To be calm and cool in a situation.
Let the cat out of the bag.	●	●	To get the point right away.
Fish out of water.	●	●	Someone is daydreaming or not paying attention.

Synonyms and Antonyms

Synonyms are words that mean the same as another word. Antonyms are words that mean the opposite of another word. Both can be useful in figurative writing.

For example, bad is an antonym for good because they have opposite meanings. But good and great are synonyms because the mean the same thing or something very similar.

Examples of Synonyms:

pretty = gorgeous
mad = angry
cold = freezing

Examples of Antonyms:

pretty ≠ ugly
mad ≠ happy
cold ≠ hot

■ Circle the words in each sentence that are synonyms.
  Or underline the words if they are antonyms.

❶ Lou ate a hot bowl of soup.

  Claire ate a cold bowl of ice cream.

❷ The dog's bark was loud.

  The cat's purr was quiet.

❸ The school day began at 8 o'clock.

  Afterschool sports start at 4 o'clock.

■ **Read the passage. Circle the synonyms that come after the bold words.**

Marco woke up bright and early. Today was the day his father would take him to see the new lamb that was born on the farm. Marco was so **excited** he almost forgot to brush his teeth! He was thrilled to get to see the newborn lamb. His mother made him stop and eat a **large** bowl of oatmeal before he could head to the barn.

"But it's huge, mom!" he said. "I can't eat the whole thing." His mother agreed to let him save some for later. He jumped out of his chair and **hurried** to the door. He quickly put on his boots and ran outside. His father was waiting for him at the entrance to the barn.

"Come on in and be **quiet**, Marco." His father said. "The lamb is sleeping." Marco walked in silently and peered over the fence. He could see the **little** lamb asleep in the hay.

"It's so tiny!" Marco exclaimed and he and his father stood side-by-side watching the little lamb.

■ **Write an antonym for each underlined word in the sentence to make it more true.**

❶ Gerald was <u>happy</u> his team lost the game.

❷ Kim was tired and wanted her brother to be <u>louder</u> so she could sleep.

❸ Mary opened her present. It was an <u>old</u> pair of shoes!

❹ Alfred won the race because he was the <u>slowest</u> runner.

❺ Cindy's couldn't pick up the box because it was too <u>little</u>.

Brain Break
Illustrating Idioms

Idioms can be hard to understand since the words in each phrase don't mean the same thing on their own as they do together. Illustrations can help readers understand what an idiom means.

■ Draw your own interpretation of each idiom below.

"When pigs fly."

"Cost an arm and a leg."

"In the same boat."

"Fish out of water."

Mindfulness Break!

Recognizing and acknowledging your emotions is an important part of practicing mindfulness. As you complete the wheel below, remember that everyone experiences these emotions, emotions are always changing, and there are no "good" or "bad" emotions.

■ Use the wheel below to draw a moment and time when you may have felt the listed emotion.

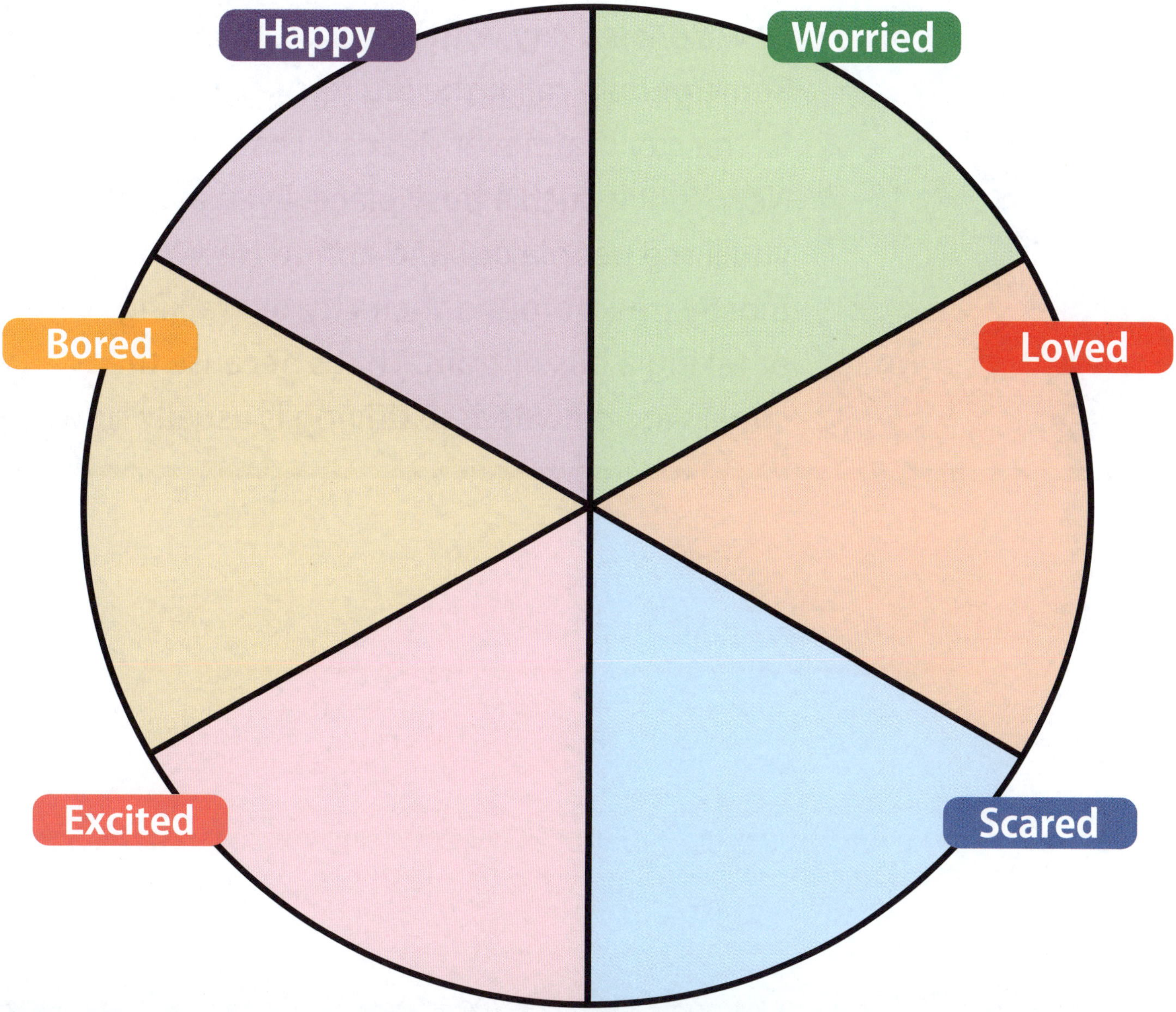

Happy

Worried

Bored

Loved

Excited

Scared

Informational Writing: Gathering Facts

Informational texts share facts about a topic. A writer tells their reader the most important or interesting facts that they want to share with their reader. The reader should learn something from an informational text.

■ Read the text below. Then write three facts you learned below.

New York is a city with many nicknames. Some people call it the Big Apple. Others call it "the city that never sleeps." That's because New York is such a busy place. Even at night you'll see people out and about! New Yorkers mostly travel around their city by walking, or taking a bus or train. That's because the streets are crowded, so driving is usually slow.

1

2

3

■ In a few activities, you will write your own informational text about a place that interests you. You can choose a place that you are interested in traveling to, or a place that you learned about in a book or movie. You can even choose your own hometown. You will gather information about that place. Write four facts about your place below. Have a parent or guardian help you research online if needed.

Some questions to consider:
What language is spoken there?
Is it a city or rural area?
What foods do people eat?
What plants and animals live there?
Are there any historical facts you should know about this city?

Place：

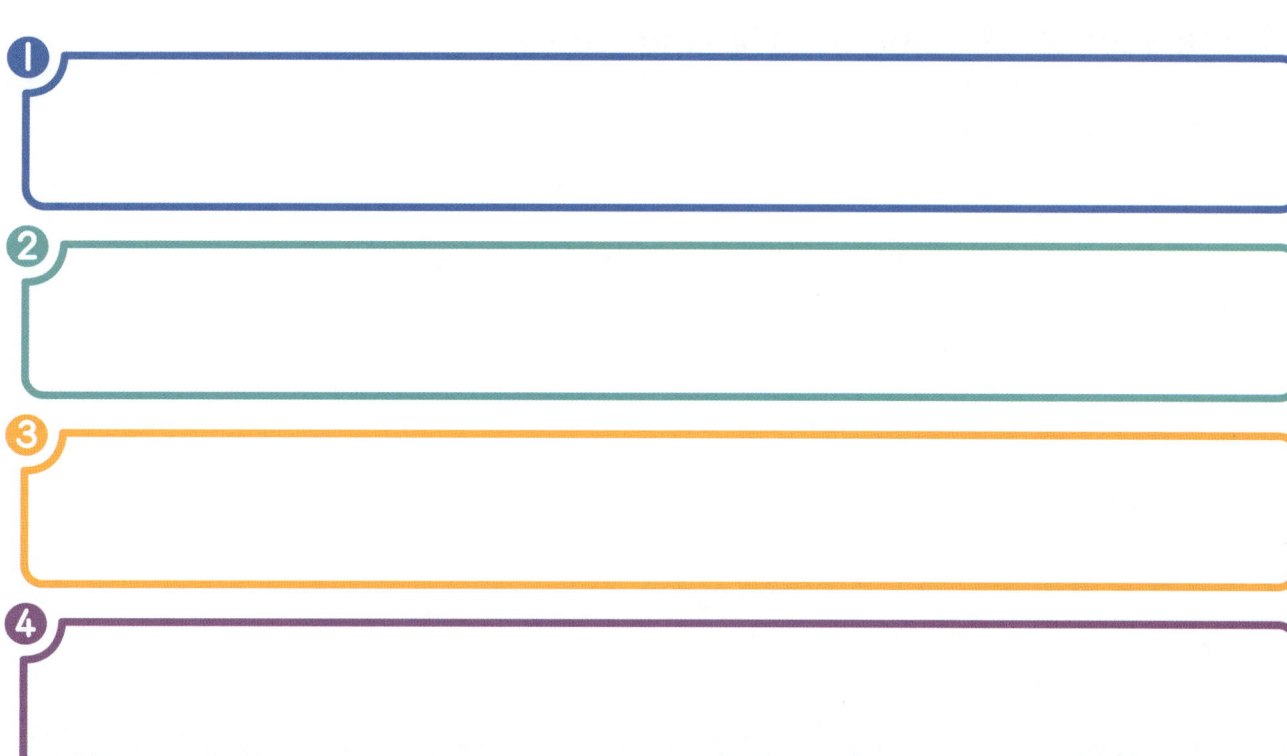

Informational Writing: Linking Words and Phrases

KEY POINTS

Linking words are words that join two or more ideas and show how they relate to each other. They are an important tool that writers use to make their ideas connect together smoothly. Some linking words include: another, for example, also, because.

Examples: The Golden Gate Bridge is a famous landmark. Another famous landmark is Mount Rushmore.

Many big cities have trains that run underground. For example, Washington, DC has a metro system.

Paris also has a metro.

It's best to visit Chicago in the summer because winter is very cold there.

■ Write a sentence using each linking word.

1 another

_____

2 also

_____

3 for example

_____

4 because

_____

■ Practice using linking words to join the facts that you wrote in previous activity (page 201). Use at least four linking words.

1

2

3

4

Informational Writing: Structure

An introduction and conclusion will help make your text feel more satisfying to read. A good introduction gets the reader's interest and tells them what the text will be about. A strong ending gives the reader a sense of closure instead of ending in the middle of an idea.

■ Read the text below. Circle the introduction and underline the conclusion.

If you are a movie lover, then Los Angeles is the city for you! Los Angeles is home to Hollywood, where many movies and TV shows are filmed. If you visit, you can tour some of the studios and see some places you might recognize

from watching TV. You may even spot an actor walking by! You'll also see the famous Hollywood sign. It's a must-see for any movie fan!

■ Draft an introduction and a conclusion for your informational text.

Introduction

Conclusion

Writing an Informational Piece

■ Write an informational text about a place of your choice. Make sure to use facts, linking words, an introduction, and a conclusion.

■ Draw a picture of the place you just wrote about.
   Be sure to include details from your writing.

Mindfulness Break!

Gratitude is feeling thankful for the people and things in your life.

■ Draw or write something you are grateful for in each box.

Addition and Subtraction with Decimals

■ Add.

①
```
   1.5
 + 0.3
 ─────
```

②
```
   0.9
 + 4.3
 ─────
```

③
```
   5.2
 + 7.8
 ─────
```

④
```
   3.64
 + 1.24
 ──────
```

⑤
```
   5.78
 + 2.17
 ──────
```

⑥
```
   6.39
 + 8.71
 ──────
```

⑦
```
   4.73
 + 3.10
 ──────
```

⑧
```
   2.66
 + 2.19
 ──────
```

⑨
```
   4.73
 + 6.57
 ──────
```

⑩
```
   2.30
 + 5.16
 ──────
```

⑪
```
   3.5
 + 8.62
 ──────
```

⑫
```
   7
 + 4.89
 ──────
```

■ Subtract.

❶
  6.4
− 0.2

❷
  3.7
− 1.9

❸
  1.0
− 0.8

❹
  5.42
− 5.22

❺
  5.42
− 3.19

❻
  2.24
− 2.17

❼
  7.81
− 6.50

❽
  2.63
− 0.70

❾
  1.29
− 0.3

❿
  8.50
− 5.17

⓫
  6.4
− 4.81

⓬
  3
− 1.58

Multiplication and Division with Decimals

■ Multiply.

①
$$\begin{array}{r} 2.3 \\ \times\ 3 \\ \hline \end{array}$$

②
$$\begin{array}{r} \overset{1}{0.6} \\ \times\ 2 \\ \hline \end{array}$$

③
$$\begin{array}{r} \overset{2}{5.5} \\ \times\ 4 \\ \hline \end{array}$$

④
$$\begin{array}{r} 7 \\ \times\,0.9 \\ \hline \end{array}$$

⑤
$$\begin{array}{r} 4.1 \\ \times\ 2 \\ \hline \end{array}$$

⑥
$$\begin{array}{r} 0.8 \\ \times\ 8 \\ \hline \end{array}$$

⑦
$$\begin{array}{r} 6.2 \\ \times\ 5 \\ \hline \end{array}$$

⑧
$$\begin{array}{r} 6 \\ \times\,0.7 \\ \hline \end{array}$$

⑨
$$\begin{array}{r} 2.14 \\ \times\ 2 \\ \hline \end{array}$$

⑩
$$\begin{array}{r} 6.31 \\ \times\ 3 \\ \hline \end{array}$$

⑪
$$\begin{array}{r} 8.37 \\ \times\ 7 \\ \hline \end{array}$$

⑫
$$\begin{array}{r} 5.42 \\ \times\ 5 \\ \hline \end{array}$$

■ Divide.

① 3)6.3 ② 2)4.4 ③ 6)12.6 ④ 8)24.8

⑤ 0.
6)4.2 ⑥ 7)2.8 ⑦ 7)5.6 ⑧ 9)8.1

⑨ 3.
2)7.6 ⑩ 8)9.6 ⑪ 4)14.4 ⑫ 7)22.4

Converting Decimals to Fractions

KEY POINTS

$$0.5 = \frac{5}{10}$$

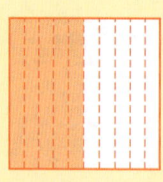

0.5 represents that there are **5 tenths** or $\frac{5}{10}$

$$0.05 = \frac{5}{100}$$

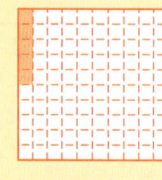

0.05 represents that there are **5 hundredths** or $\frac{5}{100}$

$$0.45 = \frac{45}{100}$$

0.45 represents that there are **45 hundredths** or $\frac{45}{100}$

■ Convert each decimal to a fraction, and each fraction to a decimal.

① $0.1 = \dfrac{\boxed{}}{10}$

② $0.7 = \dfrac{\boxed{}}{10}$

③ $0.03 = \dfrac{\boxed{}}{100}$

④ $0.09 = \dfrac{\boxed{}}{100}$

⑤ $\dfrac{2}{10} = \boxed{}$

⑥ $\dfrac{6}{10} = \boxed{}$

⑦ $\dfrac{1}{100} = \boxed{}$

⑧ $\dfrac{8}{100} = \boxed{}$

■ Convert each decimal to a fraction, and each fraction to a decimal.

❶ $0.35 = \dfrac{\boxed{}}{100}$

❷ $0.42 = \dfrac{\boxed{}}{100}$

❸ $0.51 = \dfrac{\boxed{}}{100}$

❹ $0.19 = \dfrac{\boxed{}}{100}$

❺ $0.68 = \dfrac{\boxed{}}{100}$

❻ $0.77 = \dfrac{\boxed{}}{100}$

❼ $\dfrac{17}{100} = \boxed{}$

❽ $\dfrac{33}{100} = \boxed{}$

❾ $\dfrac{64}{100} = \boxed{}$

❿ $\dfrac{58}{100} = \boxed{}$

⓫ $\dfrac{99}{100} = \boxed{}$

⓬ $\dfrac{26}{100} = \boxed{}$

Converting Fractions to Decimals

Convert a fraction to a decimal

You can convert a fraction to a decimal by dividing the denominator by the numerator.

$$\frac{1}{5} = 1 \div 5 = 0.2 \qquad \frac{3}{4} = 3 \div 4 = 0.75$$

Another way: Multiply both the numerator and the denominator by the same number so that you get a fraction whose denominator is 10 or 100. (Remember **equivalent fractions**.)

$$\frac{1}{5} \times \frac{2}{2} = \frac{2}{10} = 0.2 \qquad \frac{3}{4} \times \frac{25}{25} = \frac{75}{100} = 0.75$$

■ Convert each fraction to a decimal.

1 $\frac{1}{2} = \boxed{}$

2 $\frac{2}{5} = \boxed{}$

3 $\frac{4}{5} = \boxed{}$

4 $\frac{3}{4} = \boxed{}$

5 $\frac{1}{4} = \boxed{}$

6 $\frac{3}{5} = \boxed{}$

■ Color the bars or the unit squares to show the amount represented by each fraction.

① $\dfrac{1}{2}$

② $\dfrac{2}{5}$

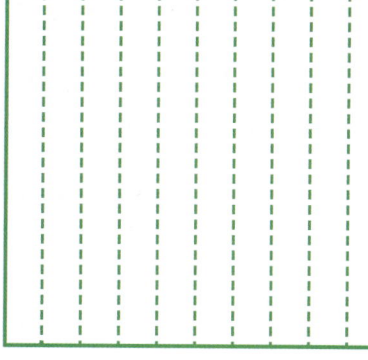

③ $\dfrac{1}{4}$

④ $\dfrac{2}{4}$

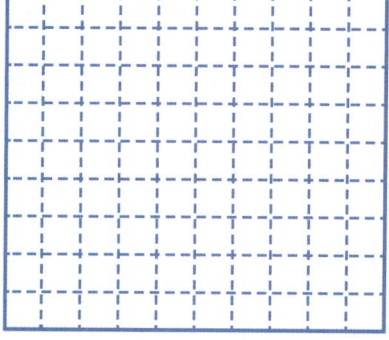

⑤ $\dfrac{4}{5}$

⑥ $\dfrac{3}{4}$

Decimals and Fractions

■ Circle the correct fraction for each blank on the number line.

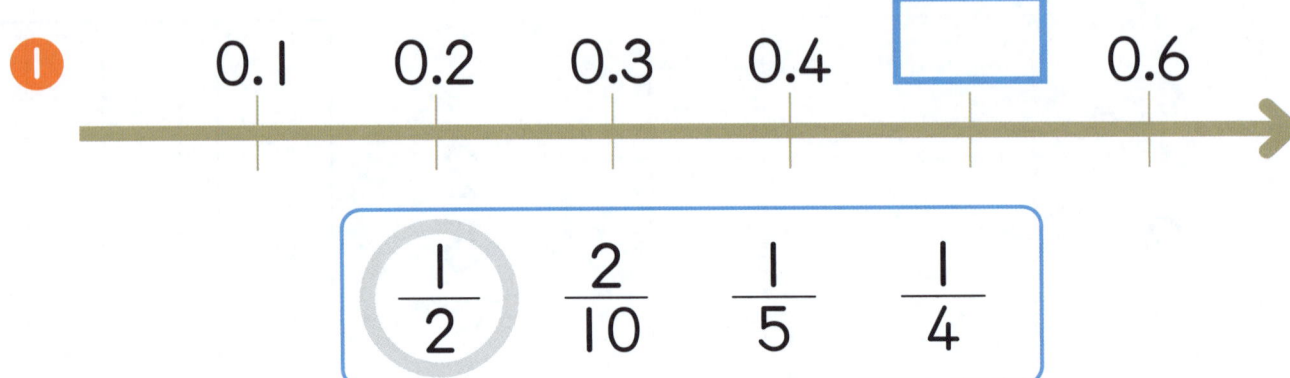

❶ 0.1   0.2   0.3   0.4   [   ]   0.6

$\frac{1}{2}$ $\frac{2}{10}$ $\frac{1}{5}$ $\frac{1}{4}$

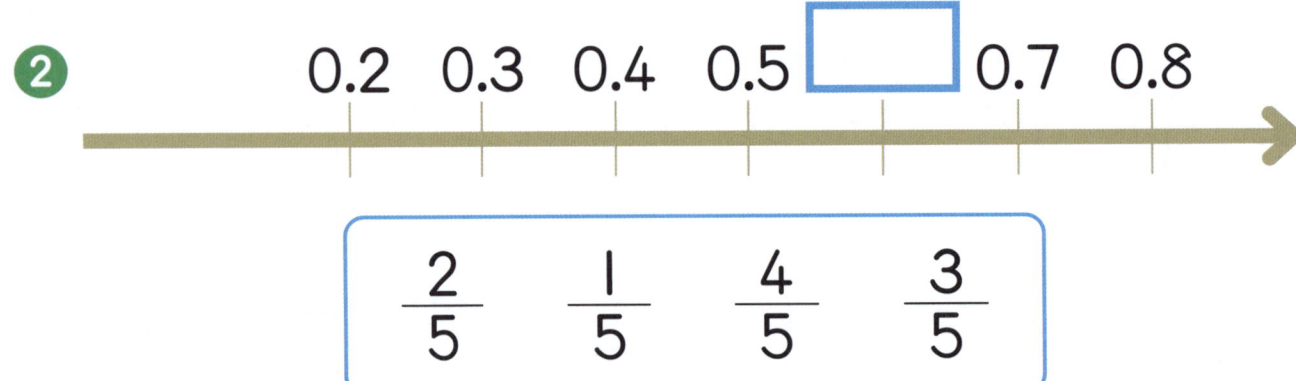

❷ 0.2 0.3 0.4 0.5 [   ] 0.7 0.8

$\frac{2}{5}$ $\frac{1}{5}$ $\frac{4}{5}$ $\frac{3}{5}$

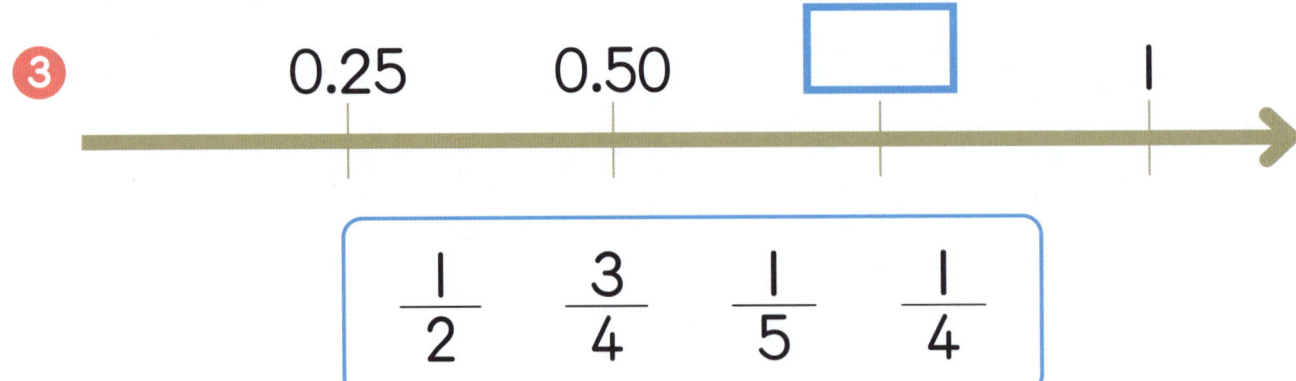

❸ 0.25   0.50   [   ]   1

$\frac{1}{2}$ $\frac{3}{4}$ $\frac{1}{5}$ $\frac{1}{4}$

■ Write a check mark (✓) in the box if what each kid is saying is correct.

1

I used 0.8 feet of ribbon for a gift for my friend Ursula. That means it is $\frac{4}{5}$ of a foot.

2

I used 0.25 gallons of water for watering my plants today. That means it is $\frac{2}{4}$ of a gallon.

3

I ate 0.4 pints of chocolate ice cream when I got home after school. That means it is $\frac{2}{5}$ of a pint.

Brain Break
Data and Graphs Quiz

■ These are line graphs of this year's average temperatures in Town A and Town B. In the blank next to each child, write "A" if they talk about Town A, or "B" if they talk about Town B.

Town A

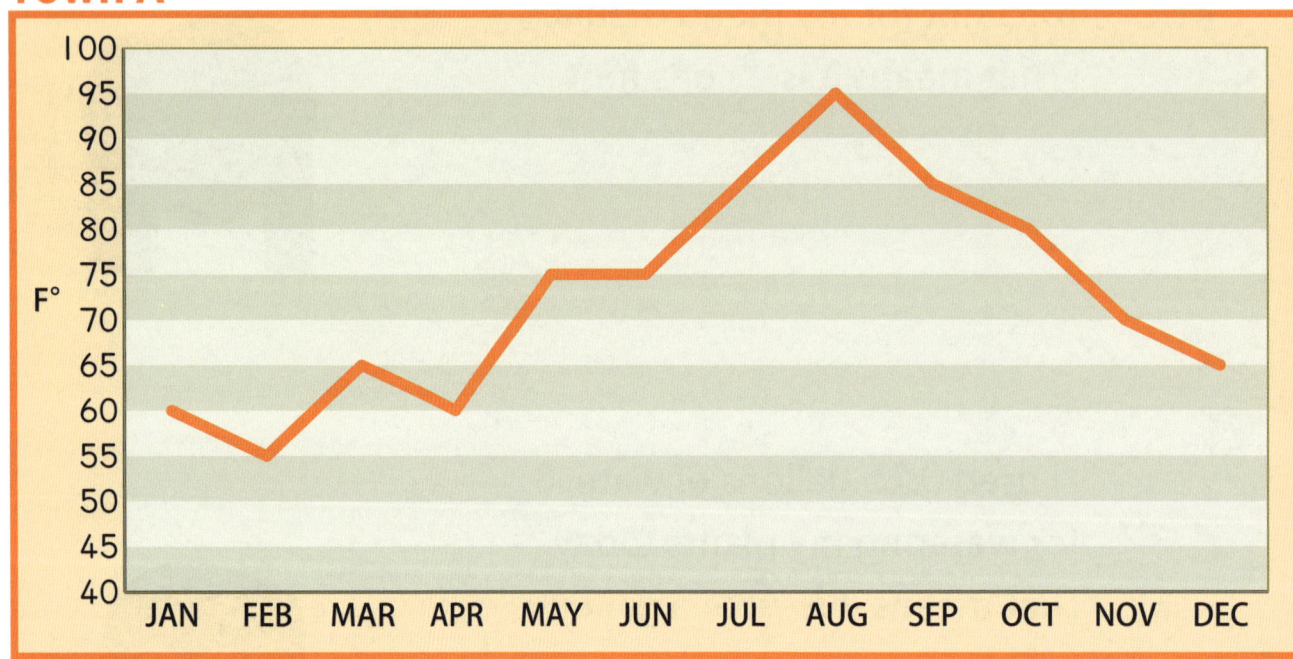

Town B

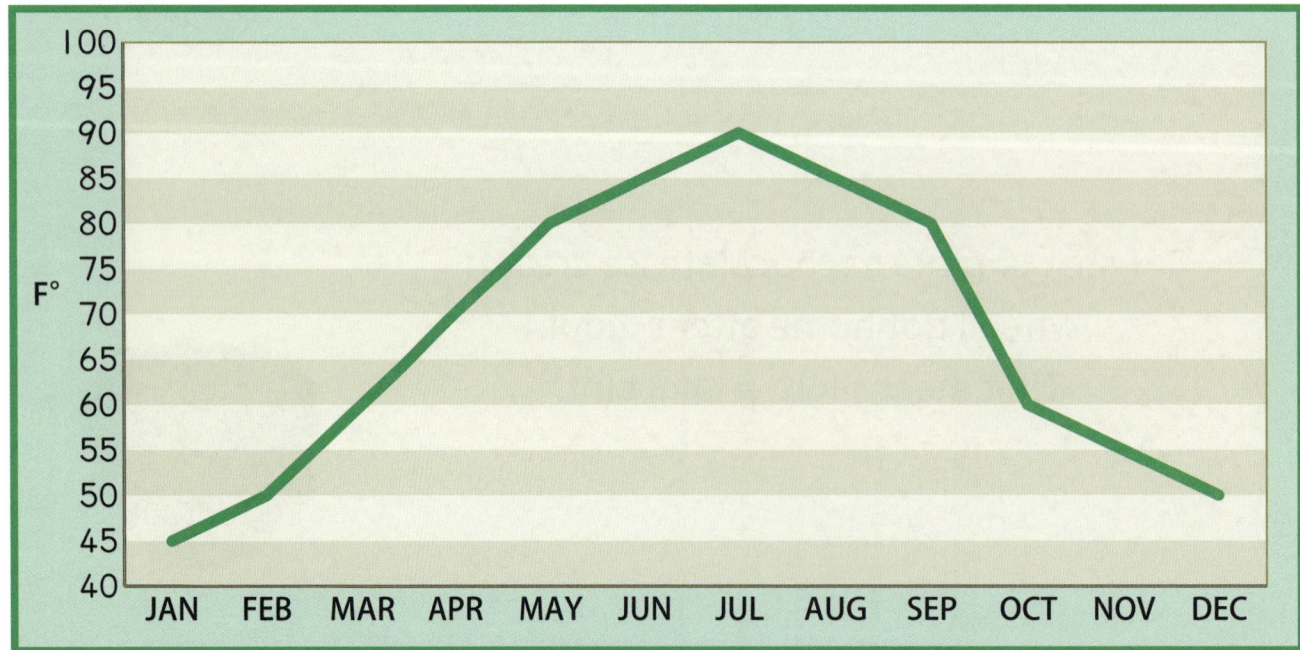

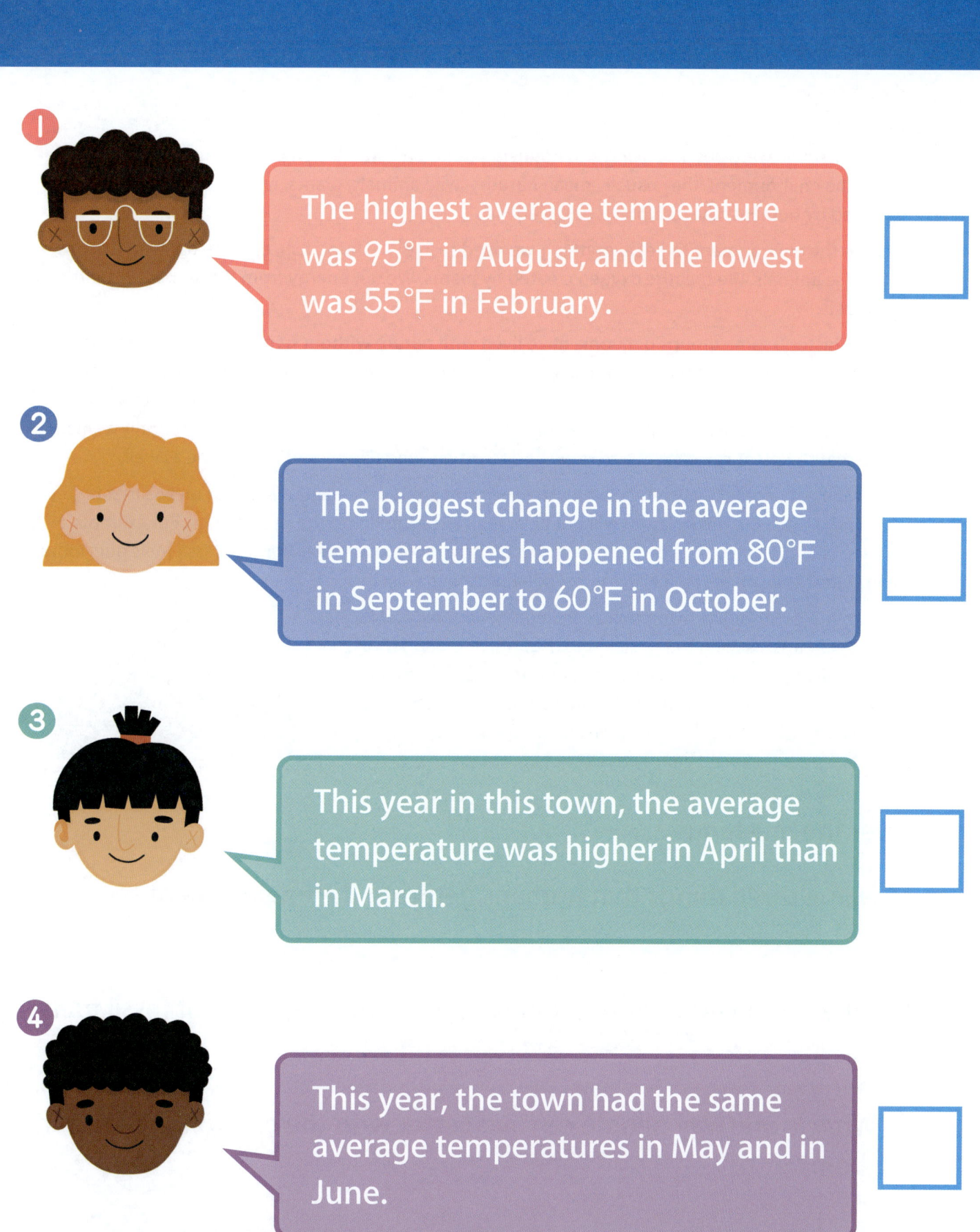

1. The highest average temperature was 95°F in August, and the lowest was 55°F in February.

☐

2. The biggest change in the average temperatures happened from 80°F in September to 60°F in October.

☐

3. This year in this town, the average temperature was higher in April than in March.

☐

4. This year, the town had the same average temperatures in May and in June.

☐

Our Environment

The environment is every physical living and nonliving thing on Earth. When people talk about protecting the environment, they usually mean nature – wild animals, plants, waterways, and land that is less impacted by humans, like rainforests and wetlands.

Humans use the environment to get everything we need to live. We hunt, fish, and use the land to grow food and raise animals. We breathe oxygen created by plants. We get energy from the sun, wind, water and fossil fuels.

Throughout history, some groups of people have lived with nature without harming it. Many groups of indigenous people take what they need to live from nature by fishing, hunting, gathering, and farming but do not overuse resources. For example, they farm in one area for some years, then move to another area and allow the first area to recover. When gathering food or medicinal plants, they take only a small portion so that the plant can continue to grow and so others who need it can have some as well.

The way that most people today interact with the environment is unsustainable, which means that if they continue doing the same things, Earth will not be able to keep providing the same things. For example, driving cars, taking planes, and powering factories all use a lot of fossil fuels. Burning fossil fuels puts more carbon into the atmosphere, which increases global warming.

Global warming harms many living things, including humans, and is melting the ice caps, causing the sea level to rise, which is dangerous for everyone living near the coasts. Additionally, fossil fuels are a non-renewable resource, which means that humans are using them much faster than Earth can create them. Humans need to switch to renewable resources like solar and wind energy to fix these problems.

■ Answer the questions.

❶ Name three things that humans get from the environment.

_____

❷ Why should humans use renewable resources instead of fossil fuels?

_____

❸ What is one way people can live better with the environment around them?

_____

■ Fill in the blanks to complete the statements.

❶ The [   ] is every physical living and non-living thing on Earth.

❷ The environment provides everything [   ] need to survive.

❸ [   ] people have been able to live in harmony with the environment for thousands of years.

❹ Using [   ] [   ] is unsustainable for the environment and can cause future problems for humans.

❺ [   ] [   ] is the process where burning fossil fuels cause Earth's temperature to rise.

❻ Humans need to find more [   ] resources to help sustain Earth.

Pollution

KEY POINTS

Pollution happens when the earth is dirtied by harmful substances. The main kinds of pollution are air, water, and land pollution. Pollution can be caused by natural and man-made actions. Humans pollute Earth by burning fossil fuels. But a volcano can also pollute the air with ash and gases when they erupt.

Air pollution happens when harmful gasses and particles are released into the air. Most air pollution is created when fossil fuels like coal, gas, and oil are burned. Wildfires and volcanic eruptions also pollute the air, and so do harmful chemicals released into the air from factories. Air pollution contributes to global warming. It can also cause acid rain, which harms living things. It can cause cancer and asthma in people and other animals.

Water pollution is when harmful chemicals, trash, sewage, or other substances are in waterways like the ocean, rivers, and underground reservoirs. Cities and factories sometimes dispose of waste in waterways. Chemicals used on farms can also cause water pollution because rain washes them into creeks and rivers. Water pollution hurts animals and plants that live in the water and can also make water unsafe for humans and other land animals to drink.

Land pollution is when trash and harmful chemicals are on the land. This pollution can harm animals that live there. It can also get into food plants that grow there, which can hurt the people and other animals who eat them.

Pollution is all over the world, but many places that used to be very polluted are now cleaner than they used to be, like rivers that used to be dangerous to swim in but are now safe. There are ways we can reduce pollution. Electrical plants, factories, and cars use fossil fuels. We can reduce air pollution by using more renewable resources like solar, wind, and hydroelectric power instead of burning fossil fuels. Governments can require factories to be more careful about what they release into the air, water, and land. Farmers and scientists can work together to find ways to help crops grow without polluting waterways.

■ **Answer the questions.**

❶ What creates the largest amount of air pollution?

_____

❷ What harm does water pollution cause?

_____

❸ What is one solution for reducing pollution created by humans?

_____

■ Match the type of pollution to a cause and a solution.

Air Pollution

Factories and people dumping trash and chemicals into water sources.

Carpooling and biking to work can help limit this pollution.

Water Pollution

People over farming and spilling hazardous waste into the land.

Requiring the government to make factories and people be more careful about not polluting water.

Soil Pollution

Burning fuel that sends smog and chemicals into the air.

Finding other ways to dispose of waste so it doesn't pollute the land.

Managing Waste

When trash, also called waste, is collected from homes, businesses, and government buildings like schools, it is brought to landfills. In the past, trash was often piled up in open areas and burned once the pile got too big. This released many harmful pollutants into the air, water, and land.

Today, landfills in most countries are designed to contain waste and keep it from contaminating, or dirtying, water, air, and land. Landfills have layers of plastic, stone, and soil separating the landfill from the rest of the environment. After trash is collected, it is disinfected and compacted so that it takes up less space. The compacted trash is put into the landfill and covered with a layer of soil. The soil makes the landfill less smelly and keeps the trash away from animals like rats. More trash and soil are added until the landfill is full. After that, more soil is added so plants can grow on top.

There is a system for collecting any liquids that seep through the layers so that they do not contaminate the soil and water. There is another system for collecting methane, a dangerous gas that is given off when garbage decomposes. These systems are a big improvement compared to the landfills of the past, but they are not perfect. Areas near landfills often have more air, water, and soil pollution. This is dangerous for humans and other living things and can cause disease.

Governments, companies, and individuals should work to create less waste. We can keep using what we already have instead of buying new things. Companies can create packaging that uses less plastic. We can try to eat all the food we buy before it goes bad instead of throwing it away.

■ Answer the questions.

1 What is a landfill?

2 Why do landfills have systems to collect liquids that seep through the soil?

3 What is one thing you can do to help create less waste?

■ Write true or false for each statement.

1 Landfills are places where waste and trash is dumped.

2 Landfill are safe and do not cause any pollution.

3 Landfills have layers of plastic, stone, and soil to help keep the harmful waste from contaminating the land around it.

4 Some landfills compact the trash down once they are full and layer soil on top to allow plants to grow over the waste.

5 Landfills can produce methane gas which is helpful for the environment.

6 Humans need to work on finding ways to produce less waste to help the environment.

Recycling and Composting

KEY POINTS

Some trash can be recycled or composted instead of being sent to landfills. This can help conserve resources and reduce the amount of waste in landfills. Recycling is when existing things are turned into new things. For example, old newspapers can be recycled at a factory and turned into new paper towels. Glass, metal, and paper, including cardboard, are fairly easy to recycle. They can be turned into new glass, metal, and paper products. This means fewer trees need to be cut down to make paper products, less metal has to be mined, and less sand and other materials have to be used to make glass. It still takes energy to recycle metal, glass, and paper, so it is better to reuse than recycle, but recycling these products is helpful for the environment.

Many kinds of plastic can be recycled, but it is much more difficult than recycling paper, metal, or glass. The plastic that results is often poor quality, and the process can release harmful chemicals and other pollutants. Plastic is made from fossil fuels, so its production is not good for the environment.

Composting is a way of recycling old food and yard waste like grass clippings. Fruit and vegetable peels, egg shells, old food, coffee grounds, and more can be composted and turned into a nutrient-rich mixture that helps plants grow! You can compost at home with an adult's help or contribute compost to a garden or city-wide program. You can write to your local government to ask them to start city-wide composting and recycling if they do not already. You can also write to companies and ask them to sell products that use paper, metal, or glass packaging instead of plastic.

■ Answer the questions.

❶ What materials are easier to recycle?

❷ What materials are harder to recycle?

❸ What can be turned into compost?

■ Sort the items below into Recyclable, Non-recyclable, and Compostable.

glass bottles	metal can	newspaper
batteries	leftover vegetables	paper plate
plastic soda bottle	an old coat	sneakers
a baseball	dead plant	old Christmas tree
plastic bag	broken mirror	can of hairspray

Recyclable	Non-recyclable	Compostable

Brain Break
Science Journal 4

Create a plan for reducing waste in your home. Ask your parent or guardian for help as needed. Use the questions below for help!

- How can I reduce the things I throw away at home?
- Is there anything I can recycle or upcycle in my room?
- Can I compost my leftover dinner?

My Waste Reduction Plan:

Unit 4

Art Break!

■ One way to reduce waste is to recycle! Many every day items can be recycled or upcycle into art. Give it a try! Create a collage out of scrap paper and other materials from around your home.

The US Government

A democracy is a type of government that is ruled by the people. In representative democracies, people vote for representatives whose opinions are closest to their own. These representatives should try to make the government do the things the people they represent think are important. The US is a democracy with three branches of government, each with different powers. There are checks and balances in the system so that none of the branches can become too powerful.

The legislative branch is made up of the Senate and the House of Representatives, together called Congress. The legislative branch makes laws and can declare war. It can also impeach presidents and federal judges if they have broken laws. Laws start as bills in committees, or smaller groups of representatives or senators. If the bill is created in the Senate, then the Senate votes on it. If more than half of the senators vote yes, it goes to the House of Representatives and they vote on it. If more than half of them vote yes, then it goes to the president for approval. If a bill starts in the House of Representatives, they vote on it first, then the Senate. If the president approves the bill, then it becomes a law.

The executive branch is made up of the president, the cabinet, and departments. The executive branch can recommend laws to Congress. It can also veto laws that Congress passes. This means that if the president doesn't agree with a law that Congress passes, the president can stop it from becoming a law unless two-thirds of both the Senate and the House of Representatives vote to make it a law. The president is the commander-in-chief of the US military. The president can send soldiers to fight in wars, but the president cannot declare a war on another country – only Congress can.

The third branch of the US government is the judicial branch. The judicial branch is made up of courts with judges. The president chooses all federal judges and the Senate approves or rejects judges. Judges decide if people or companies are guilty or if they owe money to others, sometimes with the help of a jury. The Supreme Court can also decide if a law goes against the US Constitution. If a state or federal law contradicts the US Constitution, they can declare it unconstitutional. In that case, it is no longer a law.

■ **Answer the questions.**

❶ What is a democracy?

❷ What are the three branches of US government?

❸ What is the purpose of the system of checks and balances?

■ Read each statement and write which branch would check the decision.

> **legislative branch**   **executive branch**   **judicial branch**

1 The president makes an executive action. This branch can declare it
unconstitutional.

branch

2 The president vetoes a new law. This branch can override the veto.

branch

3 The congress declares war on another country. This branch can send
soldiers to fight in that war.

branch

4 The president appoints a new Supreme Court judge. This branch can
approve or reject the candidate.

branch

5 If the president does something unconstitutional or illegal, this
branch can decide to impeach them.

branch

6 If the legislative branch proposes a new law, this branch can decide
if it is unconstitutional.

branch

US Constitution

Constitutions are documents that state the laws for a country or state. They describe how the government should work and how power should be shared. The United States Constitution is the oldest constitution in the world that is still in use. It was written 1787 at the Constitutional Convention in Philadelphia. It became the law of the US in 1789 after most of the new country's thirteen states had approved it.

The US Constitution explains how the country's government works, with the legislative, executive, and judicial branches. It establishes the US as a democracy, or a government that is controlled by the people. Originally, only white men who owned a certain amount of land were allowed to vote. Today, most adult citizens can vote.

The US's founders wanted states and the federal (whole country) government to share power. Right after the Revolutionary War, the thirteen states ratified the Articles of Confederation. This document gave the states a lot of power and the federal government very little power. This made it impossible for the federal government to collect taxes or enforce any laws. This didn't work well, so the founders met again and wrote the US Constitution to replace the Articles of Confederation. The US Constitution gives certain rights to the states and other rights to the federal government.

The US Constitution can be changed, but it is difficult. Three-quarters of states and two-thirds of the Senate and House of Representatives have to approve any changes to the US Constitution. These changes are called amendments. Only twenty-seven amendments have been passed in the more than two hundred years since the Constitution was written. Some of the most important amendments ended slavery, gave Black people full citizenship, gave Black men the right to vote, and gave women the right to vote.

■ **Answer the questions.**

❶ What is the purpose of a constitution?

❷ What was the problem with the Articles of Confederation?

❸ What is an amendment?

■ Write true or false for each statement.

1 The US Constitution is the oldest constitution in the world still in use.

2 The US Constitution explains how the country's government works.

3 The US Constitution states that today only white men can vote.

4 The US Constitution was written to help balance the amount of power the states and the government had.

5 The Articles of Confederation replaced the US Constitution.

6 It is very easy to make changes to the US Constitution.

7 Changes to the US Constitution are called amendments.

Bill of Rights

After the US Constitution was ratified in 1789, many people were worried that it did not give individual citizens enough rights. They worried that the federal government could abuse its power. The first ten amendments, or changes, were written to fix this. These ten amendments are also called the Bill of Rights because they list rights of people under US law.

The **first amendment** gives people freedom of religion to practice or not practice any religion they want. It guarantees people freedom of speech as long as their speech does not cause physical harm to others. It gives freedom of the press, which means that journalists can report on what is happening without worrying that the government will punish them if they expose something bad that the government is doing.

The **second amendment** gives the right to bear arms. This means that people are allowed to own weapons in case they need to defend the United States from enemies.

The **third amendment** states that people cannot be forced to house soldiers. The British had forced colonists to house their soldiers, so the new country wanted to make sure that wouldn't happen in the United States.

The **fourth amendment** says that the government cannot search people's homes, bodies, or other things without a good reason. This is why police have to have a warrant from a judge that says they have a good reason to suspect someone before they are allowed to search a person's home.

The **fifth amendment** gives people rights if they are accused of a crime, including that the government has to go through a legal process before punishing them.

The **sixth amendment** also gives people rights if they are accused of a crime, like the rights to a fair trial and to a lawyer.

The **seventh amendment** says that people can go to court for civil cases, where one person or company says that another person or company owes them money.

The **eighth amendment** says that punishments for crimes have to be fair and cannot be "cruel and unusual."

The **ninth amendment** says that the Bill of Rights does not list every right that people in the US have. Just because the Bill of Rights doesn't say it, that doesn't mean it isn't a right of the people.

The **tenth amendment** says that any powers that the federal government doesn't have automatically belong to state governments. This was to keep the federal government from being too powerful.

■ Fill in the blank with the correct amendment.

1 This amendment gives people the right to bear arms or carry weapons.

amendment

2 This amendment says that punishments have to fit crimes.

amendment

3 This amendment gives people the freedom to practice whatever religion they want without being persecuted or harmed by another group.

amendment

4 This amendment gives people rights if they are accused of a crime.

amendment

5 This amendment says that any powers that the federal government doesn't have automatically belong to the states.

amendment

6 This amendment says that the government cannot search homes or bodies without a good reason.

amendment

7 This amendment says that the Bill of Rights does not cover all the rights a person has.

amendment

8 This amendment gives people the right to go to court for money if someone owes them.

amendment

US States

When adults vote, they get to vote for local, state, and federal representation. Depending on the election, they might vote for the mayor, the school board, and the city council for local elections, the governor, state representative, and state senator for state elections, and the president, representative, and senator for federal elections. A person who runs to be elected is called a candidate.

Local representatives decide local laws and how money is spent in a city or town. State representatives decide state laws and how money is spent in the state. Federal representatives decide laws for the whole country and how money is spent in the whole country. All of these elected officials should try to represent the desires and beliefs of the people who live in the areas they represent. People running for local or state offices will often campaign to show and tell the voters about what changes they will make if elected. What a candidate believes in and wants to change can effect how many people vote for them.

Most adult US citizens (18 or older) are allowed to vote if they have completed their voter registration. People who are born in the US are automatically citizens. Immigrants can vote if they have been naturalized, or become US citizens through an official process. Some citizens are not allowed to vote because of crimes they were convicted of, or found guilty of, in the past. This depends on the crime and the state in which they live.

The president and vice president are elected through the Electoral College, a system of indirect representation. There is a winner-take-all system in almost all states, meaning the candidate who gets the most votes in a state gets all of the state's electoral votes. If one candidate gets 50.5% of the votes and the other gets 49.5%, the candidate who got 50.5% will get all of the state's electoral votes. States with more people have more electoral votes, which is why California has fifty-four electoral votes and Wyoming only has three. A candidate needs 270 electoral votes to become president.

■ **Answer the questions.**

❶ **Who is allowed to vote in the United States?**

_____

❷ **What is the Electoral College system?**

_____

❸ **Who do people vote for in local elections?**

_____

■ You are running for class president at your school. Fill in the boxes below with your campaign information.

I am running for: _____

My campaign slogan: _____

My promises	I will change

Vote for me because	What I believe in

Brain Break
Crossword Puzzle

■ Use the clues to complete the crossword puzzle.

Across

❶ This branch of government contains the court system.

❸ This is a person who serves in Congress.

❺ The Senate and the House of Representatives make up this.

Down

❷ The US has this type of government.

❹ The leader of the US and head of the Executive Branch.

❻ This body votes on new bills and laws.

❽ This branch of government makes the laws.

❿ The president is part of this branch of government.

Mindfulness Break!

■ Color the picture. Focus only on coloring and breathing.

Jigsaw Puzzles

■ Fit the missing pieces in the puzzle.

Ⓐ

Ⓑ

Ⓒ

Ⓓ

Ⓔ

Ⓕ

Ⓖ

Ⓗ

❶ ☐ ❷ ☐ ❸ ☐ ④ ☐

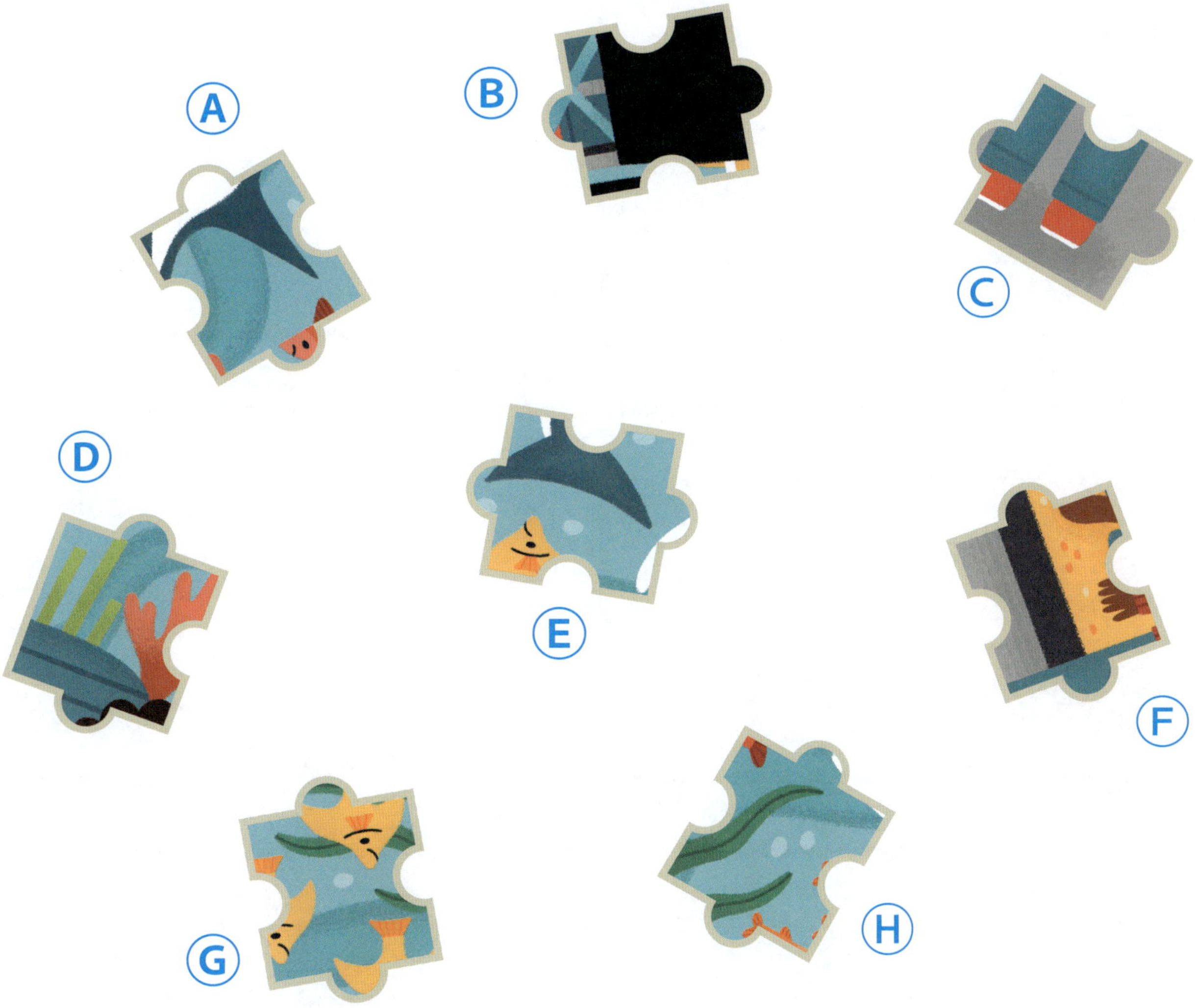

❺ ☐ ❻ ☐ ❼ ☐ ❽ ☐

Maze Puzzles

■ Which maze can reach the goal? Write one of the letters Ⓐ to Ⓓ in the box for each.

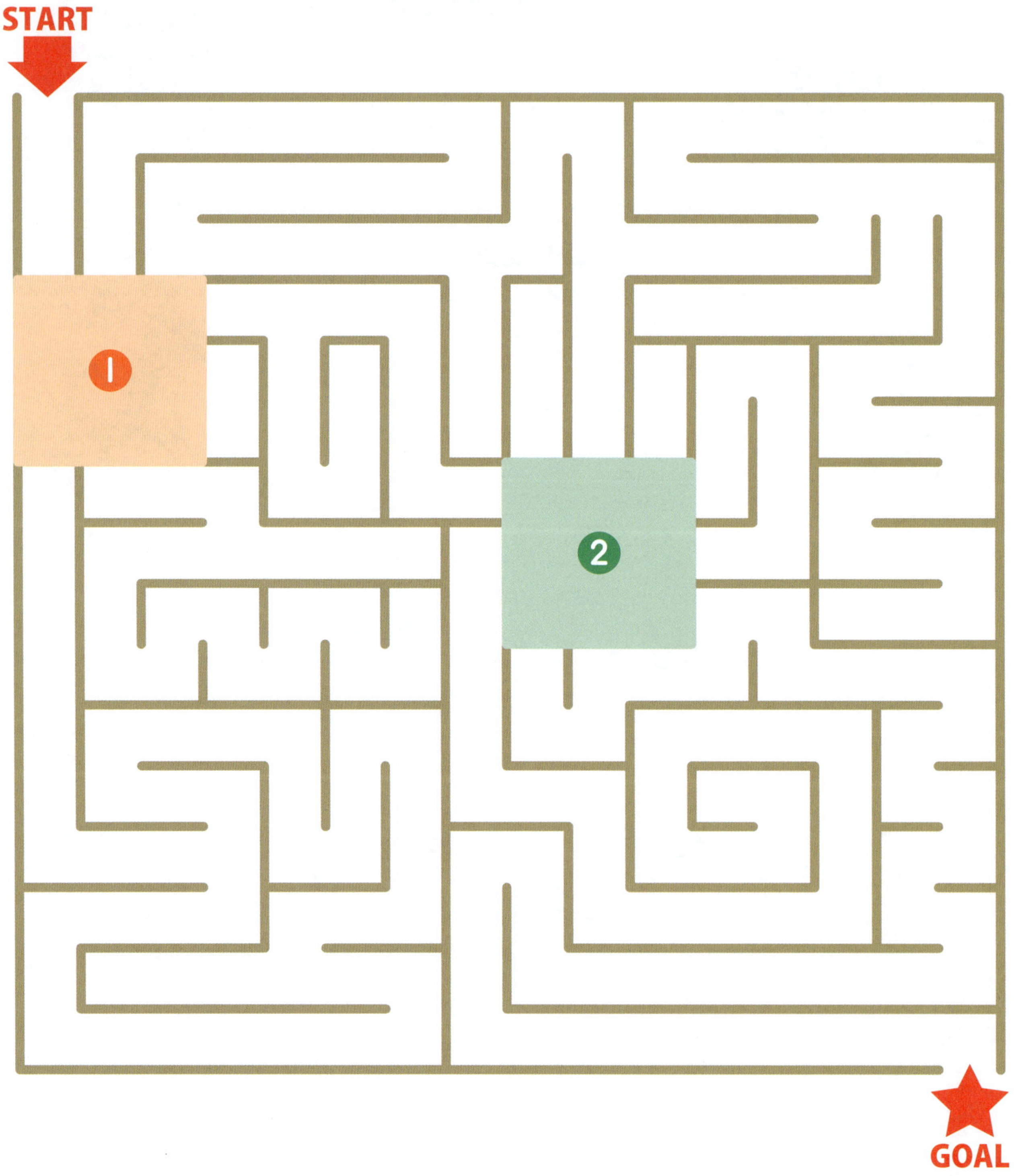

START

1

2

GOAL

1 **A**  **B**

C  **D**

2 **A**  **B**

C  **D**

Combination of Shapes

■ Write a check mark (✓) on the shape that can be made using all the shapes in the box.

①

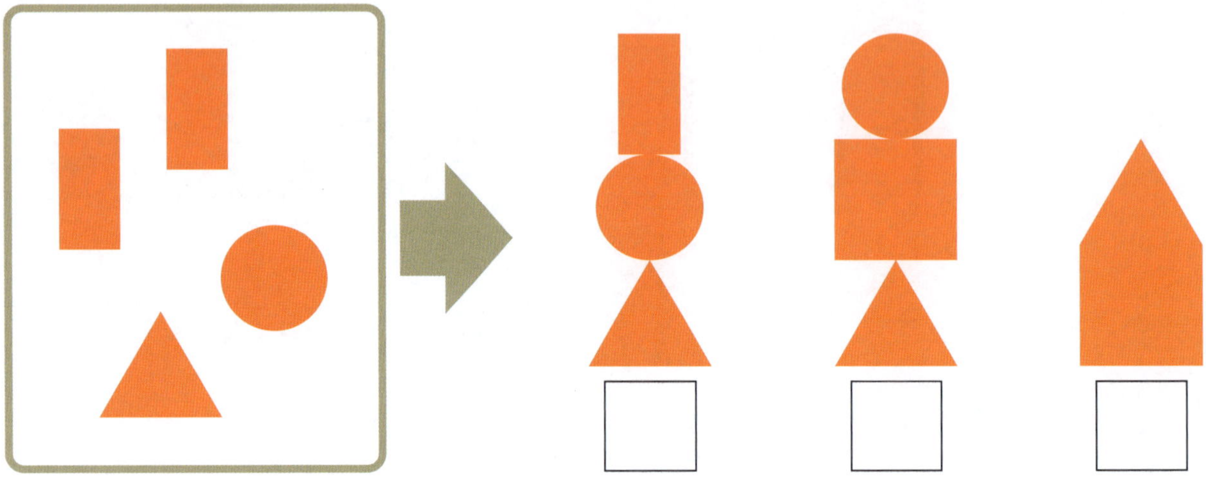

②

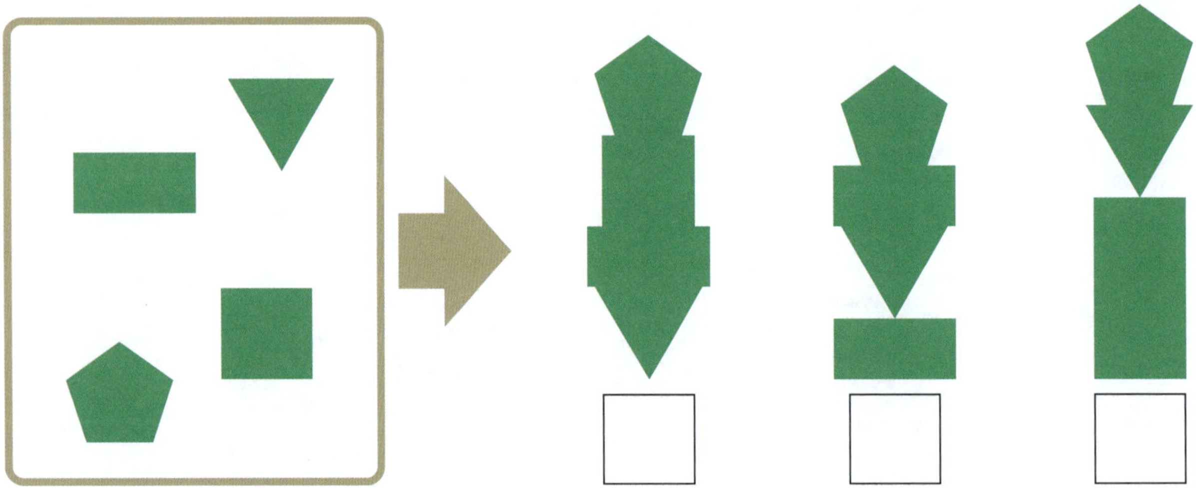

③

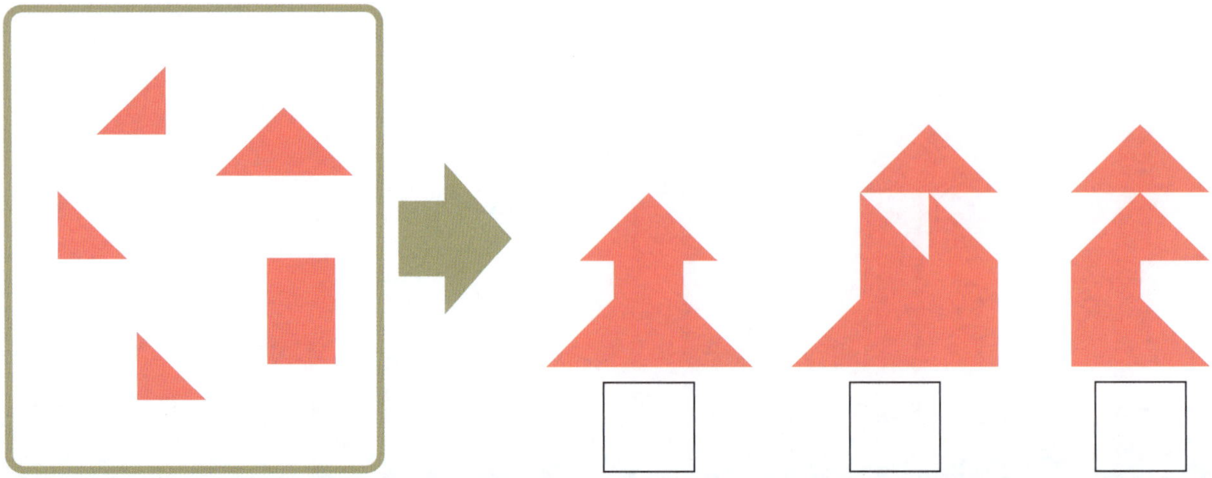

4

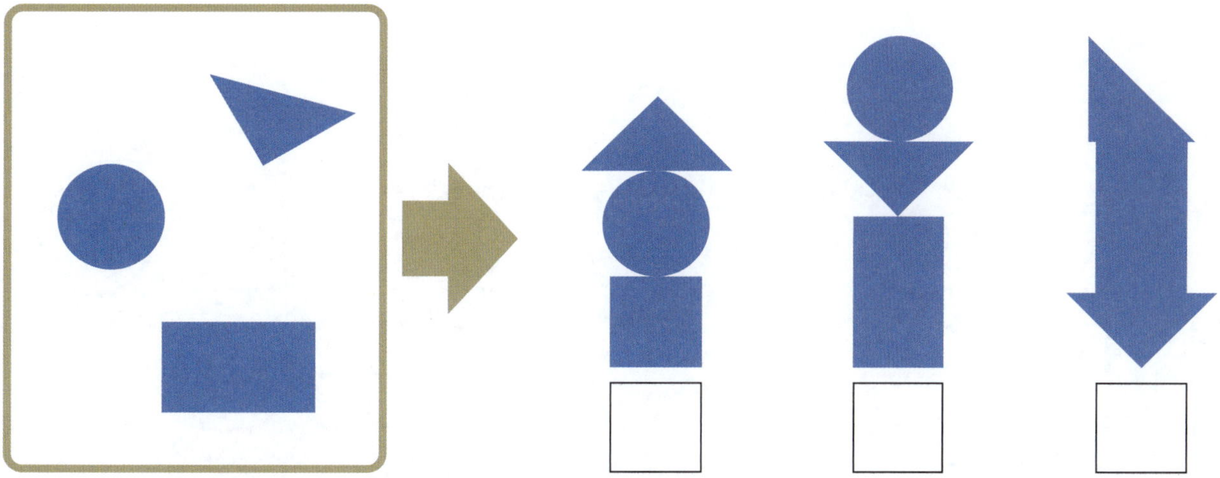

5

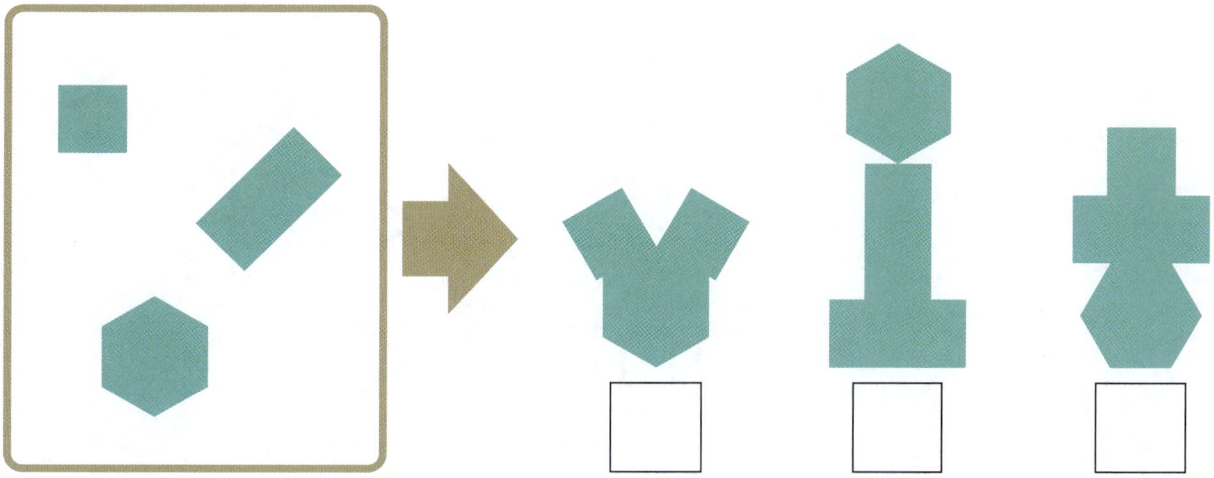

6

Spot the Difference

■ There are five different marks on the left and right pages.
  Find and circle them on the right hand page.

Physical Education Break!

It's important to move your body and exercise!
Try this fun activity below to break up your studying!

■ Complete the exercise for each letter to spell your name.

Spell Your Name Exercise Game!

A-B-C	D-E-F	G-H-I
15 Jumping Jacks	15 Arm Circles	5 Lunges to the Left

J-K-L	M-N-O	P-Q-R
15 High Knees	Run in Place for 60 Seconds	5 Lunges to the Right

S-T-U	V-W-X	Y-Z
15 Toe Touches	10 Jump Jacks	5 Sit Ups

Unit **5** Table of Contents

Use this page to keep track of your progress throughout the book. Place a check mark in the box when you have completed a section.

■ Fill in the blank with the correct word from the Word Box.

Word Box

ancestor	tradition	fragile	peculiar	shabby

❶ Every year Greg's family does a 5K race after Thanksgiving. It is a

family [　　　　　　　　].

❷ The recipe was passed from Mina's [　　　　　　　　　　] to her

mother.

❸ Kevin had to be careful with the family heirloom because it was

[　　　　　　　　].

❹ Aja's favorite dish is white rice with ketchup. Her brother thinks it is

[　　　　　　　　].

❺ Quentin thought the old farmhouse was cool but his sister thought it

was [　　　　　　　　].

■ Use the context clues in the passage to determine the meaning of the underlined words.

Daniel's grandparents came to celebrate the Lunar New Year with his family. He was excited to see them and learn more about the holiday <u>traditions</u> they do each year. Daniel's grandparents gave him a red envelope full of crisp new money. This was one of the traditions of Lunar New Year. Then, his grandfather told him stories of his <u>ancestors</u> that used to celebrate this holiday many, many year ago. He told Daniel that praising their ancestors is an important part of Lunar New Year. Daniel also helped his mother and

 grandmother make dumplings for dinner. His mother told him to be careful with the dough because it was <u>fragile</u>. Finally, Daniel's family ended the night by lighting fireworks to scare off evil spirits and bad luck in the New Year. Daniel thought this was a <u>peculiar</u> reason for fireworks but he enjoyed it all the same.

tradition

ancestor

fragile

peculiar

Vocabulary 2

Growing your vocabulary is essential for success as a reader and writer.

■ Fill in the blank with the correct word from the Word Box.

Word Box

| eager | humble | concentrate | sturdy | frantic |

❶ Hank was [ ] when he received his achievement award.

❷ Anna needed to [ ] when studying so she went to her bedroom and shut the door.

❸ Gil lost his lucky socks before the big game. He was [ ] as he looked around his room for them.

❹ The bench Samson built was very [ ]. It could hold a lot of weight without breaking.

❺ Laurel couldn't wait for the concert to start. She was [ ] to see her favorite singer perform.

■ Use the context clues in the passage to determine the meaning of the underlined words.

Brandon asked his dad to teach him how to build a rocking horse for his little sister's birthday. He was very eager to start and woke his dad up early in the morning on a Saturday. Brandon's dad showed him how to measure and cut the wood pieces. He had to concentrate carefully when cutting out the horse's head because it was a difficult shape. His father helped him sand the edges for safety. Then, showed him how to level the rockers to make sure the horse was sturdy enough to support his little sister. Finally, Brandon painted the horse brown and tied a big ribbon around its neck. When he gave it to his sister, she was very happy and gave him a big hug! Brandon was humble about his hard work and just gave her a big smile back.

eager

concentrate

sturdy

humble

Multiply-meaning Words

KEY POINTS

Some words sound and are spelled the same, but have different meanings.

Fly can be a noun meaning the name of an insect. Or it can be a verb like "a bird can fly."

It is important to pay attention to the other words in a sentence to help find the meaning of multiple-meaning words.

■ Circle the meaning of each underlined word.

1 We knew the bread was old because it had <u>mold</u> on it.

   a. a spore growth on food

   b. a container to be filled with plaster to make an object

2 David helped his sister pick the <u>squash</u> in the garden.

   a. to squish something

   b. a type of vegetable

3 Stacy had to <u>log</u> the runners times from the race.

   a. to record information

   b. a cut down tree intended for building or burning

4 Bradley and Samantha went to the movies for their first <u>date</u>.

   a. a current day, month, and year

   b. an event where a couple spends time together alone

■ Write a word from the box that fits both sentences.

Word Box

| right | change | tear | patch | trunk | fan |

1 Ryan found a lot of spare [_____] in the couch.

After swimming, we need to [_____] our clothes.

2 Stella opened her grandmother's [_____] to find a blanket.

The elephant sprayed water with its [_____].

3 Eddie did the [_____] thing and returned

the wallet he found on the sidewalk.

My house is on the [_____] side of the road, not the left.

4 In the summer, we use a [_____] to stay cool.

Jeff was a big [_____] of baseball.

5 The movie was so sad she shed a [_____].

After falling off his bike,

Pedro found a [_____] in his new jeans.

6 We picked pumpkins at the pumpkin [_____] in the fall.

Mickey had to [_____] his coat after he found a hole in it.

KEY POINTS

An affix can be added to a word to change the meaning. An affix can be a prefix like *dis-* that goes at the beginning of a word or a suffix like *ing* and go at the end of a word. The word the affix is added to is often called the root word.

Example: Adding *un* to the word *remarkable* changes the meaning from something unique to something common, *unremarkable*.

Liam's singing voice was remarkable.

VS.

Liam's singing voice was unremarkable.

■ Choose the correct affix to complete the sentence.

Word Box

dis-   re-   un-

❶ Quinn was always late for work. He was [　　　　　] reliable .

❷ Kelsey never listened and always [　　　　　] regarded the rules.

❸ Mikayla was tired after soccer practice. She needed to rest and [　　　　　] charge .

■ Read the passage. Write the meanings of the bold words with affixes in the lines below.

On Saturday, the kids from Troop 214 gathered for their first hiking trip. They had planned the adventure the previous week, but when they arrived at the start of the trail they quickly realized they were **unprepared**. Mia couldn't find her water bottle and Sam had **misplaced** the map! They had only packed one snack per person and no one remembered to bring the first aid kit. "This is not what we expected," Mia said looking around at her friends. "Maybe we should try again next weekend?"

But the group decided to keep calm and try the hike anyway. After walking for a half hour, they realized Sam's map didn't have the right trails marked. They didn't know which trail to take! Sam suggested they **regroup** by resting next to a large rock to check the map again. They felt a little scared because the path ahead was **unknown** to them.

"Why don't we **retrace** the path and go back to the start of the trail to ask for help?" Mia said. Her friends agreed. With a new plan, they were ready to try again.

❶ **unprepared**

_____

❷ **misplaced**

_____

❸ **regroup**

_____

❹ **unknown**

_____

❺ **retrace**

_____

Brain Break
Matching Multiple-meaning Words

■ Match the pictures to the words to show each words multiple meanings.

mouse

nail

match

bat

date

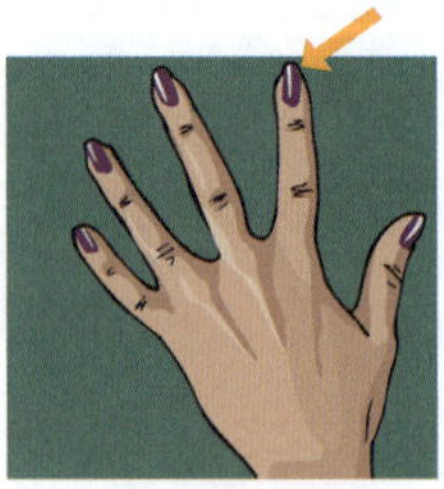

bark

Mindfulness Break!

■ Meditation can be an important mindfulness tool. Read the steps below and try meditation!

Let's Start!

❶ Pick a quiet place and get comfortable!

❷ Sit up straight, but stay relaxed.

❹ Close your eyes and take a deep breath in and then let it out.

❸ Think about what your arms and legs are doing. Try to keep them relaxed.

❺ Focus on breathing, in and out.

❻ Notice when your mind starts to wander and try to bring it back to your breathing. Focusing on breathing in and out.

Bonus: You can also try a mantra to focus on while breathing like, "Today will be a good day!"

❼ When finished, open your eyes and bring your mind back to the present and what's around you.

Opinion Writing: Stating an Opinion

KEY POINTS

In an opinion text, the writer states a clear opinion and provides facts and reasons to support their opinion. The reader should be able to understand the writer's opinion and why they feel that way. The first step in writing an opinion piece is to decide what your opinion is and state it clearly.

■ Read the text below. Then write the author's opinion below.

Cooking is an essential skill, and I believe everyone should learn how to cook in school. Cooking at home is cheaper and healthier than getting take-out all the time. It is also more convenient, because you don't have to leave your home. If you learn how to cook in school, then you can help your parents out at home. You will also be prepared to take care of yourself when you're an adult. Since all kids need to learn this, it isn't fair to make them figure it out on their own. We should all be able to learn from a teacher so that we can grow up to make our own food at home.

■ In a few activities, you will write an opinion piece of your own. On this page, you will give your opinion on four topics. Then you will choose the opinion you want to write about. You can choose to write about one of the topics below, or a topic of your choice.

Topic ❶ Is screen time bad for you?

Topic ❷ Would you rather be able to fly or be invisible?

Topic ❸ Should kids have to do chores at home?

Topic ❹ What is the best place you can go on a field trip?

Opinion I will write about ...

Opinion Writing: Providing Reasons

It's not enough for an opinion text to just have an opinion! Opinion pieces also need to have reasons to back up the opinion. Reasons help the reader understand why the writer feels the way they do. They may also persuade the reader to feel the same way.

■ Underline the reasons in the text below:

Some people think recess is just a fun time of day that isn't important. But I believe that recess is actually one of the most important parts of school. During recess, we have a chance to play outside and joke around with our friends. If we didn't have this time, we would feel more stressed all day long. Recess is a time to meet new people and make friends, which is also very important. This helps us to have fun and welcome new students. Finally, recess allows us to take a break from our schoolwork. When we are done with recess, then we are ready to go back and learn more instead of feeling tired!

■ Fill out the outline below to plan your opinion piece. Include four reasons that support your opinion.

Introduction

Opinion Statement

Reason

❶

❷

❸

❹

Conclusion

Opinion Writing:
Linking Words and Phrases

You can use linking words and phrases to connect your opinion and reasons. This makes the relationship between your ideas more clear. Here are some common linking words:

in addition to ➡ adds another idea
for instance ➡ gives an example
in order to ➡ shows a reason for something

■ Fill in the correct linking phrase from the box.

Word Box

in addition to	for instance	in order to

❶ We went to the store [_____] to get the things we needed to make dinner.

❷ [_____] to being a talented musician, she is also an amazing dancer!

❸ You can learn a lot from a book. [_____], I recently taught myself how to play chess!

■ Write two sentences for each linking phrase.

❶ in addition to

-
-

❷ for instance

-
-

❸ in order to

-
-

■ Use your outline to write your full opinion piece. Don't forget to include an introduction, opinion statement, reasons, and a conclusion.

Brain Break
Fun Opinions!

■ If you could change one thing about your school, what would it be? Why?

Mindfulness Break!

Setting goals is an important step to achieving the things you want. You can use mindfulness to help you figure out your goals, how to set them, and how to achieve them.

■ Use the chart below to set some goals for your current school year.
List the steps needed to achieve them.
Record if you meet your goals in the future.

My goal:	My goal:	My goal:
The steps:	The steps:	The steps:
Did I achieve my goal:	Did I achieve my goal:	Did I achieve my goal:

Line *PQ*

A **line** has no endpoints and extends infinitely in both directions.

Line segment *PQ*

A **line segment** represents the bounded area of a line. It has two endpoints with a determined length.

Ray *PQ*

A **ray** is a portion of a line that has one endpoint but extends infinitely in a single direction.

■ Use points *A* to *L* to draw each line, line segment, or ray.

❶ Line *AB*   ❷ Line segment *CD*   ❸ Ray *EF*

❹ Line *GH*   ❺ Line segment *IJ*   ❻ Ray *KL*

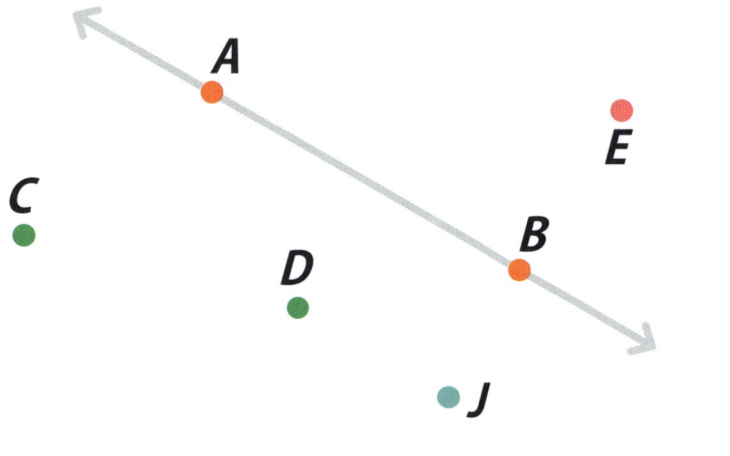
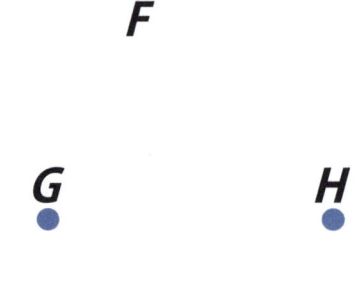

Parallel lines *l* and *m*

l ⟷
m ⟷

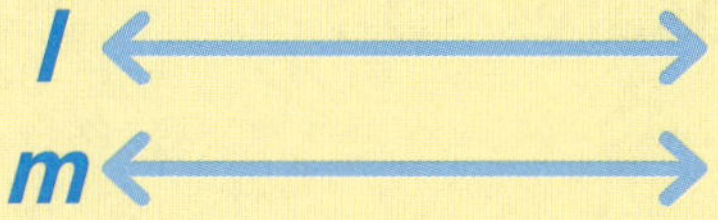

Two lines are **parallel** when they do not intersect, which means they will never meet or cross.

Perpendicular lines *l* and *m*

l ↑
⟵ □90° ⟶ *m*
↓

Two lines are **perpendicular** when they intersect and create a right angle, 90°.

■ Circle the parallel lines in red, and the perpendicular lines in blue.

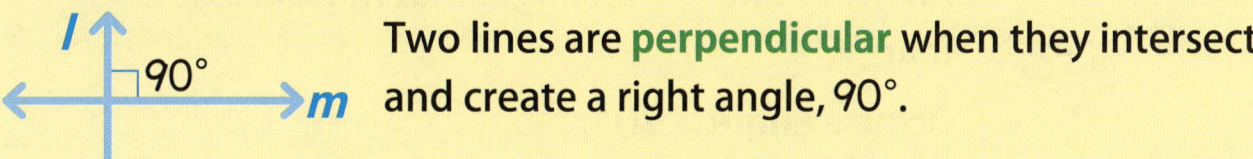

❶   ❷

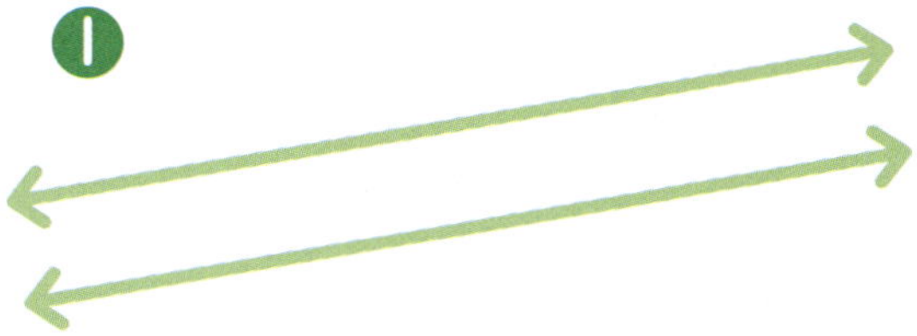

❸   ❹   ❺

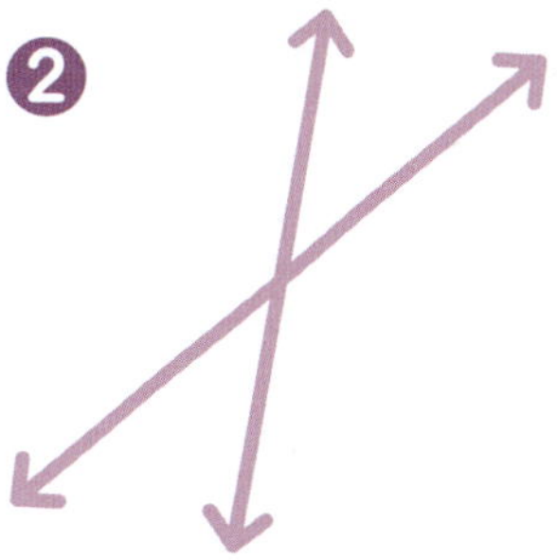

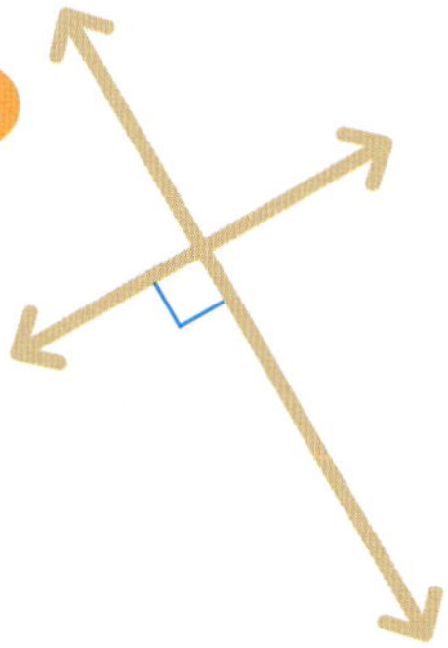

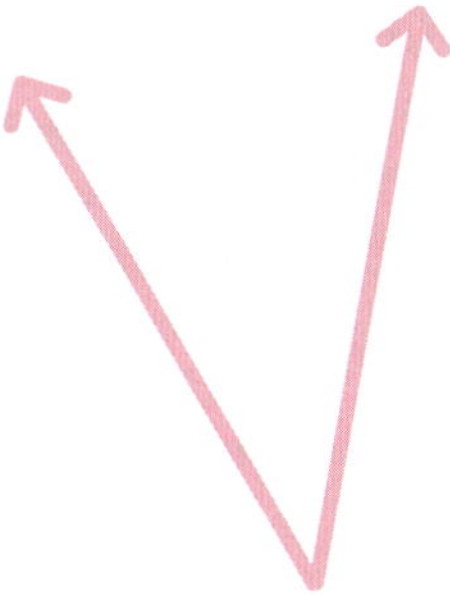

❻   ❼

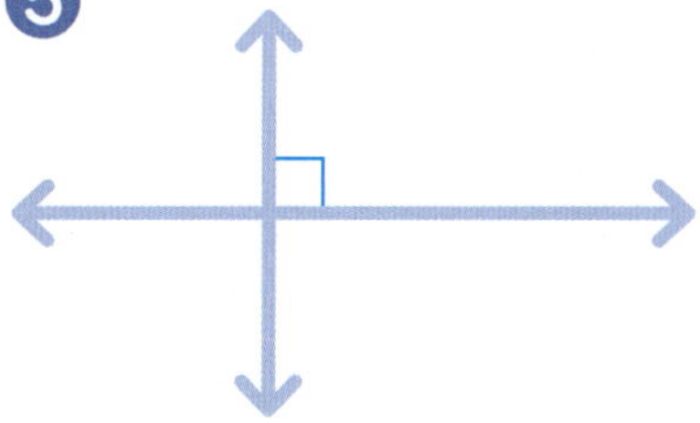

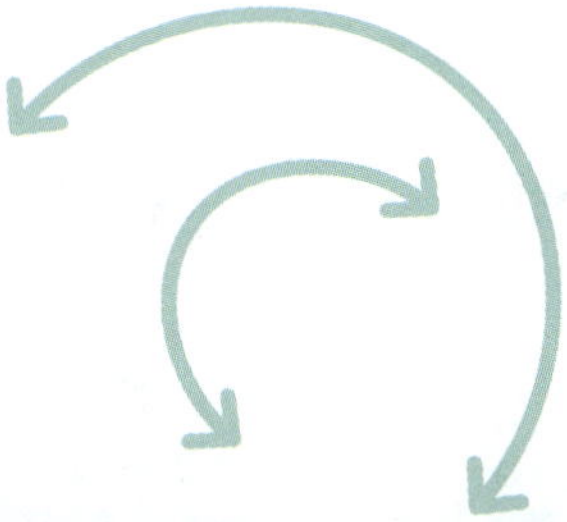

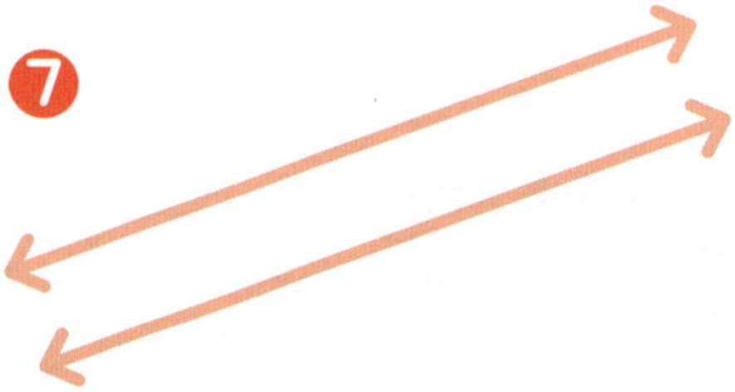

Angles

KEY POINTS

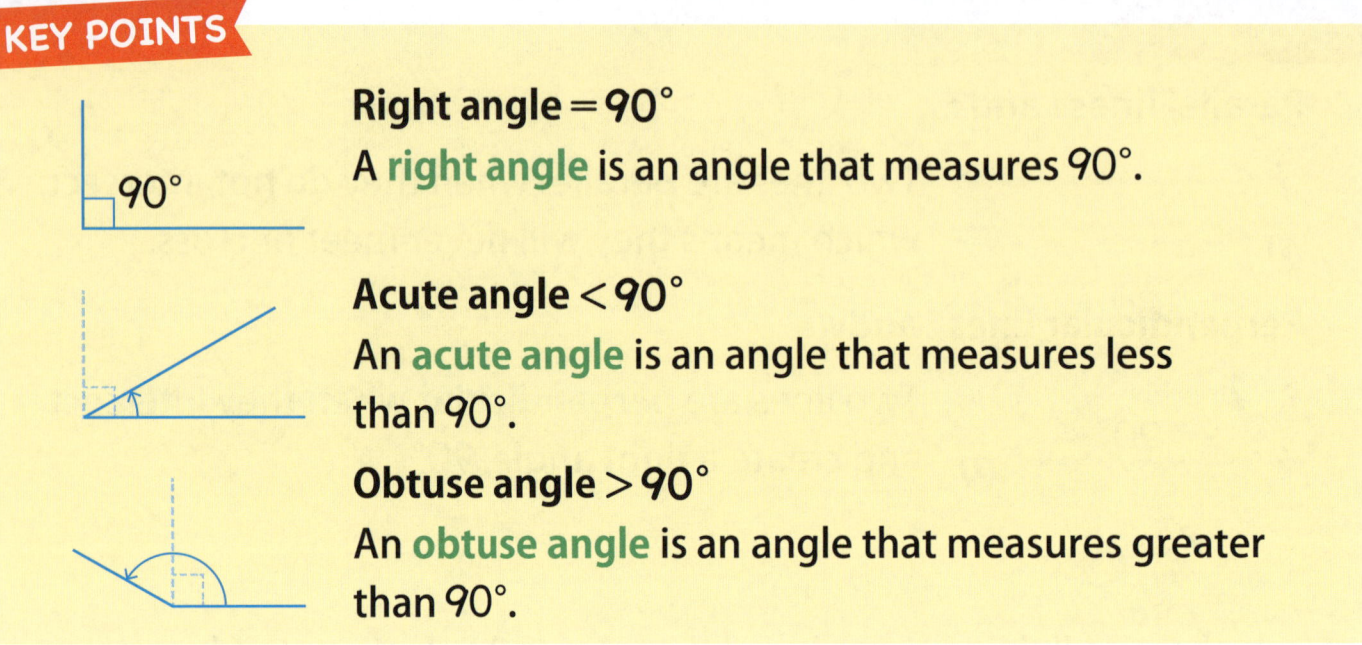

Right angle = 90°
A **right angle** is an angle that measures 90°.

90°

Acute angle < 90°
An **acute angle** is an angle that measures less than 90°.

Obtuse angle > 90°
An **obtuse angle** is an angle that measures greater than 90°.

■ Sort the angles into the categories below. Write the number of each angle in the boxes.

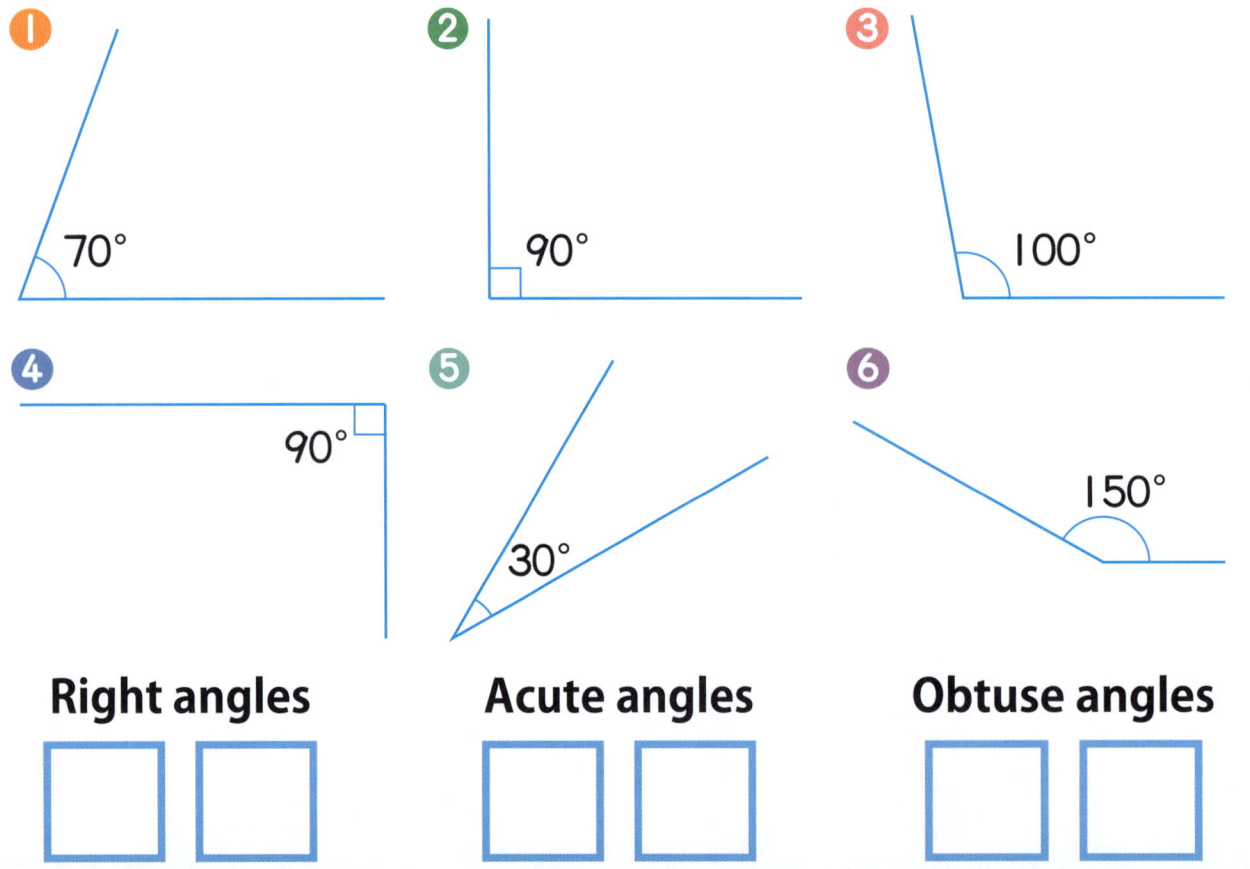

1 70°

2 90°

3 100°

4 90°

5 30°

6 150°

Right angles

☐ ☐

Acute angles

☐ ☐

Obtuse angles

☐ ☐

■ Write the name of each angle. Use "right", "acute", or "obtuse."

❶
_____ **angle**

❷
_____ **angle**

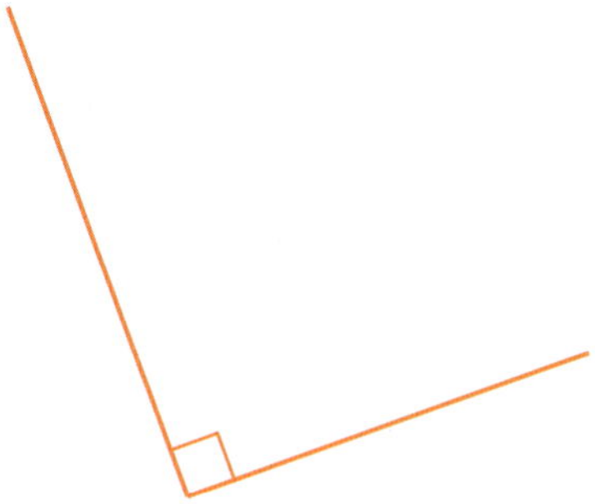

❸
_____ **angle**

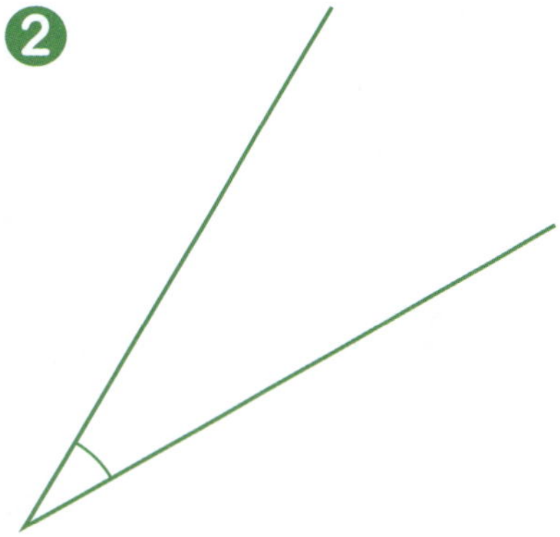

❹
_____ **angle**

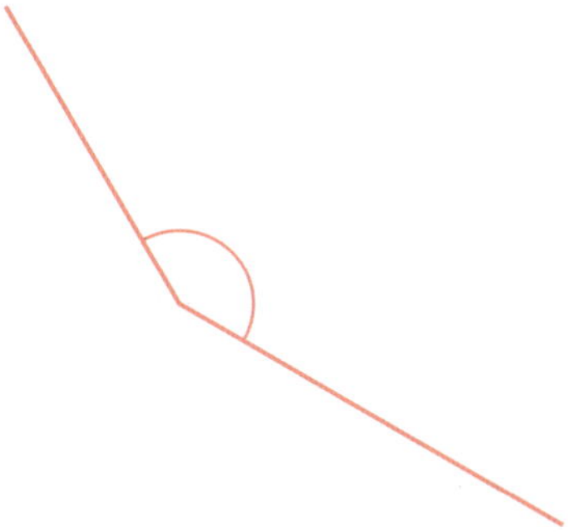

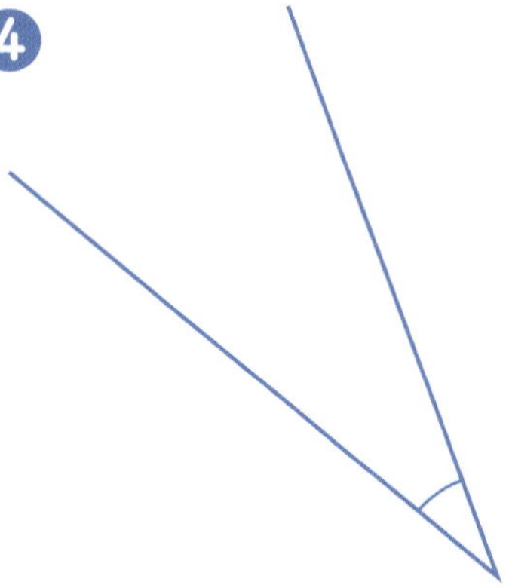

❺
_____ **angle**

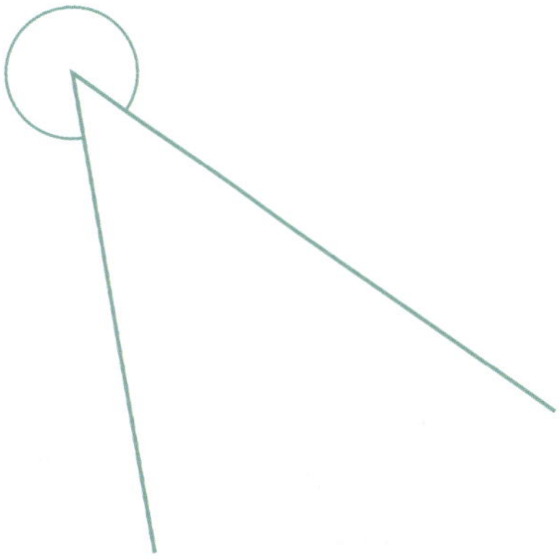

❻
_____ **angle**

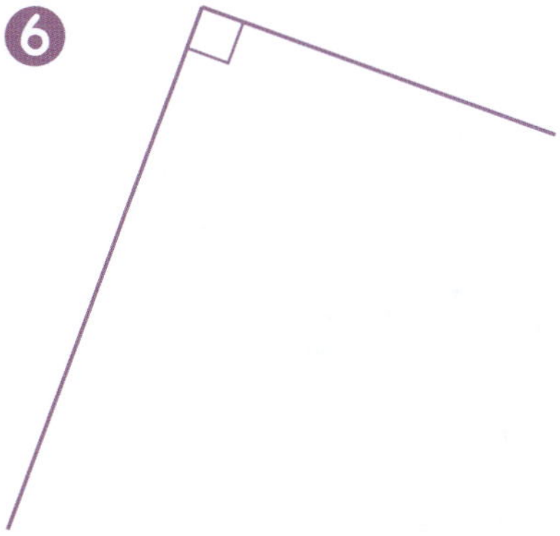

❼
_____ **angle**

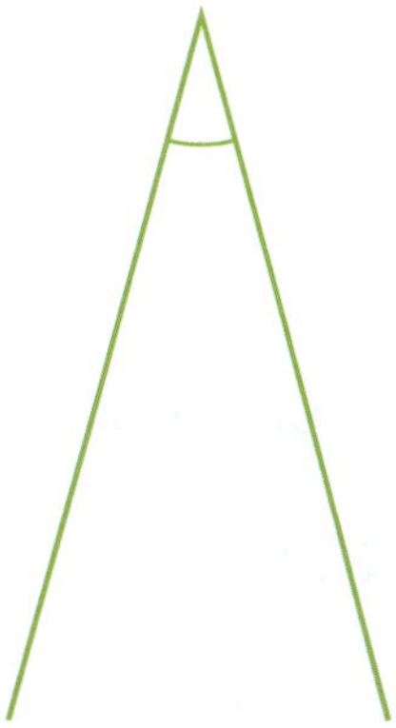

❽
_____ **angle**

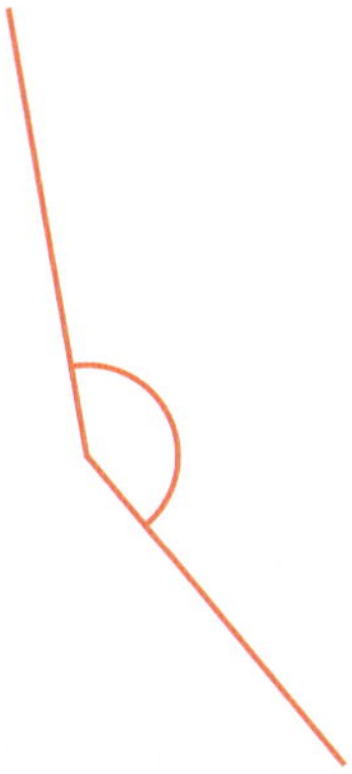

Polygons

■ Use the Word Box below to write the name of each polygon.

①

②

③

④

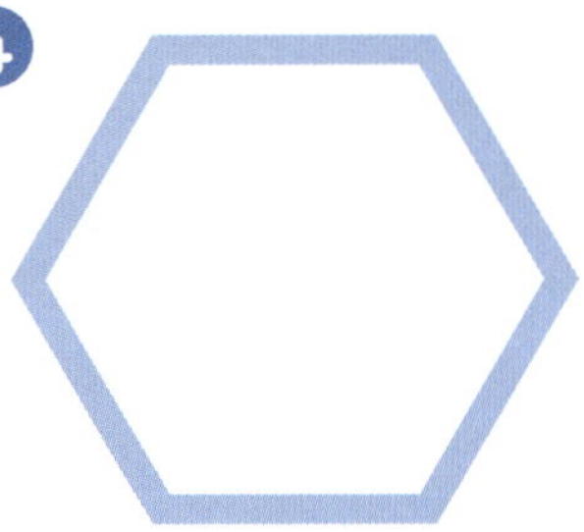

⑤

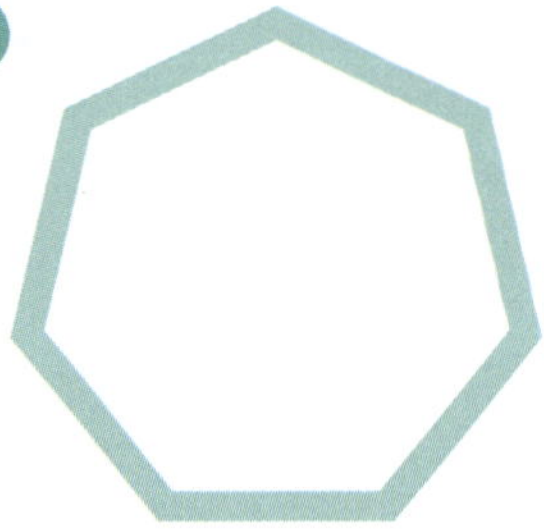

⑥

⑦

⑧

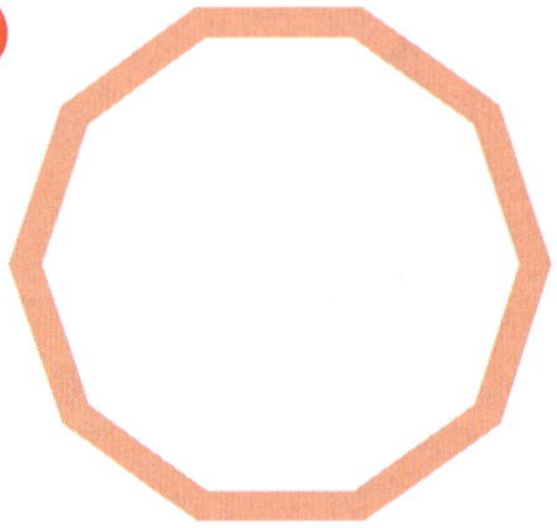

⑨

triangle	quadrilateral (quadrangle)
pentagon	hexagon
heptagon	octagon	nonagon
decagon	dodecagon

■ Fill in the correct numbers to complete each statement.

1 A triangle has

[ ] sides, [ ] angles, and [ ] vertices.

2 A quadrilateral has

[ ] sides, [ ] angles, and [ ] vertices.

3 A pentagon has

[ ] sides, [ ] angles, and [ ] vertices.

4 A hexagon has

[ ] sides, [ ] angles, and [ ] vertices.

5 An octagon has

[ ] sides, [ ] angles, and [ ] vertices.

Traits of Shapes

A **rectangle** is a quadrilateral with four right angles.

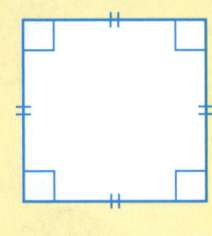

A **square** is a quadrilateral with four right angles and four equal sides.

A **quadrilateral** (or **quadrangle**) is a polygon with four sides.

■ Write the name of each shape.

_____

_____

_____

_____

_____

_____

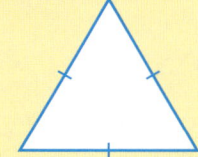 An **equilateral triangle** is a triangle with three equal sides.

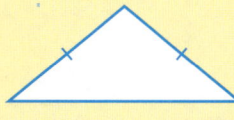 An **isosceles triangle** is a triangle with two equal sides.

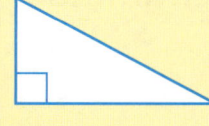 A **right triangle** is a triangle with a right angle.

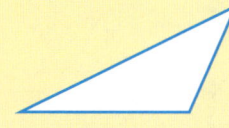 A **scalene triangle** is a triangle without any equal sides.

■ Write the name of each shape. Use "equilateral", "isosceles", "right", or "scalene."

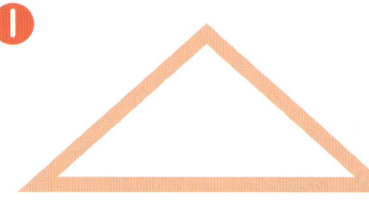

_____ triangle

_____ triangle

_____ triangle

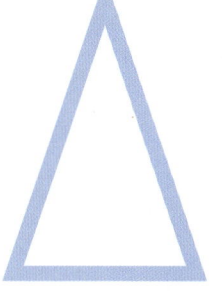

_____ triangle

_____ triangle

Area

Area of a rectangle = Length × Width
Area of a square = Side × Side

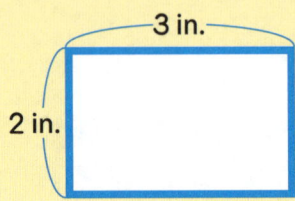

$2 × 3 = 6$ square inches
$= 6$ in.^{2}

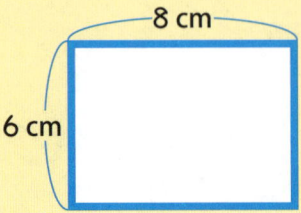

$6 × 8 = 48$ square centimeters
$= 48$ cm^2

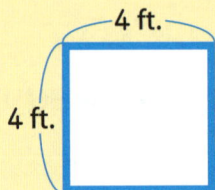

$4 × 4 = 16$ square feet
$= 6$ ft.^{2}

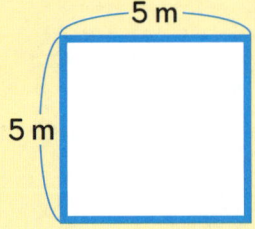

$5 × 5 = 25$ square meters
$= 25$ m^2

■ **Find the area of each shape.**

1

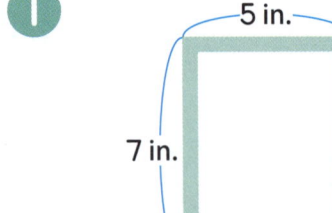

_____ in.^{2}

2

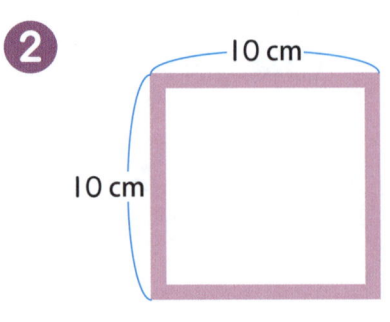

_____ cm^2

■ Circle the shape that has the largest area.

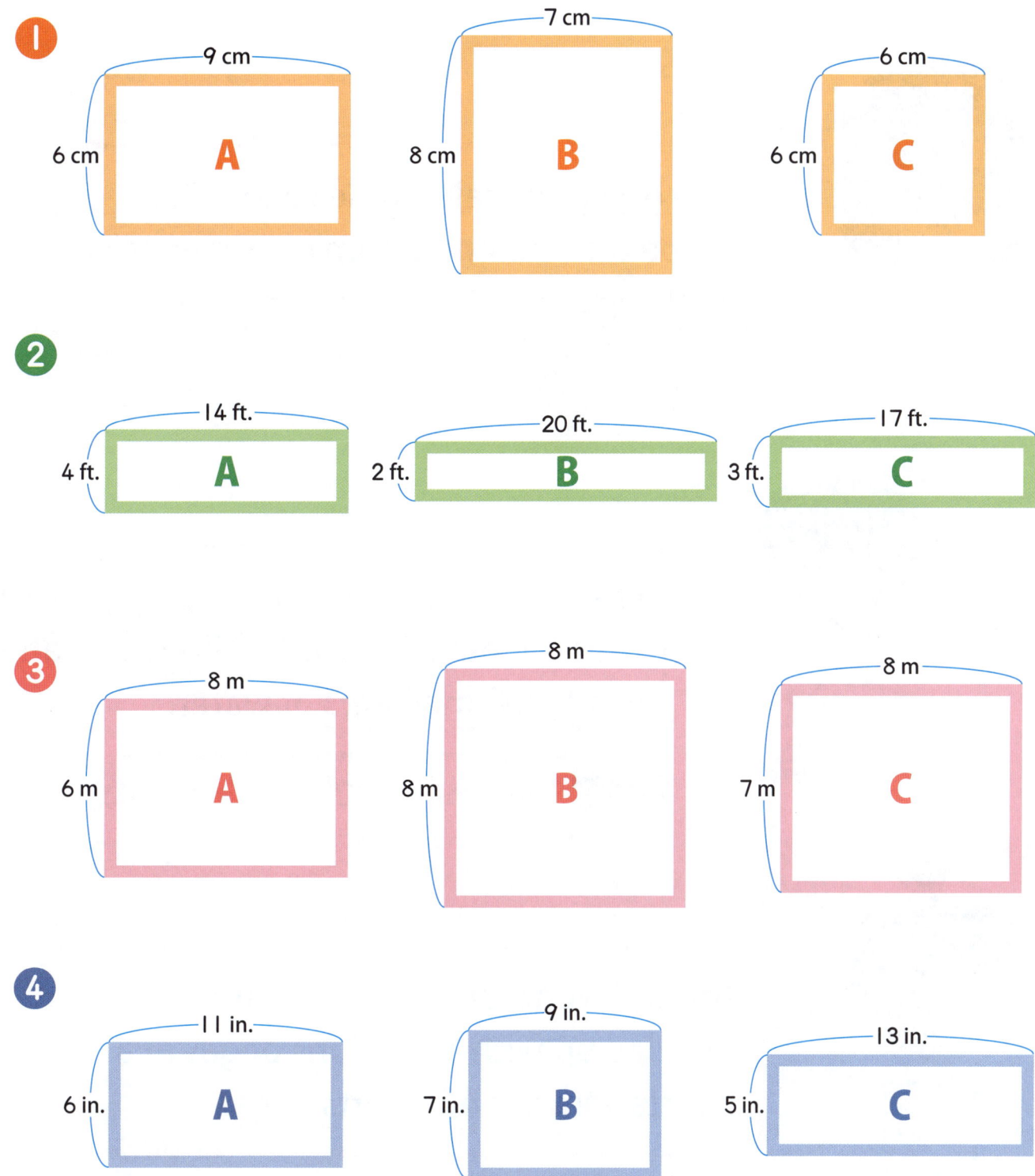

1

A — 9 cm, 6 cm

B — 7 cm, 8 cm

C — 6 cm, 6 cm

2

A — 14 ft., 4 ft.

B — 20 ft., 2 ft.

C — 17 ft., 3 ft.

3

A — 8 m, 6 m

B — 8 m, 8 m

C — 8 m, 7 m

4

A — 11 in., 6 in.

B — 9 in., 7 in.

C — 13 in., 5 in.

Brain Break
Measurements Quiz with Word Problems

■ Write a check mark (✔) in each box for those who have correctly converted the measurement.

①

> I am going to make some cakes. The recipe that I learned from my sister calls for 2 cups of milk. It is 16 ounces of milk.

Fact 1 cup (c) = 8 ounces (oz.)

②

> I researched how much water my family uses per day. We use 100 liters of water. It is 1,000 milliliters of water.

Fact 1 liter (L) = 1,000 milliliters (mL)

③

> Today, I went for a drive with my father. He filled up with 10 gallons of gas at a gas station. It is 40 quarts of gas.

Fact 1 gallon (gal.) = 4 quarts (qt.)

4

I measured the width of the schoolyard in a math class, and found it to be 50 yards. It is 150 feet.

Fact   1 yard (yd.) = 3 feet (ft.)

5

I joined the tennis club in my town, and bought a 24-inch tennis racket. It is a 3-foot tennis racket.

Fact   1 foot (ft.) = 12 inches (in.)

6

I am going to participate in the 2,000 meter run at a sport event in our city. It is 2 kilometer run.

Fact   1 kilometer (km) = 1,000 meters (m)

Energy

In science, energy is defined as the ability to do work. In this definition, work means using force over a distance - for example, pushing a shopping cart down the aisle at the grocery store. Energy makes machines move or do work. Energy also makes living things grow. Plants gather energy from the sun and turn it into food through photosynthesis. Animals eat plants or other animals and get energy from them.

Energy cannot be created or destroyed, only moved and transformed. Moving energy is called energy transfer. Energy is often transformed when it is used. It changes form. Some of it can change to heat or sound energy. Light is a kind of radiant energy. Radiant energy travels in waves. Other kinds of radiant energy, like x-rays and radio waves, are invisible to us. We can see light energy. It can travel across empty spaces. The sun gives off radiant energy, including light. Light bulbs and burning candles also give off light energy.

Sound energy is moving energy that is produced by the back and forth vibration of an object. Drums, trains, people's voices, and thunder all give off sound energy. Heat, or thermal energy, is produced when molecules and atoms (the tiny particles that make up an object) move. The faster they move, the more heat they give off. Fires, radiators, and boiling water give off thermal heat.

■ Answer the questions.

1 What is the scientific definition of energy?

_____

2 Can energy be created or destroyed?

_____

3 Name two things that give off sound energy.

_____

■ Fill in the blank to complete each statement.

❶ Energy is defined as the ability to do ⬚ .

❷ Energy makes ⬚ move or do work.

❸ Energy makes ⬚ ⬚ grow.

❹ Plants gather energy from the ⬚ .

❺ Animals get energy from eating ⬚ and other ⬚ .

❻ Energy cannot be ⬚ or ⬚ .

❼ Light, heat, and ⬚ are forms of energy we use every day.

Electrical Energy

Electrical energy is the energy produced when tiny particles called electrons move back and forth. Lightning is an example of electrical energy in nature. Lightning is what you see when a large number of electrons move through the air at the same time.

Humans have learned how to use electrical energy to power things that we use, like printers and refrigerators. To make electrical energy, humans use generators to change other kinds of energy into electrical energy. Inside a generator, wire coils move past magnets, which make the electrons in the coils move. The movement of the electrons is the electric current. Wind, moving water, steam from burning fossil fuels, or other energy sources can be used to move the wire coils past the magnets inside the generator, to change other forms of energy into electrical energy.

Electric current is sent through power lines to homes, schools, hospitals, businesses, and more. This electricity is used to power lights, dishwashers, computers, electric cars and trains, ventilators in hospitals, and so much more. If an electrical circuit is connected to a source of power, the electrons will move as long as the circuit is closed, which means that it has no gaps. If there is a gap in the circuit, the electrons will stop moving. Light switches work by opening and closing a gap in a circuit.

■ **Answer the questions.**

❶ What is electrical energy?

_____

❷ What makes the electrons in metal coils in generators move?

_____

❸ Name three things you used electricity for today.

_____

Date

Great Job Sticker

■ Circle the objects that run on electrical energy.

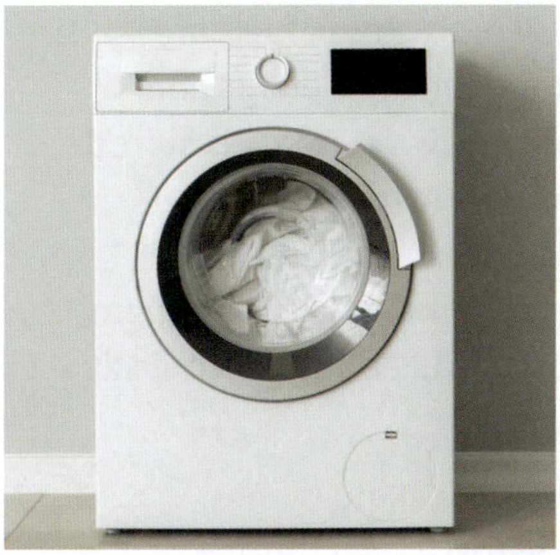

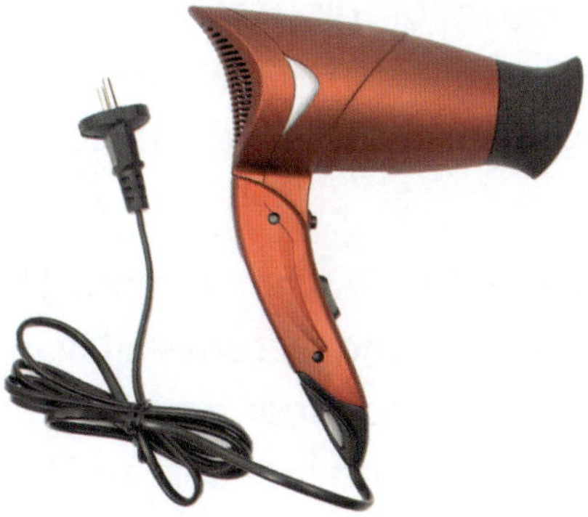

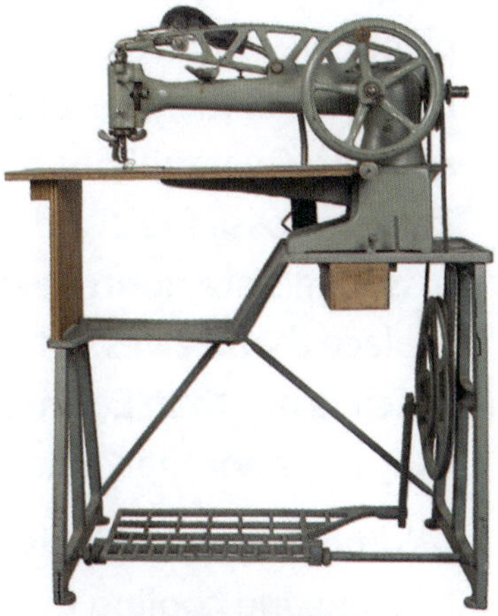

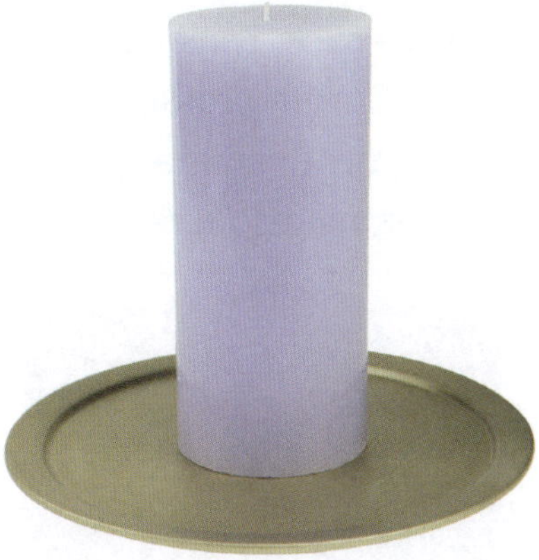

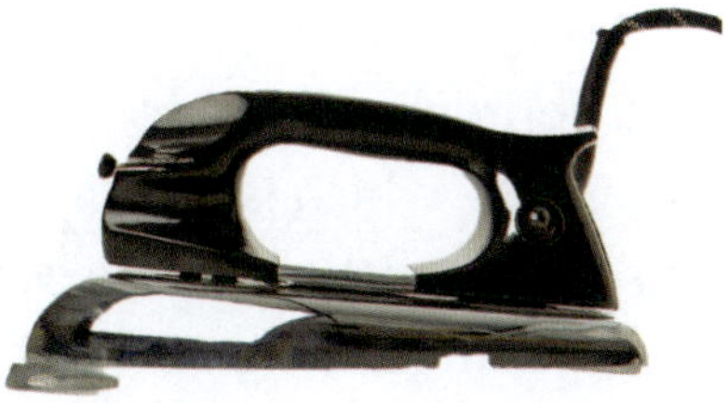

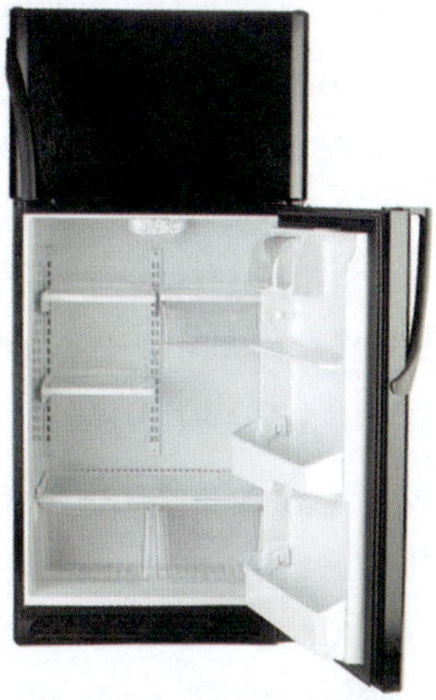

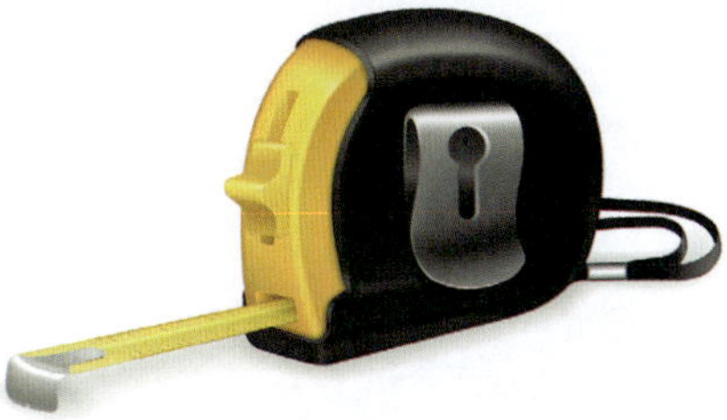

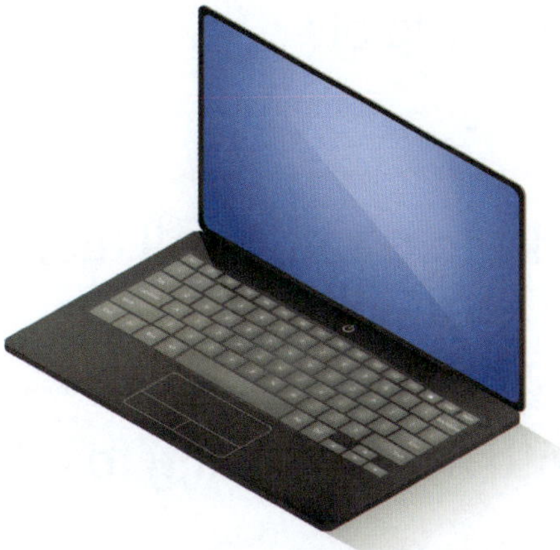

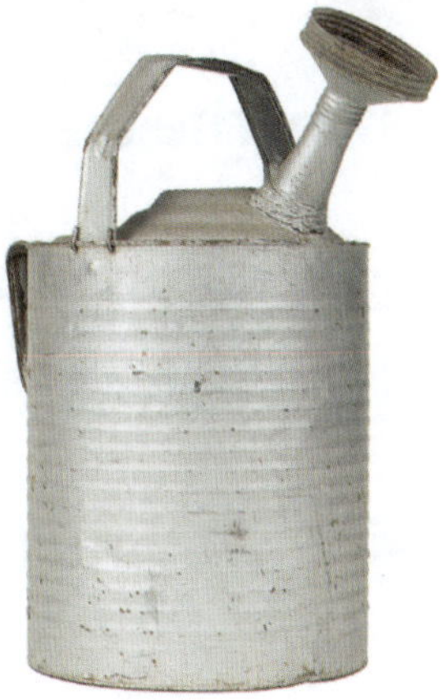

Other Forms of Energy

People use oil, coal, and natural gas to heat buildings, run cars, fly planes, and create electricity, among other things. Oil, coal, and natural gas are all fossil fuels. Fossil fuels are called fossil fuels because they are created from fossils – the remains of ancient plants and animals. Over millions of years, they turned into coal, oil, or natural gas. Their energy is stored in these fossil fuels and humans can use that energy when they burn these fuels. However, fossil fuels are nonrenewable resources, or things that are used up faster than they can replace themselves. It takes millions of years to create fossil fuels and humans are using them much faster than Earth is creating more of them. People need to be careful about how quickly they use nonrenewable resources.

Additionally, fossil fuels also create pollution when burned. Driving cars, taking planes, heating and cooling buildings, and powering factories all use a lot of fossil fuels. Burning fossil fuels puts more carbon into the atmosphere, which increases global warming. Global warming harms many living things, including humans, and is melting the ice caps, causing the sea level to rise, which is dangerous for everyone living near the coasts. Burning fossil fuels, especially coal, also creates air pollution, which is bad for humans and other animals, causing asthma and other diseases. Humans need to switch to clean, renewable resources like solar and wind energy to reduce the effects of climate change and reduce pollution.

Nuclear energy is also considered a nonrenewable energy resource. It uses radioactive materials like uranium, which is a nonrenewable resource found in the Earth. It also creates nuclear waste, which can be harmful to people and other living things living near it.

■ Answer the questions.

❶ What are fossil fuels made of?

_____

❷ How long does it take to create fossil fuels?

_____

❸ Name two issues with humans using fossil fuels.

_____

■ Write true or false for each statement.

1 Oil, coal, and natural gas are all fossil fuels.

2 Fossil fuels are made from fossils or the remains of plants and animals from long ago.

3 Humans can create fossil fuels in a factory.

4 Fossil fuels need to be burned to be used as energy.

5 Fossil fuels are a renewable resource.

6 Fossil fuels create pollution when burned.

7 Nuclear energy comes from radioactive materials.

Renewable Forms of Energy

Humans use energy created by nonrenewable resources like fossil fuels as well as renewable resources like the sun, wind, and water. Renewable resources are things that cannot be used up, like sunlight, air, water, and wind. Although they cannot be used up, it is possible to make them harder to use. For example, if we pollute water, it is harder to clean so that it is safe for us to drink again or use to water plants.

Renewable energy sources never run out and do not have to be burned. Solar energy comes from the sun and is collected by solar panels. Wind energy is collected by wind turbines that spin when there is wind. Hydroelectric power is created from naturally flowing water like rivers. It collects the gravitational energy of naturally flowing water and stores it so people can use it to produce electricity. It currently creates more energy than all of the other renewable energy resources combined!

Regular people can also choose to use renewable energy. Some people have solar panels on their houses or buy renewable energy from their power companies. People can also use fewer fossil fuels by walking, riding a bike, taking public transportation like the bus or subway, or carpooling instead of driving in their own car.

■ **Answer the questions.**

❶ What is special about renewable energy sources?

_____

❷ What are three kinds of renewable energy?

_____

❸ What kind of renewable energy currently produces the most energy?

_____

■ Match the renewable resources to the device used to harness it.

●   ● **Solar panels**

●   ● **Wind turbines**

●   ● **Hydroelectric dam**

Brain Break
Science Journal 5

Create a solar oven!

Supplies

- a cardboard box with an attached lid (like a pizza or shoe box)
- aluminum foil
- clear plastic wrap
- a glue stick
- tape
- a stick to prop open the reflector flap (like a wooden skewer or ruler)
- Box cutter or Xacto Knife (with adult help!)
- S'mores supplies! (chocolate bar, marshmallows, graham crackers)

Directions

1. Have an adult help you cut a three-sided flat out of the top of the box, leaving a 1-inch border around the three sides not connected to the box.

2. Glue aluminum foil to the inside of the flap and the inside of the box. Make it as smooth as possible.

3. Tape two layers of plastic wrap across the top of the opening you cut in the lid. One layer on the top and one layer on the bottom side of the lid.

4. Test your prop stick to see if it will hold the oven flap up.

5. Preheat your oven by placing it open in the sun for at least 30 minutes.

6. Assemble your s'mores in the bottom of the oven: graham cracker, chocolate piece, and a marshmallow. (Save the second graham cracker for after the marshmallow cooks.) Close the plastic wrap lid and make sure the foil flap is propped open.

7. Let the marshmallow "cook" for 30 to 45 minutes in the solar oven. Test if it is melted and place the final graham cracker on top.

8. Enjoy!

Art Break!

■ Color the picture!

Goods and Services

Goods are physical things that you can touch like carrots, coats, and cars. Services are things that people do for others, often in exchange for money. Babysitting, haircutting, fixing cars, and providing medical care are all services. Many goods and services are limited because demand is higher than supply – there are more people who want the good or service than can get it because there are not enough of the goods or services. For example, if a band is playing in a city and there are 10,000 tickets available but 20,000 people want to go to the show, not all of the people can go. The tickets have to be allocated. Allocation strategies decide how limited resources are divided among people.

There are nine main strategies, which are sometimes used in combination with each other. Different allocation strategies work better for different goods or services

- Price: the good or service goes to the person who can and chooses to pay the most. If concert tickets cost $500 each, only the people who can afford to pay that much can go.
- First-come-first-served: the first person there gets the good or service.
- Majority rule: the person to get the most votes gets the good or service, like in an election.
- Sharing: people agree to share a good or service equally.
- Force: people forcibly take the good or service, legally or not. Governments can use force to take land that they need. Thieves can use force to steal money from people.
- Competition: people compete and whoever wins gets the good or service.
- Arbitrary characteristic: the good or service is given to people who have a certain characteristic, like a certain age.
- Command: the government decides which people get a good or service.
- Random/lottery: the good or service is given out to a person or people who are randomly selected, like in a lottery.

■ Choose which allocation method is being used in each situation.

1 If there are 500 people who want to buy pizzas but only 350 pizzas to sell, so the owner increases the cost of each pizza.

2 Six people wanted cupcakes but there were only three cupcakes. They decided to cut each cupcake in half.

3 The runner who ran the race the fastest got the gold medal.

4 Two kids are running for class president. Sam gets more votes than Paul. Sam is the winner.

5 A store only has 50 copies of a new video game in stock. The first 50 people to come in get to buy the game.

6 A school holds a raffle for a family vacation. One raffle ticket is drawn and that family is the winner.

7 After a hurricane, the government limits the amount of gas each customer can buy.

Competition

A swimming race is a competition to see who swims the fastest. An art contest is a competition to see who created the best piece of art. There is also competition in our economy. When multiple companies offer the same kind of good or service, they compete against each other to get customers. Customers choose based on the quality of the good or service, the price, convenience, and other factors. For example, if you want to buy a new pair of scissors, you might know of a few different stores where you could buy them. You could choose the store with the lowest prices, the one with the prettiest scissors, the one with the strongest scissors, or the one that is closest to your house.

When businesses have to compete against each other, they have to do something to make people choose them over others. They might choose to have the lowest prices, but then they have to make sure they are still earning enough money to pay their employees and other expenses. They can try to make their product better than all the other products like them, perhaps inventing something new and exciting. They can make their stores fun places to visit with great customer service. In this way, competition can encourage companies to improve and offer better goods or services to customers.

When there is no competition, a company has a monopoly. For example, if there is only one company that provides internet connections in a town, everyone who lives there has to buy internet from them if they want internet. The company with the monopoly is not motivated to provide better or cheaper service because they do not have any competition. Monopolies are not allowed under US law, but the rules are complicated and it can sometimes be hard to stop them.

■ **Answer the questions.**

❶ What is competition?

_____

❷ What is a monopoly?

_____

■ Complete the activity.

❶ Create your own company and product or service.

My company name

My good or service provided

❷ How will you make your company stand out against the competition?

❸ What can you do to make your product or service seem more exciting?

Marketing Goods

Marketing is how companies plan to get people to buy their goods or services. They make a plan of what kind of company they want to appear to be. Maybe they want to seem athletic, artsy, studious, or playful. Companies use advertising to convince people to buy their goods or services. Advertising can make people want the things they sell, even if they don't need it and didn't want it until they saw the advertisement. Sometimes it is easy to tell that you are watching an ad, like when an ad comes on during the break in a TV show. It might tell you directly that you should buy a food, toy, or piece of clothing, or it might just show people using the product and looking happy. You should be careful when you watch ads. They sometimes show toys doing things they can't actually do, like flying. They might also show more parts than are actually included with the toy like a background or other figures.

A lot of advertising is harder to notice. If you watch a YouTube video where someone mentions that they love their shoes, it might not be obvious that it's an ad. Many companies give people with a lot of followers on social media free products or pay them to talk about their products. The people making the videos or posts are supposed to tell their followers that these are ads, but it can be easy to miss. Companies also pay for product placement, which is when a product is shown in a movie, TV show, or elsewhere. For example, a company could pay a TV show to show characters eating their brand of crackers. People watching the show would see those crackers and might think that they want those crackers, too.

It can be easy to think that if you had the product shown in an ad, you would feel happy like the actors or content creators in the ad look. Before you buy something, ask yourself why you want it, what you will use it for, and if you need it. Maybe you really do want to buy the thing you saw in an ad, but it's important to think through your purchases and not overspend.

■ **Answer the questions.**

❶ **Why do companies advertise their products?**

❷ **What is product placement?**

■ Create a marketing plan for each item below. What features of each item will you highlight? What makes each item better than the competitions? Would you do a print ad, TV ad, or social media ad for the product?

Happy Smiles Cola

Jonah's Pizzeria

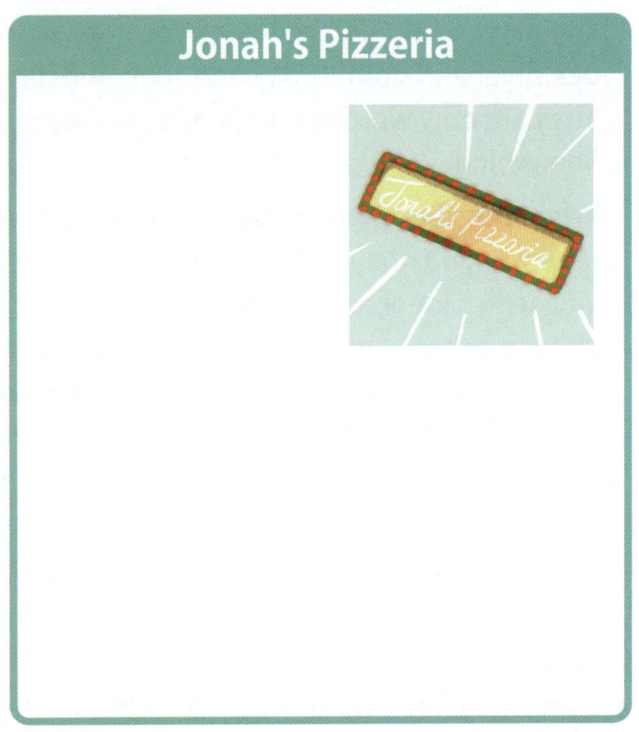

Karen's Homemade Dog Treats

Blue Bell Clothing Boutique

Saving and Investing

People started using money around 4,000 years ago. Before, people traded things with each other instead. This could be difficult – what if you wanted something from someone but they weren't interested in anything you had? With money, you can sell what you have or work to earn money so that you can buy the things you need or want. Some early money was made of precious metals like silver and gold. Today, the coins and paper used for money are not worth much on their own. They are only worth something because the government and people agree that they are worth something.

When possible, people save money. They save for retirement so that when they are older and stop working, they will still have money to live on. They save in case of an emergency when they will need a lot of money at once. They save up for big expenses, like buying a new car, sending a child to college, or going on an exciting trip. When people save money, they can earn interest. This means that if they put money in a certain kind of bank account, like a high-interest savings account, the bank will pay them some money for storing their money with them. People can also invest money. They can buy stocks, which are parts of companies. If the company does well, the person gets more money back when they sell the stock.

Sometimes people want or need to buy something but don't have enough money saved. For example, most people don't have $400,000 saved to buy a house. They might have $20,000 saved, which they use as a downpayment. The other $380,000 is borrowed from a bank through a mortgage. The person pays back this money over the next 15-30 years. They will pay interest on this money, which means they have to pay back more than they borrowed. The same is true when people borrow money to buy cars or pay for college or for medical treatment.

Before buying something, people should compare options. If you are buying a new bike, you shouldn't buy the first one you see. You should do research. How many speeds do you need? What kind of tires? Where do you plan to ride the bike? Once you decide what kind of bike to get, you can look at how much it costs at different stores and if there are any used bikes of that type for sale. By comparing prices, you can save a lot of money.

■ Answer the questions.

❶ Name two reasons people save money.

_____

❷ Why do people borrow money?

_____

■ Answer "borrow" money or "save" money to buy each item or service below.

1 A new house

2 A new car

3 A new gaming console

4 A mountain bike

5 A hospital visit for a broken arm

6 Paying for college

7 A limited edition action figure

8 New tires for your car

■ Circle the words in the puzzle below.

allocation	marketing	services
goods	competition	investing
saving	advertising	product

M	N	B	V	C	X	Z	A	G	S	D	F
A	L	L	O	C	A	T	I	O	N	H	G
T	Y	U	I	O	O	P	L	O	K	J	A
R	E	W	Q	M	A	S	D	D	F	G	D
C	X	Z	N	P	M	K	L	S	J	H	V
B	I	N	V	E	S	T	I	N	G	A	E
S	V	Q	W	T	E	R	T	Y	U	I	R
E	A	E	I	I	O	U	O	V	B	N	T
R	Q	T	H	T	E	G	N	M	H	W	I
V	A	S	E	I	A	I	U	O	T	X	S
I	Z	P	R	O	D	U	C	T	R	V	I
C	X	S	A	N	B	C	G	E	E	Q	N
E	C	F	L	O	P	S	A	V	I	N	G
S	W	D	V	F	R	T	Y	U	N	Z	B
A	S	M	A	R	K	E	T	I	N	G	M
D	F	G	H	J	K	L	O	P	I	U	N

Mindfulness Break!

Think of a place that makes you feel happy and calm. You can imagine you are there whenever you feel sad or stressed.

■ Draw a place that you feel peaceful and calm.

Unit 5 Thinking Skills

Patterns

■ Find the pattern of the sequence of each picture. Then write a check mark
(✓) below the picture that fits into the blank area.

1

2

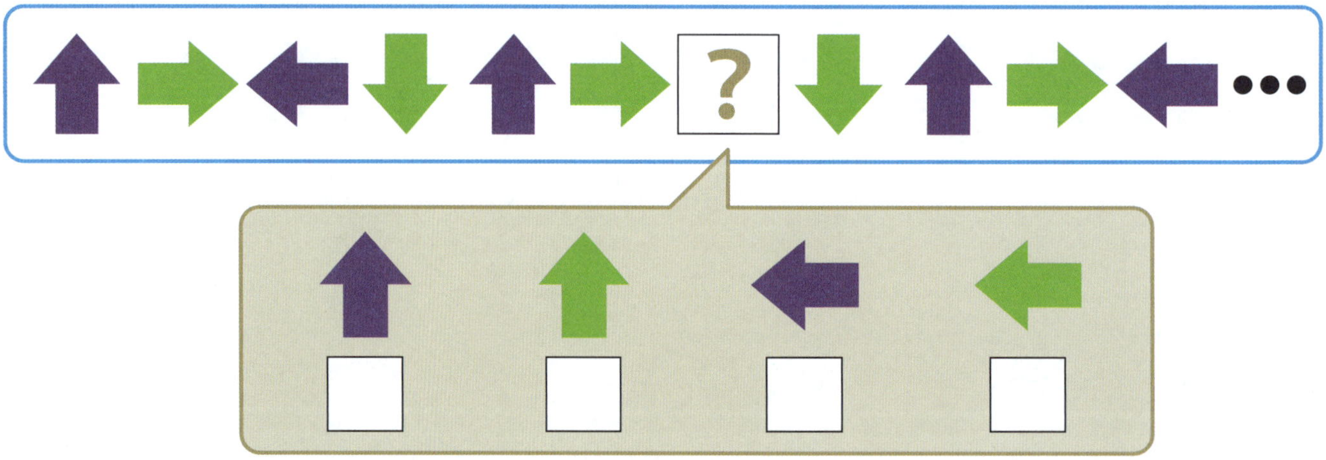

3

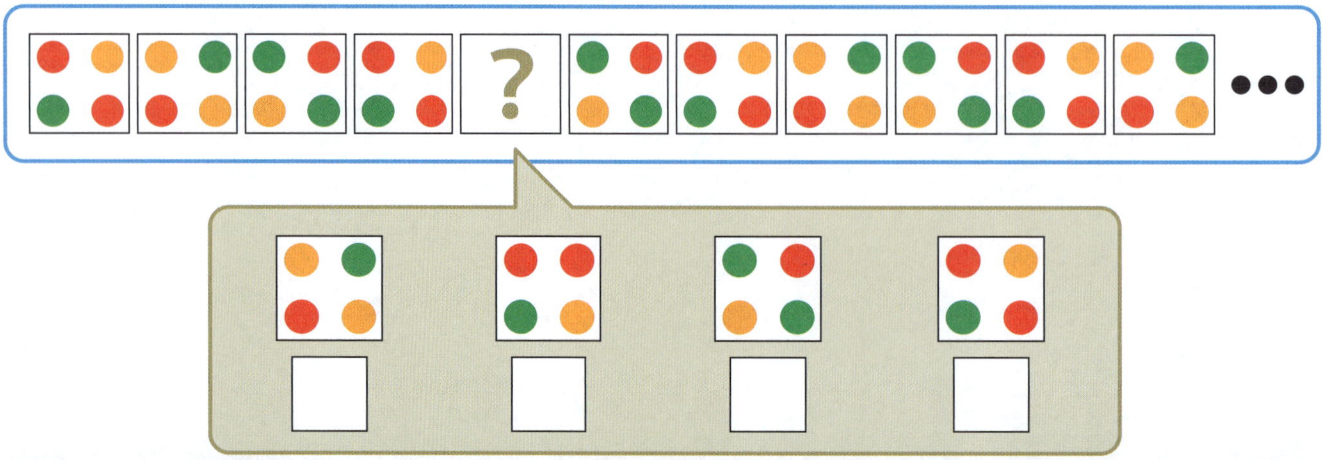

■ Use the pattern to write number in the blank area.

1 0 1 0 1 1 0 1 1 1 0 **?** •••

2 1 0 2 1 0 3 2 1 0 4 **?** •••

3 9 0 6 0 3 0 9 0 6 0 **?** •••

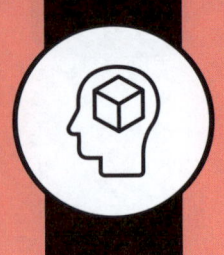

Unit 5 Thinking Skills

Word Search

■ Find and circle five sports in the puzzle.

1

H	Y	P	C	I	L	T	F	Q	E	B	D
A	B	M	J	V	L	S	R	Z	U	K	C
F	P	A	I	U	A	T	A	X	G	T	D
L	V	E	Q	Z	B	R	H	M	W	E	G
A	V	O	Z	K	T	P	Y	I	J	N	E
O	R	Q	C	X	E	B	G	H	F	N	U
J	G	N	I	I	K	S	H	S	K	I	D
B	L	T	O	L	S	S	M	G	F	S	Q
B	A	S	E	B	A	L	L	B	X	W	E
D	W	V	I	M	B	K	Y	P	N	Y	G
U	Z	E	X	C	F	S	L	W	A	O	D
R	C	T	J	S	W	I	M	M	I	N	G

    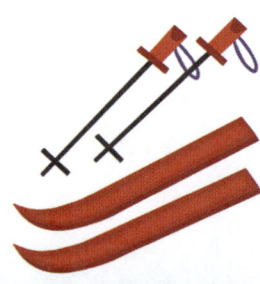

2

S	I	N	N	E	T	E	L	B	A	T	C
W	J	F	O	O	T	G	O	A	L	A	Y
I	U	W	T	V	Z	O	Q	L	X	B	C
B	A	D	N	I	N	L	O	L	V	L	L
A	K	Y	I	R	X	K	W	J	O	E	I
T	O	T	M	K	N	I	R	C	Y	C	N
N	B	A	D	P	T	O	P	O	N	Y	E
I	L	L	A	B	I	N	O	F	P	C	Y
N	R	L	B	Q	B	X	K	L	U	L	W
T	U	E	K	R	E	C	C	O	S	I	Z
O	Z	T	Q	R	J	O	U	G	Q	N	X
N	T	E	B	L	E	B	O	L	L	G	V

Creative Drawing

■ **Create two different drawings by starting with the shapes given below.**

❶

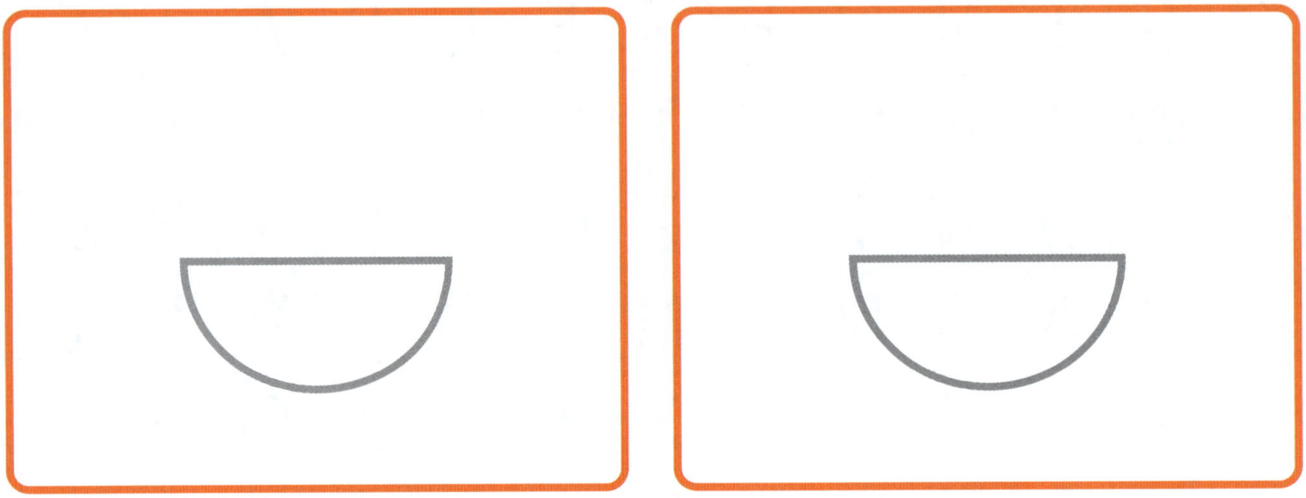

❷

❸

■ Draw a picture using the shapes given below. Imagine what they could be part of!

Combine and Creative

■ You are trying to come up with a new invention by combining the two tools in the room in the picture below.

1 Write down two items from the picture on the left hand page that you would like to combine.

2 Feel free to imagine and draw your own invention combining the tools you chose in **1**. You may add texts explanations if necessary.

Physical Education Break!

It's important to move your body and exercise!
Try this fun activity below to break up your studying!

■ Pick 5 exercises from the list and try to do them daily!
Record your progress in the chart!

10 jumping jacks	5 sit ups	5 squats
1 minute run in place		10 frog hops
1 minute yoga pose		30 seconds high knees
30 seconds marching in place		10 star jumps

Daily Exercise Plan

Exercise	❶	❷	❸	❹	❺
Monday					
Tuesday					
Wednesday					
Thursday					
Friday					
Saturday					
Sunday					

Ace Fourth Grade

Answer Key

Unit 1 Language Arts

p. 4
① that　② who　③ whom
④ which　⑤ whose

p. 5
① where　② when　③ why

p. 6
① tying　② sitting
③ biting　④ standing

p. 7
① was dancing / am/are/is dancing / will be dancing
② was talking / am/are/is talking / will be talking
③ was biking / am/are/is biking / will be biking
④ was singing / am/are/is singing / will be singing
⑤ was carrying / am/are/is carrying / will be carrying

p. 8
① there　② their　③ they're

p. 9
① two　② too　③ to
④ It's　⑤ its

p. 10
① ✗　② ✗　③ ✓

p. 11
① cute tiny new doll
② naughty young orange cat
③ old brown leather shoes
④ cool huge ancient book
⑤ small yellow wood house

p. 12
(Answers will vary.)

Unit 1 Reading

p. 15
(Answers will vary.)
Plot: Lila was playing in her yard when she saw a fawn all by itself. She wanted to pet it, but she didn't because she knew she shouldn't. It left, and she will always remember it.
Setting: Lila's backyard garden
Characters: Lila, fawn
Conflict: Lila found a fawn in her yard
Theme: It's best to let wild animals be.

p. 17
(Answers will vary.)
Beginning: Maverick struck out in his first baseball game.
Rising Action: Maverick practiced baseball.
Climax: In the next game, Maverick stepped up to bat!
Falling Action: He made it to first base!
Resolution: Maverick was proud.

p. 18
① Noah, Riley
② Coach Dan, Dillon

p. 19
(Answers will vary.)
① Emma found a rusty key.
② Emma tried the key in the lock.
③ Emma opened the door to the shed.

p. 21
(Answers will vary.)
① Friends always support each other.
② Olivia realized it wasn't right to be mean to her friend just because she was upset. Olivia realized hurting Zarah didn't make her feel any better about losing the part in the play.
③ I should be kind to my friends even when I feel upset.

p. 22
(Answers will vary.)

Unit 1 Math

p. 24
① 137　② 389　③ 788　④ 160
⑤ 351　⑥ 581　⑦ 217　⑧ 307
⑨ 516　⑩ 226　⑪ 313　⑫ 753

p. 25
① 767　② 667　③ 879　④ 291
⑤ 674　⑥ 782　⑦ 404　⑧ 628
⑨ 978　⑩ 511　⑪ 846　⑫ 933

p. 26
① 1495　② 2568　③ 4769
④ 1691　⑤ 2790　⑥ 6574
⑦ 3731　⑧ 6423　⑨ 5641
⑩ 6235　⑪ 4302　⑫ 8000

p. 27
① 4775　② 8888　③ 7877
④ 4272　⑤ 7627　⑥ 8443
⑦ 4346　⑧ 8911　⑨ 6752
⑩ 6320　⑪ 6131　⑫ 8213

p. 28
① 112　② 222　③ 545　④ 127
⑤ 218　⑥ 718　⑦ 384　⑧ 468
⑨ 197　⑩ 76　⑪ 89　⑫ 87

p. 29
① 211　② 123　③ 513　④ 318
⑤ 427　⑥ 119　⑦ 168　⑧ 238
⑨ 399　⑩ 86　⑪ 89　⑫ 67

p. 30
① 1112　② 2216　③ 5210
④ 1228　⑤ 3317　⑥ 7122
⑦ 2269　⑧ 4167　⑨ 6076
⑩ 2886　⑪ 1768　⑫ 798

p. 31
① 2324　② 1451　③ 1201
④ 1234　⑤ 2319　⑥ 1419
⑦ 2286　⑧ 3079　⑨ 4176
⑩ 1859　⑪ 2668　⑫ 759

pp. 32-33
① 3235+2146=($)5381
② 1567+4165=($)5732
③ 5368+2689=8057 (tickets)
④ 2542-1028=1514 (gallons)
⑤ 3865-2677=1188 (meters)
⑥ 4878-3989=889 (books)

pp. 34-35
① 3,246　② 50,139　③ 214,507
④ 84,170　⑤ 186,570

Unit 1 Science

p. 36
① vascular plants
② Help a plant take in water and minerals from the soil.

p. 37
① nonvascular　② vascular
③ minerals　④ sunlight / water
⑤ photosynthesis　⑥ Roots

p. 38
① sunlight, water, and air
② carbon dioxide / oxygen
③ false

p. 39
① sunlight　② oxygen
③ carbon dioxide　④ minerals
⑤ water

p. 40
① spores
② with colorful flowers and fruits
③ insects and hummingbirds pollinate plants by carrying pollen from one plant to another while feeding.

p. 41
① false　② true　③ true
④ true　⑤ false

p. 42
① For protection.
② To help conserve energy in the cold.
③ To help extra water slide off and prevent them from rotting.

p. 43

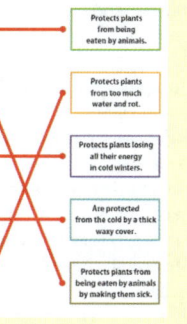

p. 44
(Answers will vary.)

Unit 1 Social Studies

p. 46
① More taxes and wanting to expand west into the United States.
② France

p. 47
① the French and Indian War.
② Boston Massacre
③ Continental Congress
④ Lexington / Concord
⑤ Declaration of Independence
⑥ Yorktown
⑦ Treaty of Paris

p. 48
① the Confederacy
② Grant / Lee

p. 49
① true　② true　③ false
④ true　⑤ false　⑥ true
⑦ false

p. 50
① France, Great Britain, Russia, Italy, Japan and the US.
② The US joined the war because Germany kept sinking American ships.

p. 51
① Assassination of Archduke Ferdinand
② Russia
③ Sinking US ships
④ Central Powers
⑤ Germany

p. 52
① The stock market crash in 1929.
② The New Deal

p. 53

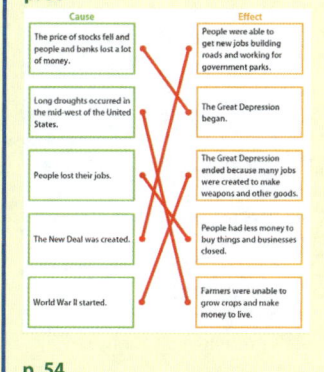

Cause	Effect
The price of stocks fell and people and banks lost a lot of money.	People were able to get new jobs building roads and working for government parks.
Long droughts occurred in the mid-west of the United States.	The Great Depression began.
People lost their jobs.	The Great Depression ended because many jobs were created to make weapons and other goods.
The New Deal was created.	People had less money to buy things and businesses closed.
World War II started.	Farmers were unable to grow crops and make money to live.

p. 54
Across
① Lee　③ Depression
⑤ Dust Bowl　⑦ Grant
Down
② Ferdinand　④ Washington
⑥ Yorktown　⑧ Allies
⑩ Lincoln

313

Unit 1 Technology

p. 56
❸

p. 57

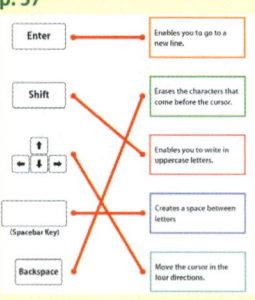

pp. 58-59
(Answers will vary.)
❶ WHAT IS YOUR FIRST NAME?
❷ HOW OLD ARE YOU?
❸ WHAT IS YOUR FAVORITE FOOD?
❹ ARE THE QUESTIONS ON THIS PAGE DIFFICULT FOR YOU?

pp. 60-61
❶ A ❷ D ❸ D

p. 62

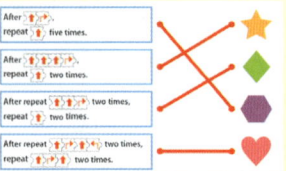

p. 63
K

Unit 2 Language Arts

p. 67
❶ ✓
❷ ✗ This book was printed in China.
❸ ✗ What does your family eat on Thanksgiving?
❹ ✗ I played soccer with my friend Emily.
❺ ✗ I jumped rope with my mom.
❻ ✓

p. 69
❶ ✓
❷ ✗ "We can practice together," my sister said.
❸ ✗ My brother asked, "Can I borrow your soccer ball?"
❹ ✓
❺ ✗ We yelled out to her, "Can we come too?"
❻ ✗ Let's pretend it's a sunny day," I said.

pp. 70–71
❶ dumlpings→dumplings
carots→carrots
bakking→baking
sprinlkes→sprinkles
degres→degrees
favorit→favorite
❷ feild→field
dinosors→dinosaurs
cristals→crystals
whether→weather
tornados→tornadoes

pp. 72-73
❶ tired→tried
trieing→trying
peddles→pedal
petal→pedal
wobbled→wobbled
❷ bitrhday→birthday
culd→could
thougt→thought
pupy→puppy
wear→where
ideo→idea
promiss→promise

p. 74
(Answers will vary.)

Unit 2 Reading

p. 76
Aidan walked through the forest with the golden light of the sun shining through the trees. After a few minutes, he reached his favorite spot. The small lake shimmered and it was surrounded by tall, thick trees that seemed to touch the sky. Their leaves rustled in the soft breeze and cast shadows on the sandy shore. The water was clear and Aidan could see the smooth stones along the bottom. He sat down on a large rock that was along the water's edge and began to set up his fishing rod. Aidan cast his fishing line into the cool, clear water. He looked out into the woods and watched a few bluejays swooping along the shore. The sun warmed the air and fed the blue and purple wildflowers. Aidan felt at peace and happy. Suddenly, there was a tug on his line and he stood up to reel it in. Out of the water popped a shiny, silver fish with water glistening off its scales. Aidan marveled at the fish before taking out the hook and letting it back into the water. It was a successful trip to his fishing hole.

p. 77
❶ a tropical island
❷ She hears the waves and tastes the salty water.
❸ Kira is excited and happy.

p. 79
❶ Ethan has to let Max go to a new family.
❷ Character vs. self
❸ Ethan knows that he helped Max find a good home, and he looks forward to helping more dogs.

p. 81
❶ first person
❷ Charlie, a dog
❸ The point of view makes it easy to understand Charlie's feelings.
❹ The reader has to figure out that Charlie is a dog.

pp. 82-83
❶ at a jumping competition
❷ Luna and Evie
❸ Thunder and Carrot
❹ third person
❺ Luna and Evie knew only one of them could win.
❻ Evie is happy for her friend to win.
❼ We should all cheer for our friends to succeed.

p. 84
(Answers will vary.)

Unit 2 Math

p. 86
❶ 6 ❷ 42 ❸ 30
❹ 8 ❺ 25 ❻ 56
❼ 36 ❽ 48 ❾ 93
❿ 32 ⓫ 84 ⓬ 75
13×6=78 (seeds)

p. 87
❶ 2 ❷ 3 ❸ 9
❹ 9 ❺ 4 ❻ 2
❼ 7 ❽ 9 ❾ 10
❽ 8 ⓫ 6 ⓬ 10
36÷4=9 (cookies)

p. 88
❶ 246 ❷ 693 ❸ 749
❹ 1684 ❺ 1268 ❻ 1569
❼ 600 ❽ 2000 ❾ 5624

p. 89
❶ 1668 ❷ 1454 ❸ 1584
❹ 1488 ❺ 1446 ❻ 1726
❼ 4431 ❽ 1216 ❾ 1375

p. 90
❶ 276 ❷ 583 ❸ 903
❹ 3360 ❺ 325 ❻ 216
❼ 468 ❽ 1139

p. 91
❶ 1564 ❷ 1350 ❸ 3901
❹ 460 ❺ 1230 ❻ 2600
27×63=1701 (stickers)

p. 92
❶ 5 ❷ 7 ❸ 8
❹ 10 ❺ 4R3 ❻ 6R5
❼ 7R1 ❽ 10R2 ❾ 9R1
❿ 8R2 ⓫ 8R1 ⓬ 7R2
⓭ 1R8 ⓮ 8R2

p. 93
❶ 22 ❷ 32 ❸ 21 ❹ 11
❺ 15 ❻ 15 ❼ 12 ❽ 13
❾ 22R2 ❿ 13R2 ⓫ 16R1 ⓬ 14R4

p. 94
❶ 216 ❷ 289 ❸ 173
❹ 164 ❺ 387R1 ❻ 244R2
❼ 154R3 ❽ 142R5

p. 95
❶ 91÷7=13 (boxes)
❷ 70÷4=17 (books); 2 (remaining)
❸ 438÷3=146 (colored pencils)

p. 96
❶ 11:00 a.m. ❷ 6:30 p.m.
❸ 2:00 a.m. ❹ 4:45 a.m.
❺ 11:30 p.m. ❻ 5:40 p.m.

p. 97

Unit 2 Science

p. 99
❶ fish
❷ mammal
❸ bird
❹ amphibian
❺ reptile

p. 100
❶ Food, water, shelter, space, and air.
❷ To protect from weather and predators.
❸ Breathing with their lungs, breathing with their gills, or breathing through their skin.

p. 101
❶ true ❷ false ❸ true
❹ true ❺ false ❻ true
❼ true

p. 102
❶ Mammals, and some fish.
❷ Fish, reptiles, amphibians, and birds.
❸ Marsupials carry their young babies in pouches until they grow.

p. 103
Egg-laying: alligator / sea turtle / platypus / hawk / snake / frog / bass / bald eagle / penguin
Non-egg laying: bear / dog / giraffe / whale / tiger / moose / horse

p. 104
❶ A physical adaptation is a trait living things inherit from their parents that helps them survive and reproduce.
❷ Omnivores have sharp and flat teeth for eating different types of food.
❸ A bear hibernating in the winter.

p. 105
❶ opossum ❷ cow
❸ lion ❹ fish
❺ horse ❻ gorilla
❼ hummingbird

p. 106
(Answers will vary.)

Unit 2 Social Studies

p. 108
1 New York City
2 The first battles of the Revolutionary War.
3 New England

p. 109
(Answers will vary.)

p. 110
1 It has rich soil and flat land.
2 Because they are the biggest freshwater lakes in the country.
3 Detroit, Michigan

p. 111
(Answers will vary.)

p. 112
1 Hot, wet summers and mild winters.
2 The Appalachian Mountains
3 Because air conditioning was made more affordable, which made living in the south more pleasant for people.

p. 113
(Answers will vary.)

p. 114
1 Because gold was discovered and many people wanted to go west to find it.
2 Because Spanish and Mexican people originally inhabited and settled in the Southwest.
3 The weather on Oregon and Washington's coast is rainy and warm.

p. 115
(Answers will vary.)

p. 116

Unit 2 Technology

p. 118
1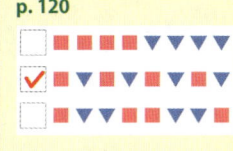
2

p. 119
1 B 2 D

---

p. 120

p. 121
1 A 2 B

p. 122

p. 123
1 B 2 C

p. 124

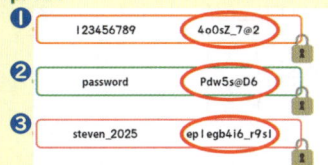

p. 125
1 true 2 false 3 false
4 true 5 true

Unit 3 Reading

pp. 128-129
1 It's fun to enjoy family traditions.
2 They are excited to celebrate.
3 Eid al-Fitr
4 It is a special day.
5 6 (Answers will vary.)

pp. 130-131
1 The Florida Everglades
2 The Everglades is a wetland ecosystem. The park is home to many different plants and animals. It is important for the environment.
3 The importance of the Everglades as a national park in the US.
4 That the Florida Everglades is an important national park and helps the environment.
5 (Answers will vary.)

pp. 132-133
B → F → D → C → A → E

pp. 134-135
1 Jazz music
2 Passage 1
3 The informational text shares information, and the opinion text gives an opinion.
4 5 (Answers will vary.)
6 positive
   (Answers will vary.)

p. 137
(Answers will vary.)

Unit 3 Writing

p. 138
Circle: I / mom / flight attendant
1 I sat in my seat.
2 I pulled my tray down.
3 I fell asleep.

p. 139
(Answers will vary.)

p. 140
1 ☒ "I love going to the movies," Hannah told him.
2 ☑
3 ☑
4 ☒ Molly looked at me and said, "Let's go outside!"

p. 141
(Answers will vary.)

p. 142
Underline: cool / like a little cloud / birds singing loudly / smelled like it was about to rain

p. 143
(Answers will vary.)

pp. 144-145
(Answers will vary.)

p. 146
(Answers will vary.)

Unit 3 Math

p. 148
1 $\frac{2}{5}$ 2 $\frac{5}{6}$ 3 $\frac{2}{3}$ 4 $\frac{3}{4}$
5 $\frac{5}{9}$ 6 $\frac{3}{8}$ 7 $\frac{7}{12}$ 8 $\frac{9}{10}$

p. 149
1 $\frac{1}{4}$ 2 $\frac{3}{8}$ 3 $\frac{2}{5}$ 4 $\frac{4}{9}$
5 $\frac{1}{6}$ 6 $\frac{3}{10}$ 7 $\frac{1}{3}$ 8 $\frac{5}{12}$

p. 150
1 = 2 < 3 =
4 > 5 =

p. 151

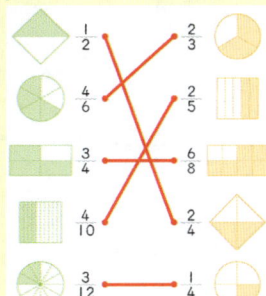

---

p. 152
1 $\frac{2}{2}$ 2 $\frac{3}{3}$ 3 $\frac{2}{2}$
4 $\frac{2}{2}$ 5 $\frac{4}{4}$ 6 $\frac{6}{6}$
7 $\frac{3}{3}$ 8 $\frac{2}{2}$ 9 $\frac{4}{4}$

p. 153
1 $\frac{1}{2}$ 2 $\frac{1}{2}$ 3 $\frac{1}{8}$
4 $\frac{1}{3}$ 5 $\frac{3}{4}$ 6 $\frac{3}{4}$
7 $\frac{2}{5}$ 8 $\frac{2}{3}$ 9 $\frac{2}{3}$

p. 154
1 $2\frac{1}{2}$ 2 2 3 $3\frac{1}{3}$

p. 155
1 $\frac{7}{3}$ 2 $\frac{8}{3}$ 3 $\frac{7}{2}$
4 $\frac{15}{4}$ 5 $\frac{12}{5}$

p. 156
1 $3\frac{2}{3}$ 2 $3\frac{1}{2}$ 3 $1\frac{3}{4}$
4 $3\frac{3}{5}$ 5 $5\frac{3}{8}$ 6 $3\frac{5}{6}$
7 $9\frac{4}{9}$ 8 $3\frac{2}{3}$ 9 $6\frac{4}{5}$
10 $7\frac{6}{7}$

p. 157
1 $2\frac{1}{4}$ 2 $1\frac{2}{3}$ 3 $1\frac{1}{5}$
4 $2\frac{3}{8}$ 5 $2\frac{7}{12}$ 6 $5\frac{1}{3}$
7 $6\frac{3}{10}$ 8 $2\frac{1}{2}$ 9 $2\frac{2}{7}$
10 $8\frac{1}{6}$

p. 158
1 1, 2, 3, 4
2 1, 2, 3, 4
3 4, 1, 2, 3

p. 159
1 B 2 D

Unit 3 Science

p. 161
1 Water
2 Land
3 core / crust / mantle
4 core
5 mantle
6 crust

p. 162
1 Igneous rocks are made from hardened magma.
2 sedimentary
3 metamorphic

p. 163
1 igneous 2 sedimentary
3 sedimentary 4 metamorphic
5 igneous 6 metamorphic

p. 164
① Minerals are made out of only one element and rocks are made out of many different ones.
② From the soil.

p. 165
① true   ② true   ③ true
④ false   ⑤ false   ⑥ true

p. 166
① Fossils are the remains of plants or animals that lived long ago and are impressed into rocks.
② People study fossils to learn about the past.
③ Fossils are formed when tiny bits of rock, soil and dead plants or animals form layers and pressure on them turns them into rocks.

p. 167

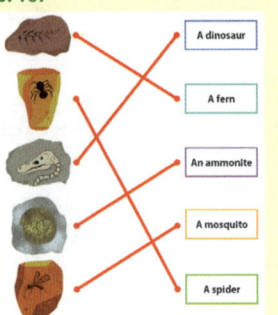

p. 168
(Answers will vary.)

Unit 3 Social Studies

p. 170
① It was easy to get water to live.
② Where a person lives affects their culture based on the resources available for food and clothing.

p. 171
① Earth's
② Water
③ water
④ fertile
⑤ Nomadic
⑥ natural resources
⑦ geography

p. 172
① Natural resources are things found in nature that are used by people.
② wood and stone
③ To power gas cars and generate electricity.

p. 173

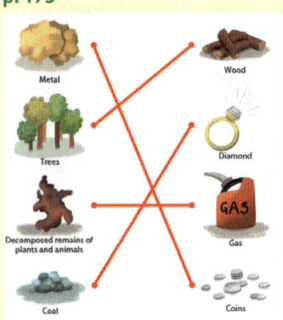

p. 174
① water and sunlight
② fossil fuels and coal
③ Renewable resources are naturally regrown or remade. Nonrenewable resources are used up to make energy.

p. 175
① renewable
② renewable
③ nonrenewable
④ renewable
⑤ renewable
⑥ renewable
⑦ renewable
⑧ renewable
⑨ nonrenewable

p. 177
① true   ② true   ③ false
④ false   ⑤ true   ⑥ true

p. 178

Unit 3 Personal Finance

p. 180
① 3.45   ② 0.68
③ 1.32   ④ 2.05

p. 181

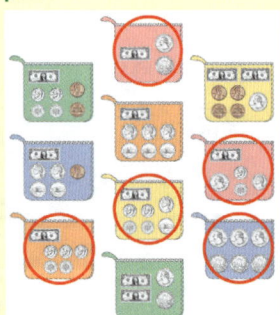

p. 182
① 0.13   ② 0.02
③ 0.01   ④ 0.11

p. 183
① Hot Dog / Orange Juice
② Hamburger / French Fries

p. 184
① Cashless   ② Cash
③ Cashless

p. 185
① Producer   ② Producer
③ Consumer   ④ Producer

p. 186

p. 187

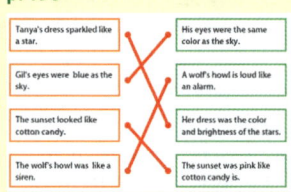

Unit 4 Reading

p. 190

p. 191
Underline: as cold as ice / jumping around like a rabbit / The stars look like sequins / the moon looks like Swiss cheese.
① very cold
② jumping up and down
③ shiny
④ containing lots of holes

p. 192

p. 193
Underline: The tent was a giant rainbow inside. / The smell of popcorn filled the air with warmth. / Then the elephants came in, each one a gentle giant. / The sky was a sea of color.
① It was very colorful.
② It smelled good and comforting.
③ They were big but gentle.
④ The sky was full of color.

p. 194
① Don't be sad about something that already happened.
② He needed to study.
③ She didn't know what to say.
④ Petra was feeling sad.

p. 195

(matching exercise with idioms)

p. 196
① Underline: hot / cold
② Underline: loud / quiet
③ Circle: began / start

p. 197
Circle: thrilled / huge / ran / silently / tiny
① upset   ② quieter
③ new   ④ fastest
⑤ big

p. 198
(Answers will vary.)

Unit 4 Writing

pp. 200-201
(Answers will vary.)

pp. 202-203
(Answers will vary.)

p. 204
Circle: If you are a movie lover, then Los Angeles is the city for you!
Underline: It's a must-see for any movie fan!

p. 205
(Answers will vary.)

pp. 206-207
(Answers will vary.)

p. 208
(Answers will vary.)

Unit 4 Math

p. 210
① 1.8   ② 5.2   ③ 13
④ 4.88   ⑤ 7.95   ⑥ 15.1
⑦ 7.83   ⑧ 4.85   ⑨ 11.3
⑩ 7.46   ⑪ 12.12   ⑫ 11.89

p. 211
① 6.2   ② 1.8   ③ 0.2
④ 0.2   ⑤ 2.23   ⑥ 0.07
⑦ 1.31   ⑧ 1.93   ⑨ 0.99
⑩ 3.33   ⑪ 1.59   ⑫ 1.42

p. 212
① 6.9   ② 1.2   ③ 22
④ 6.3   ⑤ 8.2   ⑥ 6.4
⑦ 31   ⑧ 4.2   ⑨ 4.28
⑩ 18.93   ⑪ 58.59   ⑫ 27.1

p. 213
❶2.1 ❷2.2 ❸2.1
❹3.1 ❺0.7 ❻0.4
❼0.8 ❽0.9 ❾3.8
❿1.2 ⓫3.6 ⓬3.2

p. 214
❶1 ❷7 ❸3
❹9 ❺0.2 ❻0.6
❼0.01 ❽0.08

p. 215
❶35 ❷42 ❸51
❹19 ❺68 ❻77
❼0.17 ❽0.33 ❾0.64
❿0.58 ⓫0.99 ⓬0.26

p. 216
❶0.5 ❷0.4 ❸0.8
❹0.75 ❺0.25 ❻0.6

p. 217
Example
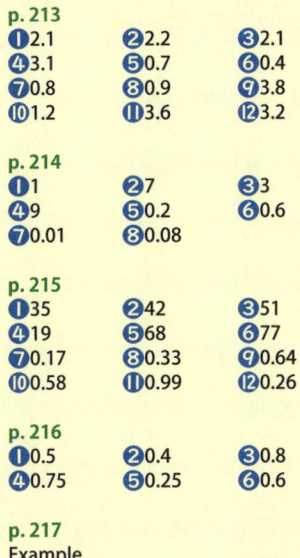

p. 218
❶$\frac{1}{2}$ ❷$\frac{3}{5}$ ❸$\frac{3}{4}$

p. 219
Place a check mark on ❶❸.

pp. 220-221
❶A ❷B ❸B ❹A

Unit 4 Science

p. 222
❶food, water and resources
❷Because fossil fuels are hard to get and take a long time to be formed again.
❸By walking or biking when they can to help limit air pollution from driving cars.

p. 223
❶environment
❷humans
❸Indigenous
❹fossil / fuels
❺Global / warming
❻renewable

p. 224
❶Burning fossil fuels, coal, and oil.
❷Makes water unusable for animals and plants.
❸Using more renewable energy.

p. 225
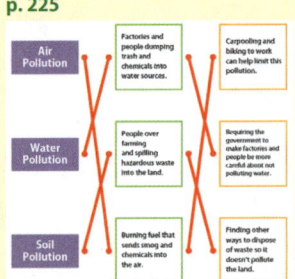

p. 226
❶A landfill is designed to contain waste.
❷To prevent dangerous liquids from getting into the soil.
❸Recycle more.

p. 227
❶true ❷false ❸true
❹true ❺false ❻true

p. 228
❶Paper, glass, and metal.
❷plastic
❸Food scraps can be turned into compost.

p. 229
Recyclable: glass bottles / metal can / newspaper / paper plate / plastic soda bottles / plastic bag
Non-recyclable: batteries /an old coat / sneakers / a baseball /a broken mirror /can of hairspray
Compostable: leftover vegetables / dead plant / old Christmas tree

p. 230
(Answers will vary.)

Unit 4 Social Studies

p. 232
❶A democracy is a government ruled by the people.
❷Executive, legislative, and judicial.
❸The checks and balance system helps ensure that none of the branches of government have more power than the other.

p. 233
❶judicial branch
❷legislative branch
❸executive branch
❹legislative branch
❺legislative branch
❻judicial branch

p. 234
❶The purpose of a constitution is to state the laws for a state or country.
❷The Articles of Confederacy gave too much power to the states.
❸An amendment is an official change added to the US constitution.

p. 235
❶true ❷true ❸false
❹true ❺false ❻false
❼true

p. 237
❶second amendment
❷eighth amendment
❸first amendment
❹fifth amendment
❺tenth amendment
❻fourth amendment
❼ninth amendment
❽seventh amendment

p. 238
❶All legal adults citizens over 18.
❷The electoral college system is an indirect system of voting that gives candidates a certain amount of votes based on the state population.
❸Mayors, governors, judges, and representatives.

p. 239
(Answers will vary.)

p. 240
Across
❶judicial ❸representative
❺congress
Down
❷democracy ❹president
❻senate ❽legislative
❿executive

Unit 4 Thinking Skills

pp. 242-243
❶D ❷A ❸H ❹F
❺C ❻E ❼G ❽B

pp. 244-245
❶D ❷A

pp. 246-247
❶
❷
❸
❹
❺
❻

pp. 248-249

Unit 5 Reading

p. 252
❶tradition ❷ancestor
❸fragile ❹peculiar
❺shabby

p. 253
tradition: something you do again and again
ancestor: family members from long ago
fragile: easy to break
peculiar: strange

p. 254
❶humble ❷concentrate
❸frantic ❹sturdy
❺eager

p. 255
eager: excited
concentrate: focus
sturdy: able to hold something
humble: not bragging

p. 256
❶a ❷b ❸a ❹b

p. 257
❶change ❷trunk
❸right ❹fan
❺tear ❻patch

p. 258
❶unreliable
❷disregarded
❸recharge

p. 259
❶not ready
❷lost
❸make a new plan
❹something they don't know
❺follow again

p. 260
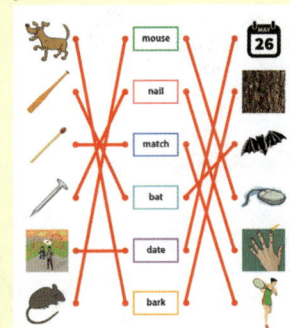

Unit 5 Writing

p. 262
Everyone should learn how to cook in school.

p. 263
(Answers will vary.)

p. 264
Underline: If we didn't have this time, we would feel more stressed all day long.
Recess is a time to meet new people and make friends, which is also very important.
Finally, recess allows us to take a break from our schoolwork.

p. 265
(Answers will vary.)

p. 266
❶ in order to
❷ In addition to
❸ For instance

p. 267
(Answers will vary.)

pp. 268–269
(Answers will vary.)

p. 270
(Answers will vary.)

Unit 5 Math

p. 272

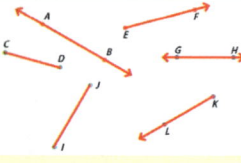

p. 273
Parallel lines: ❶, ❼
Perpendicular lines: ❸, ❺

p. 274
Right angles: ❷, ❹
Acute angles: ❶, ❺
Obtuse angles: ❸, ❻

p. 275
❶ right   ❷ acute   ❸ obtuse
❹ acute   ❺ obtuse   ❻ right
❼ acute   ❽ obtuse

p. 276
❶ triangle
❷ quadrilateral (quadrangle)
❸ pentagon   ❹ hexagon
❺ heptagon   ❻ octagon
❼ nonagon   ❽ decagon
❾ dodecagon

p. 277
❶ 3, 3, 3   ❷ 4, 4, 4   ❸ 5, 5, 5
❹ 6, 6, 6   ❺ 8, 8, 8

p. 278
❶ square   ❷ rectangle
❸ quadrilateral (quadrangle)
❹ rectangle
❺ quadrilateral (quadrangle)
❻ square

p. 279
❶ isosceles   ❷ right
❸ equilateral   ❹ isosceles
❺ scalene

p. 280
❶ $7 \times 5 = 35$ (in.^{2})
❷ $10 \times 10 = 100$ (cm^2)

p. 281
❶ B   ❷ A   ❸ B   ❹ A

p. 282
Place a check mark on ❶❸❹❻.

Unit 5 Science

p. 284
❶ Energy is the ability to do work.
❷ No
❸ Drums and people's voices.

p. 285
❶ work
❷ machines
❸ living things
❹ sun
❺ plants / animals
❻ created / destroyed
❼ sound

p. 286
❶ Electrical energy is the energy produced when electrons move.
❷ being in a closed circuit
❸ refrigerator, lights, and computers

p. 287

p. 288
❶ They are created from fossils or the remains of dead plants and animals.
❷ millions of years
❸ They renew very slowly and they are hard to collect.

p. 289
❶ true   ❷ true   ❸ false
❹ true   ❺ false   ❻ true
❼ true

p. 290
❶ It never runs out.
❷ sunlight, water, and wind
❸ water or hydroelectric

p. 291

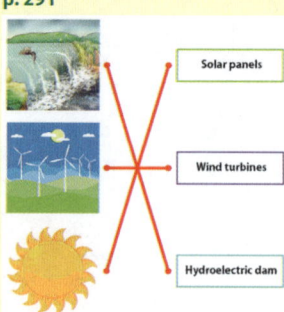

p. 292
(Answers will vary.)

Unit 5 Social Studies

p. 295
❶ price
❷ sharing
❸ competition
❹ majority rule
❺ first-come, first served
❻ random/lottery
❼ force

p. 296
❶ Competition in the economy means multiple people or companies can offer the same goods and services.
❷ A monopoly is when one person or company has all of the goods or services without competition.

p. 297
(Answers will vary.)

p. 298
❶ To convince people to buy them.
❷ Product placement is when companies place a good in a TV show or social media post to make you feel like you need to buy it.

p. 299
(Answers will vary.)

p. 300
❶ To buy something expensive or in case of an emergency.
❷ To pay for things they cannot afford to buy right away.

p. 301
❶ borrow
❷ borrow or save
❸ save   ❹ save
❺ save   ❻ borrow or save
❼ save   ❽ save

p. 302

M	N	B	V	C	X	Z	A	G	S	D	F
A	L	L	O	C	A	T	I	O	N	H	G
T	Y	U	I	O	O	P	L	O	K	J	A
R	E	W	Q	M	A	S	D	D	F	G	D
C	X	Z	N	P	M	K	L	S	J	H	V
B	I	N	V	E	S	T	I	N	G	A	E
S	V	Q	W	T	E	R	T	Y	U	I	R
E	A	E	I	I	O	U	O	V	B	N	T
R	Q	T	H	T	E	G	N	M	H	W	I
V	A	S	E	I	A	I	U	O	T	X	S
I	Z	P	R	O	D	U	C	T	R	V	I
C	X	S	A	N	B	C	G	E	E	Q	N
E	C	F	L	O	P	S	A	V	I	N	G
S	W	D	V	F	R	T	Y	U	N	Z	B
A	S	M	A	R	K	E	T	I	N	G	M
D	F	G	H	J	K	L	O	P	I	U	N

Unit 5 Thinking Skills

p. 304

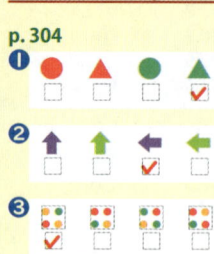

p. 305
❶ 1   ❷ 3   ❸ 3

pp. 306–307

❶
H	Y	P	C	I	L	T	F	Q	E	B	D
A	B	M	J	V	L	S	R	Z	U	K	C
F	P	A	I	U	A	T	A	X	G	T	D
L	V	E	Q	Z	B	R	H	M	W	E	G
A	V	O	Z	K	T	P	Y	I	J	N	E
O	R	Q	C	X	E	B	G	H	F	N	U
J	G	N	I	I	K	S	H	S	K	I	D
B	L	T	O	L	S	S	M	G	F	S	Q
B	A	S	E	B	A	L	L	B	X	W	E
D	W	V	I	M	B	K	Y	P	N	Y	G
U	Z	E	X	C	F	S	L	W	A	O	D
R	C	T	J	S	W	I	M	M	I	N	G

❷
S	I	N	N	E	T	E	L	B	A	T	C
W	J	F	O	O	T	G	O	A	L	A	Y
I	U	W	T	V	Z	O	Q	L	X	B	C
B	A	D	N	I	N	L	O	L	V	L	L
A	K	Y	I	R	X	K	W	J	O	E	I
T	O	T	M	K	N	I	R	C	Y	C	N
N	B	A	D	P	T	O	P	O	N	Y	E
I	L	L	A	B	I	N	O	F	P	C	Y
N	R	L	B	Q	B	X	K	L	U	L	W
T	U	E	K	R	E	C	C	O	S	I	Z
O	Z	T	Q	R	J	O	U	G	Q	N	X
N	T	E	B	L	E	B	O	L	L	G	V

pp. 308–309
(Answers will vary.)

pp. 310–311
(Answers will vary.)

318

KUMON Ace Fourth Grade

Unit 1

COMPLETED!

Unit 2

COMPLETED!

Unit 3

COMPLETED!

Unit 4

COMPLETED!

Unit 5

COMPLETED!

All Pages Completed!

Excellent Work!

CERTIFICATE
OF ACHIEVEMENT

―――――――――――――――――――

is hereby congratulated on completing

Kumon Ace Fourth Grade

_____   _____
Date   **Parent or Guardian**